# ONE OF THE BOYS

# ONE OF THE BOYS

SURVIVING DARTMOUTH, FAMILY,
AND THE WILDERNESS OF MEN

## LYNN LOBBAN

Charleston, SC
www.PalmettoPublishing.com

*One of the Boys*
Copyright © 2023 by Lynn Lobban

First Edition

Paperback ISBN: 979-8-8229-1907-5
eBook ISBN: 979-8-8229-1908-2

Dedicated to my children,
WILLIAM AND LUCY,
whom I love and respect beyond measure.

THIS IS MY STORY. It is not my mother's, my father's, my sister's, or my brother's. It is no one's story but my own. My truth as I remember it, and still know it to be. Though an occasional name has been changed, the story is true. I hope, somehow, it's helpful.

# SNEAK PREVIEW

# ESTABLISHING SHOT

*Vox Clamantis in Deserto*
"A voice crying out in the wilderness"
Dartmouth College motto

WHEN I ARRIVED at Dartmouth College in the fall of 1968 as one of its first women, I was determined to prove I was equal to any man. Just because I didn't have a penis didn't mean I was inferior. I was worthy. I deserved the same rights and privileges as men. But looking back at my eighteen-year-old self, so desperate to be more than novelty in Dartmouth's first experiment with the opposite sex, I see my confusion.

Though I was used to going into bewildering places and hacking my way through—after all, I was a child of two alcoholics—Dartmouth's wilderness presented new challenges. For as I sought to gain power on the Ivy League campus where testosterone flowed from New Hampshire trees, I was a hormonal teenage girl. While battling the status quo, I longed for the magic kiss and Prince Charming to make me whole. I screamed for equality while making Dartmouth my personal stomping ground for getting male attention, attention I feared as much as craved.

My year at Dartmouth had lasting repercussions. It affected my life in ways I could not have imagined at the time. Convinced I could do whatever I wanted after spending a year on a campus of men, I moved into Manhattan and made a life in the arts. I married, had children, divorced, and married and divorced a second time. But it's only now in sunny California, where I live as happily as I am able with my third husband, do I more fully see the truth.

When I arrived at Dartmouth College, determined to single-handedly change the world, crying in the wilderness was already my most familiar song. Dartmouth wasn't just an all-male institution, admitting women after hundreds of years of so many men, taking an experimental few to begin its journey towards coeducation in a thoughtful and measured way. Dartmouth was my hopeless cause, the father who provided wealth and privilege but should have gone to prison for what he did to me in the confines of my bed. Dartmouth was the litmus test for why my mother left me.

## INVISIBLE ART

My past runs like a movie in my head.
Memories come back in fragmented clips.
I view raw footage of my past as if I'm still in scene.
In the darkness of my psyche's screening room
I watch ancient images

played past the point of popcorn
and arrange them into some semblance of a story.

## TIME FRAME

1968 IS A year of turbulence. North Korea captures, imprisons, and tortures the crew of the USS Pueblo. North Vietnam launches the Tet Offensive, and protest against the war boils over. Martin Luther King Jr. is shot and killed in Memphis. Two months later and almost to the day, Robert Kennedy Jr. is also gunned down.

Two African-American Olympians throw their fists into the air to protest racial discrimination. Lyndon Johnson signs The Civil Rights Act of 1968. Riots break out at the Democratic National Convention, and Republicans nominate Richard Nixon who runs on law and order and wins.

Boeing introduces the 747. NASA sends three men into orbit to see the far side of the moon. Laugh-In debuts on NBC, Hair opens on Broadway, 60 Minutes premieres on CBS, and Star Trek's Captain Kirk kisses a humanoid Platonian for television's first interracial kiss.

In Rome, Pope Paul VI condemns birth control. In England, Mary Bell, a sexually-abused eleven-year-old girl, is sentenced to life in prison for murdering two young boys. And in Hanover, New Hampshire, Dartmouth College is beginning its experiment with coeducation. After catering to the educational needs of men for two hundred years, Dartmouth is letting seven women spend one academic year on its campus of three-thousand men.

## PRESS RELEASE

I MAKE NEWS in less than a month. My hometown paper, *The Jersey Journal*, publishes a story on October 6, 1968. It is my first review.

> *FRATERNITY INDUCTS GIRL ROBUSTLY*
>
> "I never had an older brother and now I've got 64 of them." So spoke Lynn Lobban of Jersey City as she was welcomed amid robust male cheers, as an honorary member of Dartmouth College's Chi Phi fraternity.
>
> The daughter of Dr. and Mrs. Robert Lobban of Jersey City is one of seven female students spending a full junior year at the all-male Ivy League institution. The Elmira College junior was selected to participate in a special students' program in the field of drama. Each of the female students in the program is considered a resident of the community and is taking courses at Dartmouth. Although the students in the program concentrate on dra-

ma studies, they will be expected to undertake other types of courses.

Joining the fraternity was more than a lark for Lynn. She is completely serious about her connections with Chi Phi and is attempting to relate her dramatic studies with fraternity activities. Her objective is to direct Chi Phi's house play.

Since this is the first time the well-established Hanover college has admitted females to its roster, it may be a little difficult for the new girl students to break through the solid "maleness" of Dartmouth. Lynn says she squirmed at convocation as an officer directed his address to the "Men of Dartmouth."

In order to have been considered for the special program at Dartmouth, the female student had to be highly qualified and have the recommendation of her faculty advisor and dean. Lynn will receive full credit for her studies at the college and return to Elmira for her senior year.

My mother and father read the paper, smiling to themselves. My mother gets a pair of scissors so she can show her friends while my father turns the page.

# RED CARPET

ON THE NIGHT of fraternal initiation, I feel more power as a woman than I have ever felt before. When the ritual for full admission into brotherhood arrives, I am ready. I've performed all my pledge duties. I've happily polished, vacuumed, and cleaned. Not just because a houseful of men is making me their own, but I have never had to do chores before.

Chi Phi Heorot, "the foremost of halls under heaven" in *Beowulf,* is not like my home in Jersey City. Heorot is sacred ground, the haven I've always dreamed of. My mother may call me terrible names, but shitbird, Heorot's moniker for pledges, feels like the highest honor.

Initiation begins in the afternoon as Heorot brothers watch twenty-one shitbirds descend into the basement. As I walk down the stairs, a brother looks up and smiles. Suddenly, I'm Audrey Hepburn descending the steps of the Louvre. Only this isn't *Funny Face.* This is serious business.

Acceptance into Heorot will not be like moving up from Brownie to Girl Scout. It won't be a matter of earning enough badges and memorizing the Girl Scout oath so I can change the color of my hat. Heorot has its own rules for entering its rarified world.

As light streams in from a small rectangular window, I notice a puke-and-beer-caked floor. The basement is ugly in the afternoon. A silver keg, its foam spilling to the floor, looms on the bar. The only woman among twenty nervous young men, I take a three-fifteen position on the shitbird clock.

"Move, shitbird, move!" a brother yells.

I shuffle along like a prisoner on a chain gang, downing a plastic cup of beer every time I circle back to the keg.

"Chug, shitbird, chug!" a brother shouts.

Walk. Chug a beer. Walk. Chug a beer. I hate beer. It reminds me of unbaked bread and male excitement at baseball games. But my fellow shitbirds don't seem to mind. Hearing them cheer every time they swallow, I think drinking in the afternoon must be more treat than trial to them. My mother would agree.

When I arrive at the keg too many times, I am dizzy. But I hold myself together. Gulping and belching, I must fly high in my flock of shitbirds because I am drinking for all women everywhere. Forget what is being asked of me is as dumb as my mother's insistence I be a virgin when I marry.

When the keg is finally drained, a brother thrusts a cigar into my hand. "Smoke this down and don't come out until you do!" he orders, cramming me into the dirty toilet along with the other shitbirds. I think of the stateroom scene in *A Night at the Opera,* only the Marx Brothers aren't here and I'm not laughing.

The room is claustrophobic. The air, revolting. I hate cigars. Whether manly rite of passage or perverse celebratory gesture, their smell is vile. The dense, disgusting smoke makes me choke. I puff and cough, and cough some more while men bump up against me. If they weren't fellow shitbirds, I'd be scared to death.

As one man after another finishes his stogie and exits the room, I am left with Mike, a man as kind as he is blond. He lifts my cigar from my hand and smokes it down, saving me from my most stubborn self. Though I hate needing help, I am grateful beyond measure.

Nauseated and freed from the toilet, I go upstairs where a brother points me to an obstacle course—sticks and empty boxes sloppily arranged on a slightly snow-brushed hill—erected in Heorot's backyard. As he opens the door, the cold air hits my face and does its best to rouse me. The sun's bright light tries to clear my head but only hurts my eyes. Coatless and confused, I stagger up the hill and stumble down in free fall. Amazed I am upright at the bottom of the hill, I hear faint fraternal cheering.

A brother calls me inside and I come like a well-trained dog. I follow to a closed door outside the meeting room where two brothers stand at attention like Royal Guards outside the palace. Staring solemnly ahead, they seem to be enjoying what feels like life and death to me.

"Shitbird Lobban!" a brother barks before he ties a blindfold round my head. "Can you see anything?" he whispers.

"No," I whisper back, wishing I could.

Pressing his heavy hands on my shoulders, he spins me around and pushes me forward on a circuitous and disorienting route that I'm fairly sure takes us back to where we started. A door closes behind me.

"Kneel, shitbird, kneel!" a henchmen orders at close range. Dropping to the ground, I pretend to be brave.

"Stick out your tongue!" he yells.

Sure. Whatever you say. Though opening my mouth in a room full of men feels slightly terrifying. I am relieved when an Alka-Seltzer, house remedy for hangovers, fizzes in my dried-out mouth.

"Stand up!" a brother yells. "Are you ready for the secret of the Chi?" he taunts.

*Are they kidding?*

Suddenly, I wonder how big this secret is, and if they're really going to tell me. Even with how far I've come, I'm not convinced they're going to accept me into their world.

"Yes! I am!" I proclaim. "But if you do anything different for me because I'm a girl, I'm going to be really mad!"

I hate calling myself a girl, but they always do, and I'm not about to cause trouble now.

A brother takes off my blindfold and my eyes adjust to a candlelit room. Heorot brothers are dressed like Franciscan monks. Their brown robes are knotted with straw-colored rope. They're wearing floppy hoods that cover their heads and hide their faces.

Happy and surprised by the soft intimacy of fraternal bonding, I feel a sweet and gentle masculinity closing in. I would be turned on if I wasn't so busy being tough. Completely mesmerized, I am relieved initiation is all-at-once religious, fairy-tale-tender, and utterly cornball.

But then someone turns me around to face a closed, full-sized casket.

My chest tightens. My mouth opens. I can't breathe.

It's 1961.

I'm in Jersey City and I'm twelve-years-old. My brother is at his boarding school, my father is passed out after a long day of doctoring and drink, and my sister and I are looking for our mother because we have to know where she is before we can sleep.

"Mommy?" we call out to her empty room.

"Mommy?" we call again, heading downstairs to the sun porch, her favorite place to drink.

But my mother isn't there. We find another dark and empty room.

"Mommy?" my sister and I take turns saying as our voices grow more strained. "Where *are* you Mommy?"

We're pretty sure she hasn't left the house. She usually doesn't take her Cadillac out of the garage when she's only wearing a nightgown. Though Hide and Seek is my favorite game because I love finding things before anybody else, this game isn't fun.

My sister goes into our father's office while I go upstairs to check the closets and look under beds. I push aside my mother's dresses and minks, and my father's custom-made suits. I lift the dust ruffles of every bed. I go up another flight of stairs and search the cold and dusty attic. I even look in the room I just know is haunted. The one with the pink asbestos padding bursting from the ceiling. But my mother is nowhere to be found.

When I rejoin my sister downstairs, we know there's only one place left to look. The basement. We take a deep breath and descend the wooden stairs. We search the laundry room where the maids do our laundry. We check the furnace room and the crawlspace where coal is stored and where we've seen rats.

"Mommy?" I whisper, as scared as I have ever been.

In a house of fifty rooms—if you count the bathrooms and closets—only one room remains. The one with the work table and tools in case my father has time to build things. The one with the unfinished dollhouse we never get to play with. The one with the two freezers.

Like canaries in a coal mine, we tiptoe in. My sister points to the top-lidded freezers sitting side by side against the wall and motions me over. I go to the one I already know is filled with packaged meats from our fancy butcher in Flemington, New Jersey. As I lift the lid, I stare down at steaks, pork chops, and roasts, neatly wrapped in peach-colored paper and tan-colored tape. The cold organization of the stacked and identified meat instantly calms me down.

But then I notice the other freezer. It's unplugged, and its lid is slightly open. I motion to my sister because I'm too afraid. Filled with dread, she walks over, grabs the silver handle, and lifts the lid.

"Mommy!" she cries out, because our mother is curled up at the bottom of the freezer.

As my sister cries, I enter *The Twilight Zone*, lost in a dimension without number. But I need to see. Looking down, I see mousy-brown-permed hair atop a large sweating body in a negligee. My mother is so drunk she can't even lift her head.

"Leave me alone," she slurs from what is clearly the best hiding place in the house.

I don't know how my sister gets her out and up into bed because I'm already in my room watching a movie. It's what I do when life becomes unbearable.

*"Are you ready for the secret of the Chi?"* a brother yells again, snapping me back to 1968 and the hallowed hall of Heorot.

With my brothers watching, there's no escape upstairs. I feel like Vincent Price in *The Pit and the Pendulum*, strapped to a slab as a giant, razor-sharp pendulum swings closer and closer to my throat. I know if what's inside this casket makes me cry or run away, I will never be a man. I pray to a nameless force as a faceless brother lifts the casket's lid.

The casket is empty.

*Empty?!?*

Though I am relieved I don't have to confront my mother or some other monster, I am outraged. How *dare* they hide the secret of the Chi from me! Men are so damn disappointing! First, they say they want you and then they don't come through! They've only been humoring me all along!

About to cry out at the injustice being done to me because I am a woman, I hear a sound at the window. I look up as the curtains part like the Red Sea. JB, a hairy, stocky brother is standing on the windowsill like a preppy Mr. Universe. Naked in all his penile glory, he is a shocking sight to see. Though his body is better than a dead or drunken one, I hope it's one I don't have to touch.

As Heorot brothers erupt in self-satisfied howling, I realize I've been spared. But wait. Is this *it?* The secret of the Chi is the *penis?* But I already know that! That's why I'm here!

As things start to feel familial and dangerous again, I'm glad I'm too drunk and overwhelmed to reason it all out. I accept the empty secret of the Chi and move on.

"You guys are so great!" I yell, flattering the shit out of them because I can't think of anything else and it seems like the right thing to do.

And with that, I am their brother and all of them are mine. It doesn't matter I pass out and miss the celebratory dinner. I am a full-fledged member of a Dartmouth fraternity. I am the woman who breaks through.

But now as I look back, I realize initiation only deepened my confusion. I believed I was one of the boys because I had gained entrance onto their playground. But initiation was only the catalyst officially thrusting me into a life-long struggle to find my power and place in a male-dominated world. A world that began in childhood.

# INCITEMENT

# ORIGIN STORY

NO OFFENSE TO those who love the place, but I hate telling people I'm from Jersey City. To me, Jersey City is like the not quite good enough family member living in the shadow of its glamorous sibling, New York. But if anyone asks, I tell them, even though their response is always the same.

"Joi-zee City!" the cute Dartmouth guy laughs, ridiculing a whole populace.

Feeling put in some subterranean place, I wait for the inevitable follow-up.

"But you don't have an accent!" he says.

That's right. I don't have that slightly dumb-sounding New Jersey accent.

"Maybe it's because I didn't go to public school," I explain, "and I never went out at night. My mother wouldn't let me."

Because that sounds equally bad, I race to mitigate the impact of my story. The words spill out like mouthwash.

"We have a house in the country, too," I assure him. "I spent every weekend and summer in Lake Mohawk."

His eyes glaze over.

"It's in Sussex County," I say, helpfully.

Nothing.

"Northwest New Jersey?"

He nods whether he knows or not because Lake Mohawk really does sound better to snobs like me.

# CHARACTER LIST

I ENTER A post-war world on a Friday, neither full of grace nor full of woe. I am loving and giving, or so the rhyme tells me and I like to believe. Born in the Margaret Hague Maternity Hospital on September 2, 1949, I arrive in a twilight of anesthesia. It is the way then. Women killing the pain of being women and letting men do it for them. I wonder if that's where it started. My mother's avoidance of pain at all costs.

My mother, Gloria Carol Larsen, is a smart, pretty twenty-five-year-old nurse from Perth Amboy, New Jersey. Her friends call her Pug because her nose must resemble a dog's though I can never see it. My father, Robert Bonser Lobban, is a forty-five-year-old surgeon from Alderson, West Virginia, who heads north after graduating from the University of Virginia's School of Medicine.

The Confederacy takes a Yankee girl.

My parents meet at the Jersey City Medical Center as attending surgeon and surgical nurse. But the story I know is that my father contracts hepatitis, has to be hospitalized, and my mother is assigned to his bed. Their love story, short on Hippocratic Oath, unfolds quickly.

My mother is surely impressed by my father's reputation, for Dr. Lobban is not just a doctor, he's a well-respected surgeon. "He does everything except the brain and the heart," I explain to my friends, knowing it leaves a lot of other important body parts.

I am also certain my mother's attraction is a monetary one. Embarrassed by her poorer background, she is glad Dr. Lobban is so handsomely paid for his surgical skills, especially in the days before what she will angrily refer to as *socialized medicine*. My mother may support Civil Rights—my father whose ancestors owned slaves and fought for the Confederacy may have reservations—but how dare this thing called *Medicare* threaten the life shc believes she deserves?

In the end though, there's a more compelling reason for my parents' coming together. My mother marries a man old enough to be her father—on December 31st so he can take the tax deduction—because she is pregnant with me. Though from the time I'm old enough to be confused by the crazy things adults sometimes say—especially under the influence—my mother yells, "You're not my first baby! Your father *killed* my first baby!"

This confuses me. I mean, who is this other baby lurking about? And how can a baby be killed before anyone sees it?

I do my best to understand. I am painfully aware I am stuck with two siblings who hate me, but I can't figure out who this *other* baby is.

Thankfully, I don't have to dwell on it. Because the next morning, my mother says something that always makes me feel better. A contrite dove in the early morning light, ashamed

of engaging in battle the night before, my mother coos in my
little girl ear, "You're my first baby. I love you more than anything."

Soothed by her declaration, I relax in her arms. Until she
says I'm not her first baby which is usually that same night.

## SCREEN TEST

I AM A starlet from an early age. My mother records my
first year as if I am Jesus come to light up the world. She takes
my picture with fancy cameras with strange and foreign names
like Leica and Hasselblad. She teaches me that life is not to be
lived as much as captured. That people are not meant to be
known as much as immortalized in fancy frames atop the baby
grand.

As I get older and can take her direction, my mother's
work grows more serious. She turns on blinding lights and
points her eight-millimeter movie camera to film the untrou-
bled moments of her offspring's lives. Mother DeMille yells
"action" and my seven-year-old self, a pointy paper hat on her
pig-tailed head, blows out birthday candles while neighborhood children cheer soundlessly around her.

Her footage is extensive. My mother shoots scenes of wintry weekends. Snowsuit-bundled children sledding down a
snowy hill. A fifteen-foot Christmas tree, panned floor to ceiling, glowing with colored lights and tinsel. A cut to sleepy children padding down the stairs, stunned by an obscenity of gifts.

Idyllic scenes of summer. Children swimming, riding bikes, hanging upside down from the cymbals and trapeze of a backyard's giant swing set. Children waking up on resurrection morning to giant rabbits at the foot of their beds. Dressed in Easter finery, children run frantically around a country house's cul-de-sac in a search for painted eggs and candy.

My mother storyboards family holidays and goes into production. A family cast of characters gather at set-decorated tables. White linen tablecloths, silver candelabra, flowers, and crystal glass. Aunts, uncles, grandparents, and cousins smile and laugh for my mother and her lens. The happy time before the drinking and dissolve.

My mother films what she needs to see, then edits it down to tell her version of our story. She herds us into the living room as my father turns out the lights. In the sound of flickering film, I stare at projected images of myself. Though I am not as happy as I look, I never complain. When I'm in front of my mother's camera or projected on her screen, I know my mother sees me.

## STAR TURN

I LOVE BEING first. Trailblazing, getting places before anyone else, is an aphrodisiac. Even if I can't always stay there, first is everything to me. I viscerally recall the year before my sister is born. A time of no edges. A blissful blending into everything. Life as one big baby orgasm.

The star of my mother's first film, I am three months old and lying on a tartan blanket of pinks and blues because my mother covered her bases. In a royal blue Best and Company dress, I am by myself. No one is holding me. But that's okay. Even though I'm a scrawny little baby, flailing around like I'm getting a series of electrical shocks, look how I smile.

Mommy and Daddy enter the frame and sit down on either side. Mommy wears a diamond-pinned rose-colored dress from Saks Fifth Avenue. Daddy wears a custom-made suit and fancy tie. He leans in to do something I'm too little to stop. He grabs hold of the bottom of my dress and lifts it up over my eyes, revealing my soggy cloth diaper and my skinny crow-like legs. He lifts my dress up, over and over again, in an early father-daughter game of peak-a-boo. Look how I laugh.

I watch this celluloid clip of Mommy, Daddy, and me, and see how much they loved me. How they loved me like they were supposed to.

## ERRORS IN CONTINUITY

BOOM! BOOM! BOOM!

My mother gives birth in quick succession. Fifteen months after I am born, my mother gives birth to my sister. Thirteen months after my sister, my brother comes along.

My world collapses with a thud.

It isn't simply more toddlers angling for maternal care. My mother starts to disappear. After fulfilling her mandate to give her husband a son, she begins to drink in earnest. Maybe it's hormonal, like postpartum depression. What do I know? I'm not the doctor in the family.

I know I don't understand this sudden eruption of family, and I am not in a place where children are allowed to express their feelings. Never sadness, and under no circumstances anger. In my white, upper middle class, Anglo-Saxon family, presentation is everything.

Children must excel and behave. They must stand up when an adult walks into a room, and ask to be excused from the table. Children are not allowed to speak their truth. It's actually not until I'm twenty-one that I find out why people may have more than one child.

"People have a second or more children, Lynn," my first therapist gently explains, "because they like having children."

"Really?" I say because I am truly shocked. "I thought it was because they were so dissatisfied with the first."

## CO-STAR

MY SISTER IS the good one, the quiet one who doesn't make noise. My sister never screams or slams her door like me who likes to take the paint off with how hard I like to slam it.

My sister is also the pretty one with silky platinum-blonde hair and a flat muscular stomach. She is the perfect skinny blond girl I always want to be.

But my sister is also the child in the middle. The one who sacrifices herself to calm our mother down. As I watch my sister try to broker an impossible peace, I would feel sorry for her, but I'm too busy hating the one my mother calls "the angel."

## MISE-EN-SCENE

THE LOBBAN MANSION sits on the corner of Gifford Avenue and Hudson—later named Kennedy after the President is killed and becomes more important—Boulevard. Gifford Avenue and the streets around it are nesting grounds for doctors and lawyers. An exclusive neighborhood of over-sized homes where the upper middle class flaunts the fruits of education, hard work, and investment.

If you count the rooms in the attic where my brother has his Lionel trains, a ping pong table, and a pool table, there are ten bedrooms. There's a huge living room, a sunporch where my mother likes to sit with a bottle and a book, and a kitchen so large two maids can work side by side. I can even roller skate there when my mother isn't home to stop me.

The living room is not really a place to live in. It's to impress those invited in for parental cocktail parties and over-produced holidays. It's a staging area for pretending things are fine. The backdrop of a successful and thriving family. For children, it's a room to pass through on your way to somewhere else.

The massive living room rug, woven with greens and pinks from Persia, covers the floor like a magic carpet. The beige brocade couch, awaiting more accomplished bottoms than mine, is wide and stiff. The coffee table, a rectangle of thick marble, is a resting place for cocktails, silver Tiffany boxes filled with cigarettes, and fancy lighters. The table's pointy corners put a painful dent in my knee when I am pushed into it by an angry sibling.

The gold and white wing chairs on either side of the coffee table sit like friends in conversation. Across the room, the Steinway Baby Grand beckons me to play a Chopin nocturne so my mother can impress her friends with her daughter's musical talents. I hate performing at her bidding and insist everyone go into the sunporch so they can only hear me yell "Sorry!" when I make a mistake.

The living room ceiling is so high I have to throw my head back to see the crystal chandeliers. The windows are tall and covered twice, with white Venetian blinds and heavy curtains so people can't see in if they are standing on the wrap-around porch or the sidewalk below. The floor-to- ceiling curtains are patterned with grapevines and grapes and make the room feel like a giant wine vat in a tomb. When I pull the curtains around me, I almost feel protected.

And there is also my father's office which takes up a whole wing of the ground floor. With its own private entrance, the office fills me with wonderment and dread. My ears fill with the bubbling sound of sterilizers that clean his scary silver instruments. My nose stings from the pervasive smell of alcohol to clean the skin before my father's stitches and shots.

Sometimes my father forgets to close the door of the examining room. When I walk past and see a woman's tiny feet in the shiny silver stirrups, and my father's hands in her undressed valley, I am so sorry I looked.

## CONCESSION STAND

MY MOTHER IS generous with the relief she provides her children. She fills the kitchen's oversized freezer—so huge and heavy I can barely lift its coffin lid—with big round gallon tubs of Breyer's ice cream, just like in the soda fountains. As I stare down at the circular containers of vanilla, chocolate, strawberry, butter pecan, vanilla fudge, and chocolate chip ice cream, I feel loved.

My mother stocks the cabinets with cakes and cookies. Graham Crackers, Oreos, Fig Newtons, Twinkies, Snowballs, and all things Hostess welcoming me in. And behind the staircase in the dark and scary cellar are heavy cases of Hoffmann Sodas stacked one on another. A never-ending supply of orange, grape, cola, black cherry, root beer, vanilla crème, and the hard to pronounce one, sarsaparilla.

I gorge on my just desserts as often as I can because sugar takes the pain away. Sugar dries up my tears. Ice cream extinguishes the fire raging in my body. I float in a sugar high where nothing really matters.

# DEPTH OF FIELD

MY MOTHER STOCKS the freezer's frosty bottom with boxes of her children's favorite candy bars. Mine is 3 Musketeers because it's not messy—I'm always spilling on myself and everyone is always laughing when I do—and because there are three strong men on the wrapper. My brother's favorite is Butterfinger which reminds me of sawdust. And my sister's is a Milky Way with a boring brown, white, and green wrapper.

I'm ten and have just wolfed down my last 3 Musketeers. I want more. Sighing at my empty cardboard box, I look at my sister's candy. There's one Milky Way left. I reach down and take it, leaving her empty box lying next to mine, hoping she won't notice.

As I creep up the back staircase to go into my room, I am gnawing through my sister's frozen candy, hoping it won't pull out my teeth.

"Lynn!" my mother calls from her master bedroom down the hall.

Oh God. Now what.

"Lynn!" my mother yells. "Come in here!"

Darn. I hope my sister hasn't already found out and tattled to my mother.

As I walk into my mother's room like a condemned prisoner, I see her fuming on her pink chaise lounge, looking like an

overweight Cleopatra. My sister is standing next to her, point-
ing her finger like I'm a witch in Salem, outed for burning.

"Did you eat your sister's candy?" my mother asks, as if
she doesn't know.

I lift my eyes to her pink ceiling and wonder what all the
pink is about. My mother is anything but girly.

*"Did you?"* my mother yells.

As my eyes dart back and forth, I'm trying to come up with
something that might save me from another spanking.

"I want the truth!" my mother demands.

Ah, the truth. I hate to lie but it seems like a good idea now.
Though I have grown to almost like the way my skin stings
hot beneath my mother's palm, I hate the raised red welts her
spankings leave on my sadly spreading bottom.

"No, I didn't!" I reply, with nougat stuck in my emerging
molars and chocolate smeared across my teeth.

Before my mother can get up to lunge at me, I decide to
cut my losses.

"Okay! Yes! I ate it!" I say, as my sister's aha mouth hits
the floor.

"But I was hungry!" I add, as if that might matter.

*"You are a fat and selfish pig!"* my mother says, convincingly
and for all time.

Her pronouncement stings. Her words, worse than any
spanking, hang in the air. The humiliation burrows deep.
Being so morally and bodily shamed in front of my sister is

life-changing. Because ever since "The Milky Way Night," it is impossible for me to tell a bald-faced lie to anyone.

I open my Five-Year Diary of childhood. I saved it because it's navy-blue leather, has a gold zipper, and says Saks Fifth Avenue and Made in England. It always looked like something I should save. I turn to January 23, 1961.

> Other people have feelings also. Do NOT eat any-
> one else's Milky Way. It will get you NOWHERE!

## REVERSE SHOT

WHEN I AM pre-pubescent chubby, and sick to death of not looking like my skinny sister, I come up with a brilliant idea. When I eat too much, I'll just throw it up.

Easier said than done. On my way to my father's office for a needed consultation, I catch him in the kitchen taking a swig of Seagram's straight from the bottle. My father looks weird when he does this in his suit and tie. And it's not the first time I've caught him sneaking a drink during his afternoon hours of saving sick people. My father does this a lot.

When he sees me, he puts the bottle back like a little boy whose mother has caught him in the cookie jar or jerking off. He mumbles something about having to go back to work. But he can't go yet. I have a life-saving question.

"Daddy, how can I make myself throw up?" I ask.

My father does not flinch, or even register surprise. He's not curious about the reason for my question.

"Put a tablespoon of salt in a glass of warm water and drink it," he says.

That sounds easy.

"Thank you, Daddy," I say, as I watch him slither back into his office.

Eager to follow his prescription, I get the salt, a glass, and head to the sink I once saw him pee in when he was too drunk to get to a bathroom. I fill the glass with hot water, add an extra tablespoon of salt because I'm so afraid of not getting it right, and gulp down the saline solution.

It feels like swimming in the ocean. My body starts to swell. The added bloat to my already bulging body makes me feel as wide and fat as an opera singer at the Met. As swollen as a dead fish washed up smelly on the shore.

I run to the small bathroom right next to the sunporch and fall down on my knees. I hang over the toilet, waiting for the heaving to begin. But nothing happens. I pretend a sound of vomiting in an effort to jumpstart the process, but relief does not come. I can't make myself throw up.

Whether my father has forgotten to tell me, or I did not hear, I honestly do not know. But I have no idea how far my fingers have to travel down my throat to expel my sugary demons. A failure at bulimia, a syndrome that won't be identified for another seventeen years, I thank my father for small favors.

# BEST BOY

THE DAY MY brother is born, *The Hallelujah Chorus* can be heard up and down the Eastern Seaboard. Like most men, my father has been waiting for a son. Someone to carry his name, move the patriarchy forward. Though I keep my name every time I marry, the perpetuation of Lobban is supposed to be my brother's job.

From my brother's first diaper change, it's obvious his gender is holier. Just by having that dangling thing between his legs, he's treated differently by both my mother and father.

He gets my father's name. He's a junior, a little replica of important things to come. Clearly, my brother will be groomed for greatness while my sister and I are already being groomed to be nice.

"It's not fair!" a voice inside cries out to no one who will hear.

I feel lacking and bare. Cheated out of something necessary for worldly success. It's not that I want that hanging thing. It seems unnecessary and in the way. I want the power that goes with it. The power I know I don't have. The power I will one day hope to get at Dartmouth College because if I can fit in there, great things will be possible for me, too.

## SUBTEXT

MY MOTHER HATES being a woman. She drinks her-
self into a terrifying oblivion in a futile attempt to drown her
red-hot resentment that men call the shots in the world. She
rages against the injustice and in a pathetic attempt at taking
control, she threatens to divorce my father.

"Who do you want to go with?" she asks. "Your father or me?"

Paralyzed by her question, I try to think it through.

"I don't know. I can't decide," I cry.

"You have to decide!" my mother yells. "Your father or
me!"

"I can't decide!" I sob, because I don't want either one of
them to hate me.

"Then go with him!" my mother says, deciding for me.
"He's got the money! He'll take care of you!"

My mother, a snake unable to shed its skin, stares with
venomous eyes. She hisses to herself, "I'm just the doctor's
*wife.*"

I don't understand my mother's self-inflicted accusation,
but her self-loathing is palpable. Obviously, being someone's
wife is as far as a female can fall.

Scared out of my little girl body, already so insufficient
and ill-formed, I abandon my gender. There is nothing good
about being a girl. Nothing good about dresses and skirts, and
having to keep your legs together so no one can get in. And

there is absolutely nothing good about the blood that gushes out of you when you get old enough to bleed.

Though I struggle like other girls to get my hair right, to lose weight so I can be as skinny as my sister and the pretty girls in the magazines, and to find the perfect pink lipstick so boys will want to kiss me—though I can't handle it for long when they do—it makes more sense to grow up and be just like my father.

## EMOTIONAL PREPARATION

MY FATHER HAS a morning ritual. He drinks a cup of coffee, smokes a cigarette after a five-minute wake-up coughing fit, takes a long shit on the toilet while he reads *The Wall Street Journal,* and then he gets up and shaves.

I stand outside the bathroom door, listening for the sound of flushing water. I knock to be polite, but my father knows it's me. I come in every morning before I go to school because my father and I are close. I'm going to be a surgeon someday. We are close in other ways, too. In ways I won't remember until I'm all grown up and my father is eighty-four and dying. Until it's safe for me to know what I'm working so hard to forget so I can stay alive.

Braving the smell of excrement and tobacco—each odor blotting out the other—I look at my father who is standing before the mirror in white boxer shorts. I love watching my father shave. Seeing my father make his skin smooth and kissable calms me down, like a Japanese tea ceremony that glues me to the present moment where everything is okay, even when it isn't.

The thick, white, shaving cream looks like the whipped cream I spray on my ice cream sundaes. I taste it and my mouth puckers in disappointment.

My father is careful with his razor, though sometimes he nicks his skin. He rips off a tiny piece of toilet paper and puts it on his chin which always looks funny when he forgets to take it off after he's dressed in his suit and fancy tie. I know he is better with a scalpel.

When my father's done, it's my turn to shave. Even though my skin is hairless and smooth and my brother is the real boy, I'm the oldest and the one who looks like my father's mother, God rest her soul. My father likes me extra for that. He was his mother's favorite, just like I am his even though I'm a girl.

Before I can shave, my father turns the razor's silver base and carefully removes the blade. He holds the red and blue striped can and with a quick push of his long, tapered finger shoots the cream into my palm. I love the hilly shape and the feel of the weight in my hand. I make a fist and move my fingers around. It's smooth and squishy like finger paint at school.

Mimicking my father, I spread the shaving cream over my cheeks and down the front of my neck. I take the razor and put it in my left hand. I turn it upside down and press it against the bottom of my neck. The pressure on my throat feels close and reassuring.

Stroke up. Stroke up. Stroke up.

Shaving feels good. Like clearing a path for something new. I turn my head from side to side in perfect imitation while my father watches with a closed-mouthed smile. He is so much easier to please than my mother.

By the time I get to Dartmouth, I'm only shaving my armpits and legs, but surely my early training by my father's side has prepared me well for manhood and the power coming with it.

## LINED SCRIPT

MY FATHER WRITES me a prescription when I am seven years old.

> Date: Feb.1958
> Name: Miss Lynn
> Address: 61 Gifford Ave.
>
> Rx: This ring belonged to my mother. It was her engagement ring. She liked it, even tho small. I hope you like it. I know you will! But consult your sister. I know both of you will do the right thing. Always do the right thing! And both of you keep your chin up!
>
> Love, Dad

I am overjoyed my father wants to give me his mother's engagement ring. I wonder if my mother knows. But I never tell my sister. As for "chin up," I guess he knows what we're going through.

## DEVELOPMENT

THE FIRST TIME I look down and see two fleshy mounds hanging off my chest, I am twelve years old. I don't know why my breasts are so big. The girls in my class are wearing training bras, but I'm already in the Olympics, way ahead in a race I didn't know I was running. No one has said anything to me, though I have caught my father staring once or twice.

I hate having to ask my mother for anything. And asking for a bra is especially mortifying. But I have nowhere else to turn. I go down the hall and stand outside her door. I hear Ricky scolding Lucy again. My mother loves *I Love Lucy*, and so do I. She makes us laugh. I wait for the commercial to come on because I need my mother to see *and* hear me.

"What do you want?" my mother says, when I open her door.

"I think I might need a bra," I say, half-showing her my chest.

An hour later, we are leaving the corset shop, and I am wearing a 34 B-sized bra with hard metal underwire that leaves red marks on my skin and feels like punishment.

Everyone is looking at my breasts now, these two big breasts that already need cupping. The girls snicker behind my back, and the boys are no longer looking at my face.

# DIALOGUE

ONE SUNDAY, WE visit my brother at Peddie, the boarding school he's sent to because my father wants to make a man out of him. He says my mother indulges him too much. I think he might be jealous because sending her only son away makes my mother sad.

As we walk around the Hightstown campus, Peddie's senior class president sees me in my blue empire dress. Cut right below my breasts, the dress is very stylish, but it makes my breasts look even bigger than they are. I round my shoulders and curve inward.

Late that afternoon, we listen to Peddie's radio station. A boy is talking about a girl who was walking around the campus. "She was wearing an empire dress," he says. "I could see her coming before she turned the corner. She was *prodigious.*"

I don't know what *prodigious* means, but I love being talked about by an older prep school boy. I think *prodigious* must be a good thing, a compliment. The boy must like me even though he is a senior, and I'm only in eighth grade.

As soon as we get home after a smelly ride on the New Jersey turnpike, I run up our shiny shellacked stairs to the Webster's Dictionary that's so big it has its own wooden stand and looks like an important statue. I turn the thin, membrane pages, searching for affirmation and dreaming of love. As my fingers move down the page, I am a miner about to strike gold.

Here it is!

*Prodigious!*

I read what defines me.

*Extraordinary.*

Yes! I think I am!

*Out of bounds.*

Wait. That doesn't sound good.

*Abnormal.*

My knees buckle beneath me.

## BACKLOT

MY MOTHER IS not without good qualities. Everyone knows how generous she is with extended family and friends. In 2017, I visit my Aunt Pauline, my mother's only sibling, to confirm that reality.

Eighty-nine, and as loving as my mother was not, Aunt Pauline lives in Tottenville, a small town at the far end of Staten Island. I love to visit her. Not just because she's the only person who can tell me things about my mother, but because I think she may really love me.

"Your mother liked to hang out with the rich kids when we were young," Aunt Pauline says. "I'd be at the soda fountain and your mother would be at the yacht club."

"You mean her taste for wealth started that early?" I say, somewhat surprised.

"Oh yes. When your mother married your father, everyone thought she was a princess," Aunt Pauline adds, as if she might have thought so, too.

Hearing this, I'm glad my observations about my mother and money are correct, but I am stunned to hear about her early greed.

"But she was really generous, right?" I counter, in an effort to mitigate my judgment.

"Oh yes," Aunt Pauline says. "Your mother bought your grandparents whatever they needed. That's how they got hearing aids. And whenever you got a new coat, your cousins got a new coat. Your cousin John wore all of your brother's clothes. He used to be the best dressed boy in PS 4."

While Aunt Pauline smiles at the memory, I remember how much my mother loved to shop. How she loved New York City. How the tiny island of Manhattan was her oasis in her dried-out Jersey City world.

## COSTUME SUPERVISOR

MY MOTHER LOVES to spend what she always calls "your father's money" at Lord & Taylor, B. Altman's, Best and Company, Bergdorf Goodman, and Saks Fifth Avenue. High-toned stores where she shops to dress her children well. Looking good is everything to my mother.

"Put that back," my mother says, moving me around like a designer getting ready to show her collection. "Try this on."

I hate the clothes my mother makes me wear, especially the gray coat and derby hat with the feather sticking out on the side. It makes me look even uglier than I am. And I especially hate my hair.

"Cut it right above the earlobes," my mother tells the barber.

I don't know why my mother wants me to look so bad. No prince will ever look at me like this.

## MEAL PENALTY

WHEN I GET hungry and my mother gets thirsty, she takes me to Reuben's on 58th Street where the waiters know our names. We push through the revolving door and are taken to a table where we watch the noisy crowd. As I sit down on Reuben's red, crackling leather seat, I feel like I'm sitting on history. I never have to look at a menu because I always have the same thing.

"My daughter will have a chicken salad sandwich on rye and a cream soda," my mother tells the old man in black who likes to flirt with her.

I love Reuben's chicken salad. The chunks of chicken swim in so much mayonnaise, they slide down my throat when I get tired of chewing. And I love cream soda because it's the sweetest in the world. My mother doesn't order much food.

"I'll have the matzo ball soup and a triple extra-dry Beef-eater martini with a twist of lemon," she says, as if our waiter doesn't already know.

My mother is always on a diet because she says she's fat. But I think she orders soup so she has something in front of her while I eat. I watch the matzo-balls float, then sink to the bottom of the bowl while my mother savors her martini.

As my lunch ends with a piece of strawberry-glazed cheese-cake shot through with confectionary steroids, my mother orders a double stinger. I try not to worry. All I'm waiting for is our visit to FAO Schwartz—my favorite store in the world—because my mother always buys me whatever I want.

## ART HOUSE

THE ARTS TO my mother are what medicine is to my father. When I am old enough not to embarrass her, my mother takes me to the Metropolitan Museum. I love the mummies in the Egyptian wing. The idea you can take everything with you when you die makes me glad I have a lot of stuff.

My mother and I also look at paintings, especially *The Skater*. Dressed in black and wearing a pointed hat, the handsome man is much younger than my father. As he balances on the ice, he stares down at my mother and looks like he's in love with her. I bet my mother would marry him if he wasn't a painting.

I like the Museum of Modern Art better because it's smaller and I don't have to walk around so much. When my mother shows me Picasso's *Guernica* and Monet's *Water Lilies*, the paintings feel just like my life.

When I first see *Guernica*, I get scared. If I could express emotion, I think I would cry. I don't know what the painting means, but I can hear people screaming. I can even hear the horse. The white, black, and gray colors remind me of the newspapers my father hides behind instead of talking. The bodies are cut in pieces like mine. Someone is throwing his arms up to God, and God can't hear him either. Someone is lying on the ground like my father when he's drunk and passed out on the floor. A woman is holding a dead baby who could have been me. *Guernica*, a name I can't even pronounce, takes my breath away every time I see it. I'm so happy to see the flowers.

When I walk into *Water Lilies*, I feel instantly better because the painting reminds me how life can also be. My mother and I sit down on a bench and let the magic of painted water wash over us. Blues, greens, pinks, and purples pour into our hearts and we are warmed by floral love. But I can never rest for long because I know *Guernica* is right around the corner.

## SOUNDTRACK

MUSIC IS THE background of our daily life. My mother turns on her Ampex, her top-of-the-line stereo, and blasts Beethoven, Tchaikovsky, Mozart, and Bach. The more my mother drinks, the louder the music gets. Aunt Pauline says our house always sounds like Radio City.

My mother loves opera and loves to sing along. I don't know why she sings with the men though, like Rodolfo instead of Mimi. Maybe it's because her voice is low and powerful like a man's. I'm glad she also loves Broadway musicals. Then I get to sing along, too.

Musicals teach me about life. Rodgers and Hammerstein make me think life is worth singing about. When Emile sings *Some Enchanted Evening*, my heart bursts with joy. I understand Emile. *This Nearly Was Mine*, too. But I think Nellie is stupid. Trying to wash a man out of your hair just sounds dumb. Julie Jordan is smarter, though not as smart as me because even before *What's the Use of Wondrin'* starts, I know the ending will be bad.

I would sing along with *The King and I*, but *Getting to Know You* sounds too friendly. I don't really want anyone to know me, though I wish I could whistle. It might make me feel less afraid.

And it would be nice to be a von Trapp child because when I sing *Do Re Mi*, I feel happy. *The Sound of Music* always puts a smile on my face. Until *Edelweiss* and I hear my mother singing along with the Captain and I hear how sad they are. It's better to hear her sing *Oh, What a Beautiful Mornin'* with Curly because morning *is* a beautiful thing. No one is drunk yet, and things really could go my way.

By the time I'm a teenager, I listen mostly to Frank Sinatra and Barbra Streisand because their voices neutralize something bad inside me. My mother must understand because she buys me all of their records, even though she comes in one night and smashes every single one because I didn't clean up my room the way she wanted.

But all in all, music helps me survive. Music is my heart link to my mother. Music is something I don't even know she is giving me.

## FORCED PERSPECTIVE

BECAUSE MY FATHER can afford it, my mother has a subscription to the opera. She sits me in a box at the Metropolitan Opera House in the days before Lincoln Center. I always go because opera makes my mother happy and no one else will. Certainly not my father. My father is tone deaf to my mother *and* to her music.

But there's a price for trying to please my mother. Opera is hard on my child-self. There are too many fat people singing in foreign languages about things I don't understand. Even after I read the wordy libretto. And every story ends up worse than it started. People are always dying. Mimi sings while she coughs herself to death. And Madame Butterfly, with the big black beehive wig, sticks a knife in her stomach because she doesn't know what else to do. Opera is depressing.

Ballet is a lot better, though I don't like ballerinas. They're too stiff and tight in their pink pointy shoes. I hate skinny girls lined up in rows. Starving robots revolving around each other, spinning in their own orbits, going nowhere. They're like the cotton candy that disappears in my mouth when we go to Madison Square Garden to the circus, or the rodeo, or the Ice Follies, or the Scots Guards with their bagpipes and plaid skirts, or that horse show with the big white horses called Lilliputians or Lipizzaners, or something like that.

I prefer the determination of the Rockettes. Women tapping. Women making noise. Women throwing up their legs and kicking their way to congruity.

I also love movies, especially on Radio City's big screen. Movies wipe out my worries. Except for maybe *Ben Hur*. Even though Charlton Heston is my boyfriend now, the chariot race is scary and the leper colony makes me cry. Probably because I feel mangled and outcast, too.

## CINEMA VERITE

THERE ARE REALITIES I try to run away from.

"I'm going to burn the house down while you're sleeping!" my mother yells after she's drunk enough alcohol to stop feeling her pain.

"No, Mommy! No!" I yell back, jumping out of bed to sniff for smoke.

"I'm going to kill you!" my mother yells, because the milk bottle has just slipped from my tiny hands, spilling milk and glass over the maid-polished floor. I run upstairs and hide in the closet at the end of the hall. Crouching behind my mother's moth-ball-smelling winter clothes, I wait until I hear her close her bedroom door.

"This isn't gold! This is junk!" my mother shouts, as she lifts up her nightgown to pee on the fruit bowl I proudly gave her on Christmas morning. As she shames me and my taste, the things I see on television seem more real.

"You're evil, mean, and ugly!" my mother says, branding me night, after night, after night.

It's hard forgetting the things my mother says and does. I'm better at forgetting what my father does because I need him to be my good parent. Every child must have one.

## VIDEO ASSIST

I LOVE MY television. My safe and scheduled universe is better than the one I have to live in. I like human beings boxed in and contained. Stories I can switch on and off. The dial on my television set is the only control I have.

Every day I come home from school, make a pre-dinner sandwich, grab a bunch of cookies, pour a giant glass of Hawaiian Punch whose very color makes me smile, and trudge up the stairs to the safety of my room. I close the door and turn on my TV because my mother lets me have one in my room.

I do my homework, write papers, and study for exams in front of my television because my TV friends are dependable. Especially Lucy, Ricky, Fred and Ethel, George and Gracie, Roy and Dale, the Beaver, Dobie Gillis, Dr. Kildare, Lassie, Flicka, the Andersons, and the Kramdens.

I also love my friends in the movies. Fred and Ginger, Mickey and Judy, Spencer and Kate, Cary, Claudette, Jimmy, Gary, Kirk, Clark, Bette, Audrey, and Marilyn. I love them because they never leave me. I watch my friends in my TV until Uncle Johnny Carson says goodnight and the screen is filled with the flag and static fuzz.

"Open a book and improve your mind!" my mother yells, not understanding I want to lose it.

Anyway, books are my mother's obsession. Except for *Jane Eyre,* and the books I have to read for school, I'm not interested in reading.

"You're going to ruin your eyes!" my mother screams, as if I care.

Blindness is a small price for having family and friends.

## BLACKOUT

I ALSO FIND solace at the theater. When I see Moss Hart's *Act One* on my mother's bed and read "The theater is the refuge of an unhappy child," I think, *exactly.*

My mother takes me to my first Broadway play when I'm sixteen. *You Can't Take It with You.* Watching actors and actresses living life onstage is thrilling. I feel alive. Sitting in the audience and laughing with other people is unmitigated pleasure.

I sit beside my mother in the darkness of the Brooks Atkinson Theater and watch Maureen Stapleton, George Grizzard, Piper Laurie, and Pat Hingle live out their heightened lives in The Glass Menagerie. Four rows ahead, and just a few feet above me, they're so close I can hear them breathe. I can even see them cry. The Wingfields may be characters in a play, but they make me feel more normal than my friends in the TV because they're flesh and blood alive. Their unhappiness is real and living right in front of me.

The theater becomes the only dark place I feel safe in. House lights dim and I am comforted by the requisite hushing of the people around me. If someone doesn't stop talking, the culprit is led away. Clear and simple boundaries. The cravings of a child.

In my holy church of make-believe, I watch life illuminated in proscribed time and space. Scenes are carefully constructed. People know what to say and what will happen next. Existence is a predictable force.

I collect *Playbills* like I save church bulletins. The bulletins remind me of God, but my *Playbills* are proof of His existence.

# ABOVE-THE-LINE EXPENSES

I ATTEND THE Bergen School for Girls, a private school at the end of our street. I go to Bergen School from the time I enter kindergarten at four years old, until I'm sixteen and graduate from high school. Bergen's motto, "Nova Spes Cum Phoebo" aka "Everyday a New Beginning," makes me feel hopeful.

Private school is most likely my mother's idea, though I'm not completely sure because my father never weighs in on anything except what medicine to take, his four years in the Philippines saving wounded soldiers, how snow tires are as good as chains when driving in the snow, and the difference between a cantilever and suspension bridge.

But private school is fine with me. Especially because my mother says bad things happen in public school. I don't know what they are except maybe picking up a Jersey City accent and getting knocked up by some Catholic boy. But mostly, I think my siblings and I go to private school because we can. The Lobban children deserve small classes where we can be seen, heard, and attended to, unlike at home. Not to mention we might get the best education money can buy.

There are boys at Bergen from kindergarten through eighth grade. I love having boys in my class. Especially Jerry Aquino in fourth grade. His mother dresses him in a boy suit and tie and when I stand next to him, his starched white shirt makes me feel buzzy inside. I also like Jimmy Hayes in seventh grade with his big boy body and easy laugh. Jimmy's the boy I spin bottles for. But the bottle always points to pimply Larry or Noel, a boy so skinny and tall, his jacket cuffs don't reach his wrists so his white shirt cuffs always look like collars.

At the end of eighth grade, I have to say goodbye to boys because Bergen's high school is only girls, and not too many girls at that. There are thirty girls in the high school, and only six in my senior class. This actually works for me. Since I have been trained from birth to be a wunderkind—well-behaved, well-dressed, well-adjusted, high achieving, and rule-abiding—it is easy to excel. I can be a large fish in the tiny Bergen pond. I can swim mightily in its waters and make my mother glad.

## DISASTER FILM

I LIED. THERE is another book I read. I read it all the time. I even hide it under my bed so no one can take it away. That would be awful because I need *The Merck Manual.* The fat black book contains an incredible amount of necessary information for my survival since deep down I know there is something terribly wrong with me.

When I open *The Merck Manual,* I'm shocked by how many horrible diseases there are. It's a wonder anyone is still alive. I don't read everything. That would take forever. Mostly the diagnosis part so I can figure out what's wrong with me. Then the prognosis part to see if I will survive. The time I think I have leukemia, I'm sad to see how short my life will be. I tend to skip the treatment part because I don't think what's wrong with me can really be fixed.

My sister gets sick a lot with asthma and bronchitis and gets to stay home from school. My father is always listening to her chest and giving her medicine and my mother is always asking how she feels.

One morning, I'm sure I have the mumps.

"Stop your faking and get dressed for school," my mother says.

The next day, I know the spots on my stomach are German Measles.

"You are such a hypochondriac," my mother says, calling me a name I don't understand.

## PROPERTY ACQUISITION

THERE'S A GUN in our house. My father operated on a Jersey City police detective who was so grateful, he gave my father a Colt 45 and a clip of bullets. I have to do something before someone gets shot and killed.

After everyone goes to bed or passes out, I sneak into my father's office. I do a quick sweep of the room because I've watched Joe Friday on *Dragnet*. When I find the gun, hidden in the back of the top drawer of my father's oak desk, I see the clip of bullets lying next to it.

I pick up the gun. It feels weighty and dangerous in my hand. I quickly put it down. I dare not take it. It is enough to steal the bullets.

With the clip in hand, I tiptoe up the backstairs to my mother's library with floor to ceiling bookcases. In full monkey mode, I climb the shelves of my mother's treasured books. When I reach the top, I drop the clip behind *The World's Great Religions* because it's the tallest book.

With the bullets safely hidden, I sneak back into bed. I can rest now. Because whoever has the gun will never have the bullets. My sister may be trying to keep the peace, but I am keeping everyone alive.

## SCRIPT SUPERVISOR

EVERY NIGHT BEFORE bed, I perform a ritual that makes sleeping possible.

I start at my door. I leave it half open so there are no surprises. I shut my dresser drawers, close my closet doors, and move to my mirrored mantle. I look at my face. I take off my National Honor Society necklace and lay it down. I take off my high school ring, and put it in the middle of the V shape the necklace makes. I take off my black and gray speckled glasses, and lay them carefully over the necklace and ring, angling them just so. If anything is not right, it's glasses, ring, and necklace back on, and it's back to the door. I leave the door half open. Dresser drawers closed. Closet doors closed. I move to the mantle. I take off my necklace and lay it down. I take off my ring and put it just right. I take off my glasses. I move to my chair and push it into my not-so-vanity table. I turn to my bed, and carefully pull down my purple flowered bedspread. But wait! The chair is not pushed in all the way. So, it's bedspread back, chair out, glasses, ring, and necklace back on.

I'm at the door. Half open. Dresser drawers shut. Closet doors shut. Shut tight. Mantle. Face. Necklace. Ring. Glasses. Chair in. All the way in. Bedspread. Folded. Neatly. Down. Yes! I kneel and say the Lord's Prayer, repeating the ending exactly three times. Our father who art in heaven—and not in my bed—Hallowed be thy name. Thy kingdom come—and not through my door—Thy will be done—and so it always is—On earth as it is in heaven—please God let me die—Give us this day our daily bread—and my cookies and my candy and my ice cream and my cake—And forgive us our trespasses—for I know I am bad—As we forgive those who trespass against us—I won't tell, I won't tell—And lead us not into temptation—it feels good sometimes—But deliver us from evil—that is me—For thine is the kingdom, and the power, and the glory. For thine is the kingdom, and the power, and the glory. For thine is the kingdom, and the power, and the glory—*is my ring in the right place?*

## ROOM TONE

I AM DESPERATE to have my own room. It's not fair my brother gets to have one, especially at the end of the hall and out of the direct line of fire. I have to share a room with my sister that's yellow, a color I hate. I have to wait a long time for privacy. It comes when I am twelve.

I think my mother moves me into the guest room because guests have stopped coming. Even my mother's best friend, Cyrene Dear, who's twenty-seven years older and owns a lot of newspapers and who we call Besta which is Norwegian for grandmother, even Besta doesn't come anymore. It's too bad because when Besta visits, my mother is on her best behavior. She doesn't drink as much or provoke my father so he can rage back like a scary monster. In fact, Besta visits are so peaceful I mark them in my diary as "The days Mommy and Daddy don't fight." It is the only page my mother rips out the night she finds my diary.

"Stand up!" my mother instructs from the head of the table as Besta enters the dining room. "Sit up straight," she admonishes, as soon as I sit down.

I lift my chest and try to feel cheerful, but the effort is exhausting. I glance down at the extra forks and spoons gleaming with silver light and feel an overwhelming burden. When I see the extra glasses for milk and water, I wish I was thirsty.

My mother, dressed in a black dress and diamond pin, sits at one end of the table. My father, in a suit and tie, is at the other. I just want the meal to be over.

"No, you may not be excused," my mother says. "Not until everyone is finished and you've cleaned your plate." Then she reminds me of starving Chinese children.

As I force down the last lima bean, I look at my mother and notice she looks friendlier in the candlelight. But when she picks up the dinner bell and rings for Lulu to take the dishes, and tells Thelma to bring in the finger bowls so we can clean our fingers with lemon water, I am sickened by the charade.

## BEHIND THE SCENES

EXCEPT FOR MY mother's bedroom, the guest room is the prettiest room in the house. I pass by it in the morning and see Besta sitting up in bed with a stack of newspapers. I watch my mother go in and serve her breakfast on a white wooden tray. Then she closes the door.

I don't know what they do in there, but they're in there for hours. Though I like Besta, I don't really understand why my mother loves her so much. Years later, I ask my father an out of the blue question.

"I remember when Besta came to visit, she and Mommy would spend hours together in the guest room with the doors closed. Do you think Mommy might have been a lesbian?"

My question is a bold one, but it's not like I remember them having much sex. Maybe twice besides the obvious three times that gave them children. The time in Jersey City when I heard the bed banging against the wall. My mother was moaning like she was being tortured. I ran down the hall to their room, but the door was locked so I looked through the keyhole. All I could see was my father's naked back going up and down on her. Then everything got quiet, and I ran back to bed. A few minutes later, my mother came to the door.

"How would you like another brother or sister?" she asked, grinning.

I didn't see the connection.

"I'll kill myself!" I said, because outside of her setting the house on fire, another sibling would be the worst thing that could happen to me.

The second time I know they had sex was during the summer at our lake house. It was a Wednesday afternoon, the day my father came up from Jersey City just to spend the day. They went into their room and locked the door. After my father left, my mother got extra drunk.

"I don't want another baby!" she started screaming. She said she was going to put an aspirin in her vagina to stop a baby which still sounds weird to me.

But those are the only times I remember them having sex. I figure if my mother was a lesbian, it might explain a lot.

"No!" my father says with uncharacteristic force. "Your mother was a healthy heterosexual!"

## MACGUFFIN

A WEEK BEFORE my twelfth birthday, my mother takes a trip to Europe with Besta. Her first and only time out of the country, she sails on the United States Lines because she's too afraid to fly.

Saying goodbye to my mother in a stateroom filled with flowers and fruit, I fear I will never see her again. I cry all the way down the plank to the pier, and as I watch the giant ship separate from the dock, I am sobbing. I don't want to be left alone with my father and my indifferent siblings. I know there will be perks with my mother away—I'm going to smoke cigarettes—it feels too dangerous to be without her. My mother must also be afraid because her first letter, written on translucent United States Lines paper, arrives within the week.

> Friday Morning 9 AM
> Dear Bob and my Kookies,
>
> The sea has been as smooth as glass and if it were always like this, I could come across in the canoe. I have just finished three laps around the sun deck and have not seen a white cap or a wave.
>
> Yesterday it was hard to say goodbye to the country, as well as all of you. I watched as we went through the narrows, and was a guide to some

people from the west who were unfamiliar with the geography and landmarks.

After lunch yesterday, I thought I would go to my room to rest, but we had lifeboat drill. The life jackets (exactly like the ones the children had) certainly don't do anything for my figure. By the time I found my station, the boat would have gone down, and my companions all come up from tourist class to the station in the lounge. One criticism of the Titanic sinking was that they concentrated on saving first class passengers, and I wondered if they would pay attention to me and my ill-dressed friends if something went wrong.

I'm glad my mother is in First Class because it sounds safer, but she sounds mean when she says lesser-dressed people might kill her.

After the lifeboat drill, I went to the cocktail lounge and had *one* scotch and soda. It cost 35 cents. Then I took a bath and rested until seven whereupon I dressed and went to dinner. They have an orchestra in the dining room, and it's all very gay. There's only one sitting at meals, and I am sitting at Dr. Sheedy's (the ship's surgeon) table for six. One couple, in their early seventies and well-preserved, are elegant and polite Jewish

people from Cleveland, Ohio. He is an industri-
alist and an avid patriot. They are fun and I like
them very much. A lone man, Dr. Dwight Hutchin-
son, is a chemical physicist with the Atomic Energy Commission who is going abroad to lecture at
Oxford and all the other great universities. He is
slight and under-nourished looking, but he must
be virile enough for he has three boys and a baby
girl who came six years after the others. Another
lone woman is a young old maid on vacation from
her secretary's job. It is the first trip abroad for all
of us.

After dinner I considered the 10 o'clock movie,
but it was Mickey Rooney and I can't bear him. I
walked around the deck. The sea was black and so
was everything else, but the stars were beautiful.
It seems fantastic to me that I shall sail for five
days before we reach land.

When I came inside and wandered into the ball-
room, I saw Senator Byrnes and his wife sitting
alone. I went over to introduce myself. They were
wonderful to me and talked a lot, and asked me
to sit with them. They are delightful and fun and
have soft Southern accents. They are both quite
elderly but obviously young in heart. He made me
like Democrats.

After I left them, I had two 35 cent scotches in the lounge and then went to my room. We had to put the clock ahead 75 minutes and by now it was 11:45 PM. I was so charged up that I took a Seconal and had a dream about Jersey City.

Following breakfast this morning, I went up to the radio room and sent a radiogram to Lynn. It cost $5.70, but I feel badly to miss her birthday.

I feel badly, too. It will be the first time I won't have a party.

I am enjoying every minute. I shall miss all of you, but I intend to enjoy myself to the fullest. I can't explain the thrill I am getting out of this. Thank you, Bob, for letting me do this. I love you very much and think it's time we stopped being mean to each other for there could be no one else for me.

Love to all, and kiss the kids for me.

Pug

I'm glad my mother sounds happy, but hearing her say she loves my father makes me think she's lost her mind.

# STANDBY

BY THE TIME my mother arrives at the Hotel Connaught in London, my letter, written on thin blue Aerogramme paper marked with eleven cents postage, is waiting.

> August 31, 1961
> Dear Mom,
>
> After you left, I went home with Kathy in her Mercadiz Benz. That car is nice, but it is too small. I am sorry that I cried, but I just couldn't help it. How was your voyage across the ocean? Did you get seasick? Have you made any new friends on the ship? How is London? I have a million questions to ask you. I saw a new kind of school shoe at Seymour's. They're only $3.95. I can't think of anything else to say except that I miss you and love you.
>
> x x x x x x
> Love, Lynn

I end all my letters with multiple kisses. I think my mother must be glad to get them. Besta must be glad too, because she sends me a postcard.

On one side of "The Royal Family at Balmoral" are a boy and girl wearing plaid skirts which looks okay on the girl, but really weird on the boy. They're sitting on a plaid blanket spread on a lawn that's even bigger than our lawn at the Lake. A tall, thin man in a suit who looks like my father, only with hair, is sitting there, too. And there's a woman wearing a dress like my mother's. Everyone is staring at the baby sitting on the man's lap.

The family looks just like mine. Everyone is posed, and the mother is barely touching the baby's fingers. She looks like she doesn't want to be there. When I turn the postcard over, I see Besta's flowery handwriting.

> Dear Lynn,
>
> How would you like to baby sit for Prince Andrew? Your mother is taking good care of me. I am sure you are taking good care of your Daddy.
>
> With love,
>
> Besta

Getting a postcard from the most important person in my mother's life makes me feel special, but I don't know what "taking good care" of my father means. I know my mother takes good care of Besta, but how am I supposed to take care of my father? He's so much bigger and smarter. Just hearing Besta say that makes me feel like I'm already doing a bad job.

# SCENIC ARTIST

AS MY MOTHER and Besta travel through Europe, my mother describes the places she's been. She writes to my father from the Victoria-Jungfrau Grand Hotel in Interlaken, Switzerland.

> Monday 1:30 PM
> Dear Bob,
>
> It is absolutely impossible for me to adequately describe this day and this place. Immediately below me is a vast green park, and rising from that are mountains (the Bernese Alps) which rise 8,000 ft. Behind them stands the "Jungfrau," 16,000 ft of snow and ice which I find hard to believe is real. It is the most magnificent sight. The air is crisp and clear, and it makes one feel like a million dollars. There are beautiful flowers growing everywhere. It is so beautiful it almost hurts.
>
> Lynn's letter was here when I arrived. She has been very faithful. I bought the girls bracelets in London, and a Swiss Army Knife for Robbie that does everything except wash dishes.
>
> This afternoon we shall take a boat ride on Lake Thun, and tomorrow we will go up the Jungfrau.

I hesitate to think of leaving the train and walking up the few steps and feet to the Summit. An extremely thin American woman did it yesterday and was winded. Others slipped and fell, and I can't see risking an accident. A few mountain sleighers went off into a crevasse yesterday, and a man was killed last week when he fell from the rises of the Wetterhorn. Some people here speak of mountains with bitterness for they have claimed many lives. One man hung by a rope (he was dead of course) for two years before it was possible to get his body down, and another who perished 50 years ago was uncovered in a snow slide, his body perfectly preserved as a young man.

Reading my mother's letter is like watching an episode of Boris Karloff's *Thriller.*

On Friday we shall go to Venice. I expect we will only stay three days and be in Paris by the 22nd. I've done so much that I can hardly believe I've only been in Europe for one week tonight. I wish Bob, that you would write to me.

I love and miss all of you!

My mother's excitement pours off the page, but I hear her loneliness about my father. When a postcard comes from Venice, she sounds even worse.

> Sept 19, 1961
> Dear Lynn,
>
> Today I crossed inside this bridge called "The
> Bridge of Sighs," because prisoners being led to
> the jail or prison were heard to sigh as they took
> their last glimpse of the outside world.
>
> Love,
> Mother

The woman I only know as Mommy has never called herself Mother before. She sounds far away. Like she doesn't
want to come home. But I need her to. I don't know why, but I
should not be left alone this long with my father.

## AUTEUR

I NAG MY father to write my mother until he finally does.
His one and only letter looks like his scribbling on a prescription pad.

> Thurs. 9/21 My dear Pug - not Plug - The storm
> passed during the night, we had no damage here.
> No school for the kids, as it was raining (we had
> very little). The wind was blowing tho this aft. Ex-
> cept for some wind, everything was ok. Took ev-
> erybody to the store for tennis shoes at 5. Am very
> glad you did not take off this Thurs. from France

& blow into the N. Atlantic storm; sea-sickness
& a very bad crossing. Trust this time next week
you (could) cross in a canoe - even tho it may be
tough. Have a good crossing. Will meet you at the
dock. Hope it's early or late - better late, so the
children can also meet you. Nothing new here.
Rather busy. A bleeding ulcer at Christ - an intes-
tinal cyst at the M.C. - maybe I was more radical
years ago than now. Now I'm conservative. Have a
very good time. I'm marking time. Will see you at
the dock. Love, Bob Sr.

I don't understand what my father means by "marking
time." Maybe he's tired of being the only parent. My mother writes one more time before she sails home on the Queen
Elizabeth II.

27 September 1961
Dear Bob,

Yesterday I went to Cunard to obtain my railroad
ticket to Cherbourg, and Besta checked on her
flights at Pan-American. Then, as all good Americans who drink, we went to Fauchon's where we
both purchased five bottles of brandy or liquors
which may be brought into the United States duty
free. Scotch and other whiskeys are much cheaper,
though by far the largest   savings are on vintage

champagne. I know you are always interested in a bargain, and it will create the nicest hangovers.

This morning I went to the hairdresser where I spoke in sign language and had my hair done. Even Lynn would not recognize me. I have not gained weight. In fact, I have lost four pounds.

I can hardly wait to see you. My love has been intensified to a plane I had not thought possible, and I am sure I have found some answers to my needed change in outlook on things.

When we meet my mother at the pier, I am as hopeful as she is for a new beginning. She lights up when she sees us, and while she gives us a hug, a pigeon shits on my father's hat. As we walk to get her luggage, she slips two gold bracelets into my father's pocket so she won't have to pay customs.

## INTERNATIONAL RIGHTS

AFTER MY MOTHER returns, I find her black leather Trip Abroad diary with a world clock embedded in its cover.

Date: September 5, 1961. Place: Aboard the SS United States. At 4 A.M. this morning, I watched as we came alongside the pier at the French Port of Le Havre. There was not much I could see from a port hole but there were a few men in dark clothes standing around watching while a crane lowered a gangway into place at some lower reach of the ship. I slept for a while and awakened at 6:45 A.M. Looking out once more, I was distressed to see a small black van from where three men unloaded a coffin, shaped in the European manner and embellished with a handsome silver crucifix. The ropes of the lifting gear were wrapped around it, but I turned away as the slow lifting of the dead body began. I vow it lies somewhere in the hold along with the refrigerated bodies of two who died en route. One a Spanish Grandee who died peacefully in his 82-year-old sleep while his wife was at lunch. He had left his native land during the Spanish revolution and I suppose he will be returned there for burial. The other that of an American on holiday who died of a heart attack at the early age of fifty leaving his wife in a state of shock and the prospect of a return to the United States on this same ship, the joy of a holiday together gone.

It is my mother's only entry to herself.

## JUMP CUT

MY BROTHER IS the lucky one. Except for the "stupid" label my mother gives him, I always want what he has. I want his room down the hall, getting to go to boarding school, his shoeshine box where he locks up all his money, his drum set to pound out his rage, and his new Swiss Army knife.

When my mother returns from Europe, she gives my sister and me 18K gold bracelets with tiny dangling charms of the places she has been. A double-decker bus, the Eiffel Tower, and a Swiss chalet. Little baby souvenirs hanging from a golden chain.

My brother gets a knife. A Swiss Army knife colored a dazzling cherry red, with a bright white cross that looks so powerful and holy it might even be able to save me. I get close to it once, when my brother and I are fighting.

We fight a lot, my brother and I. Maybe I've picked up my mother's skill and am an expert at provocation, or maybe my big sister know-it-all attitude is honestly obnoxious. But when one of our fights boil over, my brother threatens me with the Swiss Army.

"I'll cut you," my brother says.

"Go ahead," I say, sticking out my arm because I refuse to be terrorized by my pipsqueak brother.

Undaunted, my brother jabs the knife toward me. It catches on my white long-sleeved blouse. As he rips a bloodless tear, I scream as if he stabbed me and run into my mother's room.

"Stop your fighting and leave your brother alone," my mother says.

# BLEED THROUGH

I START MENSTRUATING when I'm twelve. All I know about this thing my mother calls "the curse" is that she gets it once a month and it always causes her pain, some of my friends have it, though no one really talks about it, and I'm probably going to get it, too. Thank God Carol Rokaszak, who knows about everything because she watches *American Bandstand,* is in the adjacent toilet the day my period—a word that sounds better as punctuation—pays its first visit.

Since Bergen School has no gym, on Tuesdays and Thursdays we have to trudge ten blocks to the YWCA. Tuesdays are gym days which I hate because I'm always the last one picked for basketball. Thursdays we go swimming. Even though taking off my clothes, putting on an ugly bathing suit, taking it off wet, drying off my body, putting my clothes back on, and having to dry my hair are a big pain in the ass at the end of a long school day, I love to swim.

Today, we're practicing for the Red Cross Lifesaver test. I can already flip a person on her back and save her from drowning which could come in handy with my mother someday, though she'll probably drown me before I can save her.

When practice ends, I head to the bathroom because I have to pee. I'd pee in the pool—there's probably enough chlorine to burn the skin off my body—but I'm afraid someone might feel the water getting warm.

It's not easy pulling down my wet bathing suit so I can sit down and pee, but once my cold suit is around my ankles, it feels so good to be relieved. I wish I could be relieved of so many things. I grab a few scratchy pieces of Young Women's Christian Association toilet paper out of a metal dispenser, and wiping myself in one front to back motion, I am changed forever.

"Oh no," I cry.

"Are you okay?" Carol asks, as she's flushing her toilet.

"I don't know. I wiped myself and it's *brown*."

Clearly, I missed a *Merck Manual* symptom of some terminal disease.

"It's okay," Carol says. "You just got your friend."

My *friend?*

"Don't worry. I have it, too," Carol says from the other side of the door. "Just put a bunch of toilet paper in your underpants and go home and tell your mother."

As Carol goes off to get dressed, I try to take in this allegedly normal event. I grab a wad of toilet paper as directed, stuff it into my underpants, dress as quickly as I can, and waddle home.

When I come through the front door, I'm glad my mother is home. She's just come back from a matinee of *The Happiest Girl in the World* and the album is already playing louder than I can yell. As a woman sings, "The happiest girl in the world is the one who is blessed with your love," I think, yeah, I already know this. I find my mother in the sunporch with a scotch and a book.

"I think I got my period," I say.

My mother looks up and grins. I don't know why she's so excited, like I've just told her I've been awarded the Nobel Prize. She takes me to her upstairs bathroom, opens a drawer I've never seen before, and hands me a "napkin." She says she will buy me a box of Kotex, a sanitary belt, and a few pairs of rubber pants for days when I bleed so much, I need protection from myself. Then she says, "Go tell your father."

I am not prepared for this.

"Why do I have to tell Daddy?" I ask, because I don't want to tell my father.

"Do as I say," my mother says.

As I knock, then crack open the door to my father's office, I see my father smoking at his desk. The air is thick with tobacco fog. He's writing on a patient's chart.

"Excuse me, Daddy," I say, hating to interrupt important work.

"Hello, Miss Lynn," my father says, barely looking up.

"Mommy said to tell you I got my period," I say, as quickly as I can and with as little feeling as possible.

My father stops writing. He puts out his cigarette in the ashtray filled to overflowing, and looks ahead as if something's on his mind. Then he reaches into his pants pocket, takes out a five-dollar bill, and hands it to me.

# NEGATIVE COST

WHEN I GET my period and Besta stops visiting, my mother moves me into the guest room. Wallpapered white with pink roses and climbing green vines, the room is unusual because it has two doors. Entrances or exits, depending on how you look at things. One door opens into the hallway, and the other into the TV room where I watch Peter Pan fly to Neverland and Dorothy sing herself over the rainbow because she wants to be somewhere else. The only difference between Dorothy and me is that when Dorothy goes from black and white to color, and then back to black and white, I'm still wishing I was anywhere but home.

The furniture in the room is a matching mahogany set. The tall stately dresser stands like a sentry at the door. A slant-top desk with secret compartments where I hide all my writing until my mother finds it and throws it away, is to the left of my bed. My double bed, in the middle of the room, can be seen by anyone who comes in either door. The vanity table on my right is my TV's resting place because I'm too embarrassed to use the table in any other way.

I love having my own room, except when my mother comes in and screams, "This is not your room. This is Dorothy's room! All this furniture belonged to Dorothy and your father!"

I had no idea the furniture once belonged to my father and Dorothy, his first wife who happens to live halfway down our street. Sometimes I pass Dorothy on my way to school, but I never make eye contact. She looks like a skinny crow waiting to swoop down and carry me away.

But having my own room is a good thing, even though the night my mother catches me singing *Don't Rain On My Parade* is horrible.

"Who do you think you are, singing and dancing around with that ugly fat body?" my mother screams and I jump so high I almost hit the ceiling.

I watch her exit like an actress who has just stolen the show with a walk-on part. But I don't let her silence me because singing and dancing are the only outlets I have after TV and food. Though decades will pass before I can perform with complete abandon, and then only when a director gives me permission to fly.

## CINEMATOGRAPHER

In the darkness we see a shape.
Long spidery arms,
spidery legs wobbling to the bed.
The shape pulls back the covers and sits down.
We see lines and skin,
thin folds of skin falling from a neck.
We know this shape.

We know the face, the nose, the mouth,

the eyes that do not look back at us.

We blind ourselves to what presses down

and compress it into one tiny black dot.

We hurl it back into a space so vast and empty,

it will not be seen for many years.

Until one day, when her guard is down,

she will see the dot,

full of forgotten and fragmented life,

floating before her.

All will burst forth.

She will not want to look.

She will not want to see.

She will want to gouge us out like Oedipus before her.

## FILL

I ALWAYS REMEMBER my father sleeping in my bed, but I never question why. Why, in a house full of bedrooms, he comes into my single bed in the room I share with my sister.

I remember feeling his warm bony bottom pressing against mine and how I want to move away. How I wake up smelling alcohol and cigarettes too close to my face.

I remember staring at the shadows of the buses moving on the wall and holding my breath to see if I can die.

I remember waking up in vomit in the middle of a night and my father telling me I ate too much fried shrimp at my mother's cocktail party.

I remember my father crossing the hall when I move into the guest room because I never forget the night my mother comes in and turns on the light.

## PYRO-TECHNICIAN

IN THE DARKEST time of night which is really morning, I am dead to the world and everything in it, fast asleep in the double bed my father once shared with Dorothy.

"Too bright! Too bright!" my eyes cry.

Waking up, I see my mother raging at the door. She's flicked on the overhead light.

*"Why are you sleeping with your daughter?"* my mother screams.

 I wonder who she's talking to.

*"Why are you in bed with your daughter?"* my mother screams again.

I turn my head to the left and see my father lying next to me. But before I can think too much about it, my father catapults from my bed and turns my mother's aria into a parental duet.

"You drunken son-of-a-bitch!" my father yells as if the mere implication he might be doing something wrong is pure blasphemy

Terrified he's going to kill my mother this time, I'm surprised when he doesn't even hit her. He runs past her and disappears into the darkness of the hallway.

*Daddy!*

He never comes back.

Turning and walking away, my mother never ever talks about or mentions this night. But in one electrifying moment, she banishes my father forever. It's too late for damage done, but whatever has been happening is over. And though my mother's rage feels like a jealous spouse whose husband has left her bed for another's, it is my mother who comes to my rescue. My mother who finally puts an end to it.

The next day, Dorothy's bed is moved out of my room and replaced with a single white-framed bed that my mother covers with a bedspread of lilacs.

## BOY MEETS GIRL

AFTER MY FATHER, the most important man in my life is Frank Sinatra. Our love affair begins after my mother throws my father out of my room.

The first time I see *Young at Heart,* I swoon every time Frank comes on the screen. Though there are other actors and actresses—Doris Day, Gig Young, Ethel Barrymore, and Dorothy Malone who play Laurie, Alex, Jessie, and Fran—I only have eyes for Frank who plays Barney Sloan.

Barney is my kind of guy. Tortured, talented, and completely lacking in self-esteem. As he plays a barroom piano with a cigarette drooping out of his mouth, he sings *Someone to Watch Over Me* as if the whole world is on his skinny narrow shoulders. In that instant, Frank Sinatra's voice invades my body and forever takes me hostage.

"Sometimes when you're on the outside looking in, you see some things other people can't," Barney says.

I know just what he means. I see everything too, and no one loves me either.

## STOP ACTION

THROUGHOUT MY CHILDHOOD, sorrow presses down on me like gravity gone crazy. I know my mother is also sad because she talks about killing herself all the time.

"I'm going to drown myself in the tub!" she threatens.

I glue my ear to her locked bathroom door. Terrified by the sound of water blasting from her faucets, I bang on the door until my fists are red and stinging hot.

"I'm going to jump!" my mother yells.

As she throws her leg over the banister to hurl herself over the railing so she can crack her head open on the floor below, I pull on her nightgown with the full weight of my nine-year-old Superman self.

"Let me out!" my mother screams, as my father drives our car over The George Washington Bridge.

While she pulls on the car door's handle, I press on the lock until my fingers hurt.

"I'm going to drown myself in the lake!" she says, walking in fully-clothed so her heavy raincoat can pull her down to the mucky bottom.

Suspended in the summer air, I wait in the pitch-black night, listening to the sound of lapping water. When my mother finally drags herself onto dry land, she walks right past me.

## DISSOLVE

I DON'T KNOW why my mother takes so many pills, or why one night she threatens to take all the red ones.

"I'm going to kill myself," she says in the darkness of the sun porch, holding up a vial of Seconals, the pills that help her sleep.

Her threats are nothing new, but I grow weary.

"Go ahead and take them," I say. "But if you do, I will, too."

"Go ahead," my mother says, smiling.

"I will!" I shout, taking the vial and removing six pills. "I'm just going to get some water!"

Storming into the kitchen, I put the pills on the counter and turn on the faucet. As the water runs, I pull apart each capsule. I shake the white powder into the sink and as it disappears down the drain, I rinse both sides of each pill. But when I put them back together, the sides don't fit. Each pill looks puckered and empty. I hope my mother is too drunk to notice.

With six collapsed pills in hand, I return to the sunporch ready to confront my mother who is still sitting in the dark with her pills and her scotch. I thrust out my hand, trusting she can't see.

"Go ahead and take them," she sneers.

But I can't. I'm too afraid. I don't want to swallow the pills for fear I might fall asleep and die. Instead, I accept my defeat and stomp up the stairs to watch *The Donna Reed Show* where parents love their children.

## SET MEDIC

I ALWAYS WONDER where my mother is going to take her life when she says she's going to take it. I find out in 1964 when, without announcement, she swallows all of her pills. Seconals, Libriums, and Miltowns, the drugs my father and his doctor friends give her to navigate life. I never understand why she needs so many pills. It's not like they make her happy or ever keep her quiet.

Whenever my mother does not come down for dinner, I'm glad. It means I can eat really fast and get back upstairs in time to see the end of *The Early Show*, the movie I watch every day at five o'clock. I usually miss the last fifteen minutes because the movie ends at 6:30 and my mother says dinner *has* to be at 6:15. I don't why she doesn't want me to know the ending of a story.

A few hours later, I'm watching *Peyton Place* because it makes my life feel simpler. Watching Allison MacKenzie manage her crazy life is inspiring. As the theme song is playing out the credits, I head into the bathroom to brush my teeth.

When I step into the hall, I am startled by the silence. My mother and father aren't fighting. There's no music. Not even *Stop the World – I Want to Get Off,* the musical my mother just saw and has been playing nonstop for the last three days.

I look into my mother's room. It's dark, but I can see her lying in her bed because the blinds are slightly open and the streetlight is streaming in.

"Mommy?" I whisper because I don't want to wake her.

"Mommy?" I say again because she seems a little too dead to the world.

I walk to the side of her bed. An empty scotch bottle and two empty pill bottles are lying sideways on the floor. I touch my mother's arm and shake it back and forth.

"Mommy?" I say, with impossible dread.

When my mother doesn't respond, I run and get my sister. When she sees our motionless mother, she screams, "Get Daddy!"

I run downstairs and find my father sleeping in his office on a waiting room couch. In his own drunken slumber, he is almost as hard to rouse as my mother.

"Daddy!" I yell, shaking his shoulder. "There's something wrong with Mommy! She won't wake up!"

My father jumps up in his underwear and propels himself upstairs, getting more sober with each step. By the time he sees his wife, the doctor is in full emergency mode. It feels a little like the opening credits of *Ben Casey* when a man bursts through the doors pushing a gurney.

My father checks my mother's pulse, then reaches for the phone.

"Go back to your room," he tells my sister and me. "I'll take care of your mother."

That's what I'm afraid of. Though it might not be the worst thing in the world. Some days I just want it all to be over. Every time the principal comes into my classroom, I'm sure she's going to tell me one of my parents is dead.

While my sister goes obediently to her room, I hang out in the hall. When the doorbell rings five minutes later, I run downstairs to open the door for Dr. Cangemi, my favorite doctor who lives around the corner. He's carrying his little black bag and his raincoat and hat are sopping wet.

"Hello, Lynn," Dr. Cangemi says.

"Daddy's upstairs," I quickly say.

As Dr. Cangemi rushes up the stairs, I follow behind. I point him to my parents' room. He goes in without knocking and closes the door. With nothing left but to be more afraid, I get down on my knees. Watching the rain beat against the three large windows at the top of the stairs, I think how beautiful frosted glass looks in the rain.

"Please don't let Mommy die," I say to the God I've been taught to pray to because I don't *really* want my mother to die.

Sometime later, Dr. Cangemi and my father come out of my mother's room.

"Go to bed," my father says. "You have school in the morning."

Dr. Cangemi smiles sympathetically. I hang over the banister and watch my father walk him to the door. When the door closes, my father turns and looks up at me.

"Your mother's all right. Vito pumped your mother's stomach. Now go back to bed," my father says before heading into the kitchen to drink.

## ROUGH CUT

AFTER THE NEXT night's dinner ends with my father throwing his dinner plate against the wall—barely missing my revived mother—I head to the kitchen for a dinner knife.

Tucking it into my pants, I tiptoe up the backstairs to the bathroom where my siblings and I take our nightly bath. There are no showers in our house. We get clean by lying in our own dirt.

I turn on the water, then break a cardinal rule. I lock the bathroom door. Only my mother is allowed to lock doors in our house. I will be torched if I am found out, but no one is bothering with me yet. It's too early.

I get into the tub and wash myself with a pungent bar of Ivory soap because cleaning myself seems like the right thing to do. I reach over the side of the tub and pick up the knife, sure to go missing when Lulu next polishes the silver. Angling the knife against the inside of my right wrist, I move it back and forth just like my father carving the Thanksgiving turkey. But nothing happens. My skin will not break. I try the left wrist. Still no blood. After five minutes of conscientious sawing, I am left with only welts. Raised red lines inside and across my wrists.

Thank God, my uniform jacket has long sleeves. No one at school will be able to see my botched attempt. Not that they'd notice. No one is really looking for anything there. I'm a straight A student and extremely well-behaved.

## CLIFFHANGER

SOON AFTER MY failed attempt, I come home from school and am thrilled to find a quiet house. My mother is in New York at another matinee; my father is seeing patients in his office; my sister is at her best friend's house; my brother is boarded forty-five miles away; Elouise is ironing napkins; Lulu is slicing potatoes; and JoJo, our purebred boxer, is sleeping in the backyard. I am all alone.

I skip my after-school lunch and hurry upstairs. I dump my books on my bed and don't have time to watch *The Secret*

*Storm*, my favorite soap opera, because I have to master suicide.

I walk into my parents' bedroom, really just my mother's because my father doesn't sleep in his bed anymore. He only uses the bathroom to shit and shave. On my way in, I see my mother's jewelry box.

I love her gold ornate box lined with bright red velvet. I open its latched lid and take out my mother's pearls. They smell of Arpege, my mother's favorite perfume. I love my mother's pearls. I would fondle them forever, but I have to find something sharp before someone comes home.

My father's razor is resting on the glass shelf above the porcelain sink. I have always wondered how sharp the blade has to be to scrape the scratchy stubble from his face. It's good I've watched him shave so many times because I know exactly how to lift the paper-thin blade out of its silver bed.

I go into my mother's room with the blade and stand in front of the only air-conditioner in the house. As an arctic breeze hits my face, I hold the blade between my thumb and the pointer finger of my left hand. I raise the pointer finger of my right. My nail peeks over like a rising moon. I position the corner of the blade at the top of my finger and pull down as if I'm flicking off a switch.

Blood! Bright red blood!

The cut is deep, quick, and clean. I have never seen blood gushing from a place above my waist. My menstrual blood is terrible enough, but this blood feels different. This blood is holy and more mine. Instantly grieving for my finger, I know in every part of my being that I don't want to die. My mother must be crazy.

# FIGHT SCENE

MY FATHER, THE most unassuming man during the day, goes crazy when he drinks at night, especially when my mother accuses him of sleeping with Dorothy or some other woman. His eyes bulge and he is really scary. Like Spencer Tracy in *Dr. Jekyll and Mr. Hyde* after he drinks the bubbling potion. When he turns into Mr. Hyde and starts hurting women.

One night, my mother and father's fighting crosses into dangerous territory. My brother and sister must also hear its life and death intensity because we all run down to the living room at the same time.

Our mother is lying on the floor and her mouth is full of blood. Our father is on top of her and his hands are around her throat.

"Mommy! Daddy!" we cry. "Stop it! Stop it, Daddy!"

"Go ahead and kill me," my mother taunts, enraging him more.

My father bares down.

"No, Daddy! No!" we scream, trying to pull him off.

It's not until he registers his wailing children that he finally lets my mother go.

When I come home from school the next day, my mother is not there. She's in the hospital where my father is Chief of Surgery, the hospital where no one asks questions.

## BACKUP GENERATOR

WANTING TO CONFIRM my recollection, I travel to Tottenville to talk to Aunt Pauline. As she talks about that time, I write it all down. Revealing the truth is rare in an alcoholic family, especially mine.

> Your neighbor, Agnes Cangemi, called me. That's how we found out your mother was in the hospital. Your father didn't tell us. Agnes said, "Pauline, you'd better come up here. There was a big fight last night and Pug's in the hospital." I went up with your grandmother and grandfather. When I saw your mother in her room, her tooth was out and she said, "You don't understand." And I said, "Mommy and Daddy are downstairs and Daddy wants to come up and see you." And she said, "I don't want to see him." And I said, "Well, you're going to see him." And she said, "Well, he makes me nervous." And I said, "Well, he makes me nervous, too. He's coming up. We didn't come up here for nothing."

When we went back to the house, I went brazenly into your father's office and said, "What the hell did you hit my sister for?" And your father just looked down and never said a word. Never said a word. I was furious. When your brother came home from school, he looked at me and said, "Don't you blame my father. My mother almost killed my father last night." You know your mother used to come after me when we were young. She used to stand in the pantry with the bread knife and say, "I'm going to kill myself," and our mother would say, "Go ahead."

## ZOOM SHOT

I AM ALWAYS curious about my father's first marriage. When I finally ask him about it—after my mother is gone—for once he says something interesting.

"In 1941 I was going off to war and I didn't know if I was coming back," my father says. "I was taking up a lot of Dorothy's time, so I decided I should marry her. If something happened to me, she would get everything."

I make a note to self that no love was lost in that marriage either. But just when I think the conversation is over, my father surprises me by saying more.

"I was in the Philippines for four years. When I came back, Dorothy was having an affair with someone else," he says, still seething with resentment. "I went down to Florida and divorced her as fast as I could."

I don't know what to say because I have never seen my father angry without being drunk. But I come up with a theory. My father married my mother, not just because he knocked her up with me, but because she was twenty years younger. I bet he thought he could control her.

## FIRST TEAM

MY FATHER'S MOTHER and father are dead by the time I'm born, but my mother's parents are very much alive. For me, my grandparents are a mostly loving force. They come whenever my mother calls, whenever she needs them.

I love my grandmother's pancakes, but I hate how she gets cold and angry when we misbehave. My grandfather is the fun one. He always makes me laugh. I always wonder if they know what's happening in our house. Years later, I find out.

"Your grandmother felt so badly for you kids," Aunt Pauline says. "We talked all the time about taking the three of you out of there."

"Really?" I say, shocked, but grateful they cared.

"Yes. We wanted to, but we didn't have the means. We didn't have your father's kind of money. He always told us that."

I'm glad to hear they wanted to help us, but I wish I had known. If only someone had pulled me aside and whispered, "We see what's going on, Lynn. It's not your fault."

## UNION RULES

BY SENIOR YEAR of high school, I am not only at the top of my class, I am President of the Student Council. It is my job to see the rules are followed. Every girl must wear the correct uniform. A navy-blue and gray blazer, a navy-blue or gray skirt, a short or long-sleeved white collared shirt, black loafers or white saddle shoes, and white, black, gray, or navy-blue socks.

"Nancy, you're wearing the wrong color socks." I say to Nancy because my hyper-vigilant eyes miss nothing. Nancy Lavender and I have been in school together since kindergarten and are sick to death of each other.

"It was an accident," Nancy says. "My mother mixed a green sock with a blue one when she was folding the laundry."

"I don't care," I say because I can't even imagine a mother folding laundry. "Your socks don't match. You get one demerit."

"But I never got a demerit before!" Nancy yells, and I think she will hit me, but thankfully, she's a good girl like me. "I'm telling Miss Walden!" she says.

Miss Walden, our old principal, has yellow hair and a face like a koala bear. As Nancy and I stand before her desk, Nancy tells her side of our story. Miss Walden listens, then turns to me.

"Lynn, dear," Miss Walden says. "Sometimes accidents happen, and when they do, when there are special circumstances, sometimes one has to bend the rules a little."

I can't believe my ears.

"Miss Walden," I reply, without needing to think. "I don't care about special circumstances. If we make an exception to the rule this time, *everyone* will expect special treatment. For wearing the wrong color socks, Nancy gets one demerit."

Miss Walden looks at Nancy who is so red in the face I think she will explode. "I'm sorry, Nancy," she says.

## BLACK AND WHITE

THOUGH IT'S NICE having maids—women who take care of the things you should be doing yourself—I'm always embarrassed by it. It never feels right that Irene, Thelma, Lulu, Lee, Elouise, or Hester have to make my bed after I leave for school. And it feels really wrong in the days before Civil Rights and Black Power to hear my parents call these women the "Colored Help." As if they are numbered pencils in my Venus Paradise Coloring Set.

But these women are more mother to me than my own. I collapse my head against a warm bosomy chest and as fleshy arms enfold me in an unconditional embrace, I dare not move, not even after my hair is dripping sweat. It is the only time I feel loved and cared for.

These generous women, mothering for cash and hand me downs, give a privileged white child a fleeting sense of safety in her dimmed and dangerous world.

## REVERSAL

ONE FRIDAY MORNING in the Spring of 1965, my drama class is doing improvisations in morning assembly. The Bergen School Morning Assembly consists of a Christian hymn—even though the school says it's nonsectarian—a Bible reading, the Lord's Prayer with the Catholic girls dropping out before "for thine is the kingdom," the Pledge of Allegiance, and *The Star-Spangled Banner* if it's a Monday or Wednesday and the music teacher is there to play it. When all of that is done, it's time to perform.

My drama teacher, Deborah Jowitt, comes all the way from Greenwich Village and is the coolest person I know. Miss Jowitt encourages us to take risks and I am desperate to please her. When it's my turn, I propel myself to stand in front of a room full of judgmental girls. I take cover in the body of a man.

Since I've been watching *Lust for Life* on *The Million Dollar Movie* all week long, I am filled with Vincent Van Gogh, my mother's favorite painter. I think my mother loves him because they belong to the same tortured club. I'd be in that club too, but I never want—in any way, shape, or form—to be anything like my mother.

Standing in front of an imaginary easel, I pick up a pretend paintbrush and paint swirling yellow stars in a make-believe sky. They are the stars of *Starry Night*, the painting my mother and I get lost in when we go to the Museum of Modern Art.

I hear an inaudible knock at an invisible door. With rounded fingers, I take hold of a doorknob of air and open the door to a phantom messenger. I take his fictitious note and motion him away, forgetting to close the door, allowing students and teachers to see into my private space.

As my eyes move left and right over disappearing words of unrequited love, I know I am not wanted. Not even by a prostitute. As rejection stabs me in the back, my body writhes in pain. Grabbing a knife out of the space of nowhere, I am only seconds away from becoming the world's first cutter.

With my ear held tightly between my fingers, I tug it away from my head. Then with a stroke worthy of a samurai, I slice and sever it from my body. My mouth stretches wide as an extended ear-splitting scream escapes uncensored and uncontrolled from some place deep within. As Vincent's pain mixes with mine, it hurls me to the ground. I lie on the floor in a helpless heap as students and teachers are shocked into silence.

And then, the strangest of sounds. The sound of hands coming together. *Applause.* I lift my head to hear it more fully. Amazed and delighted, I float transformed to my seat.

All day long, girls shower me with praise. Even the ones I am sure hate me. Even they have good things to say. "You were amazing," Brenda says. "You made me cry!"

As if crying is a good thing.

But the response feels cozy, like being touched. So, like a ballerina executing a perfect pirouette, I drop my plan of becoming a surgeon like my father. There will be no sterile operating theaters for me. I will slice into myself. People will be grateful for my feelings and my willingness to share them. People will be glad I exist.

## WILD SOUND

BECAUSE THERE ARE no boys in Bergen's high school, I only date in the summer at the Lake. I go to Saturday dances at the First Presbyterian Church, and sometimes sneak out to the Boardwalk where older kids go to smoke and connect.

Older boys like me. When I'm fourteen, Pumpy, who's almost eighteen, takes me to the circle where kids go to park their cars and kiss. When he thrusts his tongue into my mouth, I look out the back window of his turquoise Volkswagen bug and stare into a black sky dotted with stars, certain I am going to hell.

I don't really know what's okay. No one ever talks to me about sex. I know a penis goes into a vagina and somehow a baby comes out, but except for knowing I have to avoid this at all costs, I don't know the rules. When Pumpy puts his hand under my blouse and touches my breasts and takes off my bra, I don't know what else to do but let him.

Pumpy takes me to the Confetti Ball—the country club dance where parents don't care that gin, vodka, and whiskey bottles are on the tables with Seven-Up and Coke—and I wear a yellow chiffon dress with spaghetti straps and the highest heels I can slip past my mother. I drink at the dance because I don't have to think about what Pumpy might want to do next. But I don't have to worry. Pumpy cares about me. After the dance, he holds onto my feet while I hang out his car door and puke into the street.

## DELETED SCENE

IT'S IMPOSSIBLE TO get a good night's sleep in Jersey City. All I ever want is to fall asleep and stay there. One night, when I'm sixteen and determined to sleep, I stack three Frank Sinatra records on my stereo so Frank can serenade me to sleep.

*I've Got a Crush on You,* Frank sings. And just as I'm sinking into his sleepy warm embrace, I hear my mother yelling. I wonder why my sister hasn't calmed her down.

"Lynn!" my mother calls, as Frank segues into *You Go to My Head.*

Shit. I don't want to get up and go into her room, but if I don't, she'll stagger into mine. I leave my Frank and drag myself across the hall.

"Please stop yelling! I have to go to sleep!" I plead.

"Lynn," my mother says like a scared child, "sleep in here with me."

It's the last thing I want to do. I have an exam in the morning.

"Fine," I say, "but you *have* to be quiet. I need to sleep."

"All right," my mother says.

I get into my father's bed and pull the covers up around me. I turn away to face the door and hear Frank singing *Fools Rush In.*

"Kiss me goodnight," my mother says.

Jesus Christ.

"All right. But then you have to be quiet," I say, rolling over as my mother moves closer to me.

I give my mother a quick kiss. But my mother needs more. She grabs and holds onto me. She starts kissing me with way too much feeling. Her tongue comes out of her mouth and she licks my face and neck like I'm a bear cub in need of cleaning. Overwhelmed by strange sensations, I feel more passion coming from my mother than from the boys who touch my breasts.

As an indescribable throbbing—it feels as good as it feels terribly wrong—starts to fill the space where boys sometimes put their fingers, I pull away and jump out of the bed. I run into my room, more upset than the night my mother flicked on the light to find my father in my bed.

While Frank sings *Dream When You're Feeling Blue,* I start sobbing. I'm sure I must be a lesbian because no boy has ever made me feel the way my mother just did.

## OPTION

WHEN I AM in my early teens, my mother agrees to get help. At least I think she does.

"Your grandmother begged your father to take her to the Carrier Clinic," Aunt Pauline remembers, "but he said she had to go on her own. I forget what his reasoning was. He could have committed her, but he would not do it without her permission."

But she must have agreed once because one morning she's all packed up and ready to go to the sanitarium in New Jersey. I give her a hug before leaving for school and lean into the hope things are going to be better soon. Soon we'll be a happy family.

Walking home from school seven hours later, I am looking forward to a night free of drunken fighting. But when I walk in the door, I get an unwelcome surprise. My mother's suitcase is where I last saw it. As my heart drops into my loafers, I can almost smell my mother drinking in the sunporch. I try not to cry as my disappointment tiptoes in.

"Why didn't you go?" I ask.

My mother does not answer. Her guilty silence penetrates the air. As she stares at the carpeted floor, I start to cry. When she takes a swig from the bottle, I cry even harder. It's not until I'm hysterically flailing around the room does my mother finally register my distress.

She hoists herself off the couch and staggers to my side. But I cannot be consoled. She takes hold of my shoulders and turns me around. As she forces me to look into her eyes, I see her unfathomable pain and how she's trapped inside it. Then she asks a question that is—and will forever remain—our most honest exchange.

"Don't you know how hard it is to be a human being?" my mother asks.

Her query breaks my heart. Because I know what she means. Being human is unbearable.

When my mother cannot quiet my wailing, she summons my father. It's not until he makes me swallow a pill and puts me into bed, do I finally calm down.

## CALL SHEET

AFTER MY VAN Gogh acting conversion, I am desperate to start my life in the theater. I ask my mother if I can be an apprentice at the Gristmill Playhouse, a theater just five miles from our lake house.

"I am not driving ten miles a day so my daughter can clean toilets," my mother says.

My cheeks flush. I don't know why my mother thinks I would have to clean toilets. It makes me feel dirty inside, like she knows something I don't.

I shift to plan B. I will get a job and earn my own money so I can leave home and do what I want. I have no idea my father has put together a portfolio of blue-chip stocks for when I turn twenty-one. Right now, I think it's all up to me.

I saw an ad for checkout girls at the local grocery store and I want to be one of them. I am well-organized, hard-working, and will be an excellent packer. But when I tell my mother of my plan, she ends the discussion before it even begins.

"My daughter is not going to work if she doesn't *have* to," she says, having the last word.

I don't know why she thinks working is a bad thing. Maybe she's mad because she gave up her job to be a doctor's wife. I guess that's what women did. Sacrificed their work in the world to focus on their husbands, the running of their homes, and the accomplishments of their children. After all, at the moment, a woman can't get her own credit card, serve on a jury, open her own bank account, or take birth control pills without the permission of her husband. My mother may be President of the YWCA and the Junior Service League, but she doesn't get paid. My mother works for nothing.

My own need to work goes beyond money, independence, or ambition. I have to stop my mind. Stacking cans at the bottom of a brown paper bag sounds peaceful. Even cleaning a theater's toilets would be a welcome relief from the thoughts in my head.

## BANNED

MY MOTHER WANTED to go to college. Her parents said they would send her, but when the time came, they didn't have the money. The most they could afford was nursing school. My mother never forgave them. So, when it comes time for me to go to college, I become another drunken resentment.

"*You* get to go to college, four-eyes," my mother snarls.

"But I don't want to go to college. I want to go to a theater school," I say, because I want that more than anything.

"You are not going to a theater school," my mother says. "You have to get your degree so you have something to fall back on."

It feels like betrayal.

I see nothing good in my mother's more practical plan, nor am I assuaged by her promise to send me to The Yale School of Drama for my graduate degree. As if she can buy my way in.

Though I plead mightily, my mother does not relent. What's even worse, she makes me apply to the colleges *she* would have gotten into had her parents not betrayed *her*. And because she believes power lies behind ivy-covered walls—after all, the richest and most successful men are educated there—she makes me apply to Radcliffe (almost Harvard),

Pembroke (almost Brown), Barnard (almost Columbia), and Cornell and the University of Pennsylvania because they are already smart enough to admit women. The only reason Princeton, Yale, and Dartmouth are not on the list is because they're still all-male schools. My mother replaces them with Wellesley, Bryn Mawr, and Smith because they're Seven Sister schools and just as hard to get into.

The college process is excruciating. Though I am a straight A student—all hell breaks loose if I'm not—my SAT scores are woefully inadequate for Ivy League or Seven Sister entrance. When it comes to performing under timed pressure and inadequate sleep, I simply cannot. My mind goes crazy with multiple choice and worry. Drowning in possibilities, I fill in the dots, hoping God is directing my pencil. When it comes to magical thinking, I am a virtuoso.

Sadly, God has more important things to do than take my SAT. My scores are abysmal: 540 in English and 420 in Math. Numbers still burning in my brain.

## ROAD MOVIE

MY MOTHER LOVES our college tours. She puts me in her Cadillac Eldorado and we drive north to visit every exclusive one. I remember Wellesley College, in particular.

Though I am sick to death of girls-only schools, I have to admit—and do only to myself—that Wellesley's campus is beautiful. I think my mother loves it because it looks a little like Princeton. After she drops me at the admissions office for my interview, she goes off to walk around the campus to dream of female accomplishment.

The admissions director, sounding like Katherine Hepburn, welcomes me into her office. She tells me about the greatness of Wellesley and touts the proven benefits of single-sex colleges. Then she opens my folder. When she looks down at my transcripts and praises my grades and achievements, I think how pleased my mother will be. But then she sees my test scores.

"Your scores are very low," she says, as if I do not know. "I'm afraid they might be an indicator of future trouble. It's for your own good, but we don't want anyone coming to Wellesley who might end up committing suicide because she can't keep up."

I don't know what to say. I had no idea you could commit suicide at college. But I am certain of one thing. This is the first time I am shamed so effectively outside my family home.

When my mother comes to retrieve me, she asks about my interview.

"Fine," I say, because I dare not repeat what was said to me. The last thing I want is for her to be more ashamed of me than she already is. Besides, I would never say *suicide* out loud.

# CONTINUITY

THANK GOD, MRS. Hiatt, my English teacher and college advisor, insists I apply to safety schools. Not that any place is safe. But it sounds like a good idea.

When I tell my mother I want to apply to big universities, she says no. I have to apply to women-only colleges. Douglass College (almost Rutgers), Mary Washington, (almost University of Virginia, my father's alma mater), Sweetbriar College (all women in the South), Wells College (all women in the North), and Elmira College, Mrs. Hiatt's alma mater.

The only reason my mother and I visit Mary Washington and Sweetbriar is because my father insists. But I hate the South. It feels slow and half-asleep. Seeing the segregated bathrooms in West Virginia when I was younger and realizing that Lulu or Elouise couldn't use the same bathroom as me, enraged me then, and enrages me now. Southerners must be idiots.

In the Spring, when the Ivy League and Seven Sister rejection letters come pouring in—one after another to my mother's barely hidden dismay—and when the waiting lists are not decided in my favor, I end up at Elmira, a women's college in upstate New York that sounds as second-rate as me.

## LONG SHOT

I DON'T WANT to go to school with just women. I'm not interested in being educated enough to find a good husband so I can make smart babies. I want to learn how to live in the world alongside men. I want to learn how to compete. I decide to enter a beauty contest.

I put on my purple bikini and walk to the other side of the lake to enter the Miss Upper Lake Mohawk contest. When I get there, the girls are already lining up and everyone is wearing a one-piece bathing suit. But I put on this bikini because the top holds my breasts up better. Not to mention the open space between my breasts where you can see some skin looks kind of cool. My mother doesn't know about this suit. She's so drunk now she's stopped caring about my clothes.

When it's my turn, I walk up and down the beach in front of the three judges. As my toes dig into the sand, I hold my head high because I have been tiptoeing around my room with three books on my head for weeks. As the lake water wets my feet and a hot breeze billows through my hair, I feel good about my chances. When the judges go behind the bushes to decide who will win, I am sure it must be me. But they do not call my name. Not even for fourth runner-up.

Defeated and dismayed, I walk back home. When I get to the top of the driveway, I see my father mowing the lawn. Cutting grass, pushing seaweed out from our private beach, raking leaves, and shoveling snow are my father's break from keeping people alive. I hate to interrupt him, but I have to tell someone what happened.

When my father sees me, he turns off the mower. As I share my disappointment, blaming my loss on my bikini, my father gives me a sympathetic, yet mischievous look. Smiling, he pokes his finger into the empty space between my breasts.

## PRESENTER

I MAY HAVE lost the crappy beach contest, but Miss Sussex County is a much bigger deal. A preliminary to Miss America, this contest is not just about looks, it's about talent and intelligence. It knows girls have more going on than how their bodies fit into a bathing suit. And this time I'll be smarter. I'll wear a one-piece. Miss America never wears even a two-piece, much less a bikini. What was I thinking?

I buy the required white bathing suit even though it makes me look fatter. I don't need to get the white evening gown because I have one from my high school graduation. The six of us carried long-stemmed roses—just like beauty queens—and wore long white evening gowns and white, full-length gloves. The only difference between graduation and this contest is we got diplomas instead of crowns.

I work really hard to prepare for the contest. I walk around in my high heels like Miss Delaware or Miss South Dakota. I practice *Claire de Lune* on the piano though I have

to cut a few measures to fit it into the two-minute talent al-
lotment.

On the night of the contest, I'm glad my mother doesn't
come. I have enough to worry about. I'm going to be judged
for Swim Suit, Evening Gown, Talent, and Intelligence. I don't
need my mother's fear of my failure knocking me off the runway. I am anxious enough on my own.

When my name is called, I parade up and down the runway, first in my bathing suit, and later in my evening gown. I
pivot like they've showed me. I put my right foot out and turn
to the left so everyone on one side of the auditorium can see
me, then turn to the right so all the others can see. When it's
time for talent, I apologize out loud to Debussy for shortening
his piece, then play like I have never played before. It must go
well because I am one of five finalists.

Sitting on the stage with four other girls, I am hopeful, but
worried. Mary Sheridan, who has long, platinum-blond hair,
is not prettier than me, but she's tan, athletic, and has really
white teeth. When Mary Sheridan smiles, the sun shines. But I
may be smarter because when the host asks me a soul-search-
ing question to test my intelligence, the question isn't that
hard.

"What kind of work do you want to do in the world and
how do you think it might benefit others?" the Bert Parks look-
alike asks.

Though I am definitely going to be an actress, I just aced
a course in sociology at St. Peter's College because I really *do*

want to help sad people. So I pretend I don't want to act, and answer in a way I think they want to hear.

"I'm going to study sociology and psychology so I can help others," I say, looking at the judges. "There are so many people suffering in the world. I'm going to become a social worker so I can make peoples' lives better."

In my moment of Miss America aspiration, I almost believe what I'm saying. But I must have made the right choice because it finally comes down to Mary Sunshine and me.

As the audience holds its collective breath, I am so apprehensive that when my name is called after first runner-up, I think I have won. It's only when the crown is placed on Mary's yellow head that I fully understand.

Oh, it's nice hearing I won the talent part, but first runner-up sounds like almost, but not really good enough. I do get a trophy though. But it's not "Miss Congeniality." Mary wins that one, too. I get the "Lynn Raynor Traveling Award," named after a Miss Sussex County who died of leukemia when she was twenty. It's given to the girl who puts the most effort into the contest. In a year I have to give it back.

As I'm leaving the hall with my flowers and traveling trophy, one of the judges pulls me aside.

"Grow your hair and come back next year," he says. "I promise you. You will win."

I smile half-heartedly at the leering man and don't tell him that I wouldn't come back to his bullshit contest for a million dollars. No one will ever again get to decide if I look good

enough to win some stupid prize. I will never put my ugliness
on the line again.

# RUSHES

BEFORE I AM dispatched to a college of twelve-hundred
women, I need to talk to my mother about the night she licked
my neck. Since a conversation isn't possible after three o'clock
in the summer of 1966, I catch her as she's passing through the
basement on her way to change out of her bathing suit so she
can start her warm weather drinking.

"Mommy?"

"What?" my mother says, not wanting to be detained.

"I have to ask you something."

"What is it?" she says.

"I don't know if you remember, but a few months ago
when you couldn't sleep, you asked me to sleep in your room."

"Yes?

"Well, you wanted me to kiss you goodnight and when I
did, you started licking my face and my neck and it kind of
felt—"

"I must have thought you were your father," my mother
says, hurrying up the stairs.

## ACT DROP

THE FIRST TIME I see Elmira College is the day I'm dropped off to begin my freshman year. I hate it on sight. There's too much gray and Horseheads, the neighboring town, does not inspire confidence. What's worse is that I'm put in a room in the basement with three other girls who also waited too long to decide.

Before my parents drive back to Jersey City, my mother hands me a letter.

"Read it after we leave," she whispers, giving me a rare hug.

I watch my father's Pontiac disappear down the street, and open the letter. It's written on Holiday Inn of Elmira-Horseheads stationery.

> September 10, 1966
> Dear Lynn,
>
> I hope you will be able to sleep tonight and won't fall out of bed. It is all very exciting, and although I am sad at having to part with you, I am proud and happy you got into such a good school, all on your own.

A *good* school? Since when? Elmira was at the bottom of her list.

> We'll go to church tomorrow and I hope you will
> not forget God and his son Jesus. I know that I
> pretend that I don't care, but I really do. I talk to
> Jesus every day despite my bad behavior at times.
> I love you very much, and nothing is too good for
> you. You are to call if you are lonely or if you need
> anything.
>
> Love always,
> Mom

I bet she says that because she doesn't have to live with me anymore. As for Jesus, I wish he was giving her better advice.

## BABY SPOT

MRS. HIATT, MY ally throughout high school, is not like other teachers. Mrs. Hiatt makes me think. The books she assigns make my brain explode. Like *Trout Fishing in America* by Richard Brautigan, and *Second Skin* by John Hawkes.

When I hand in my first short story, *Dark Clouds Overhead*, Mrs. Hiatt is curious and encouraging. So, when I get to Elmira and am instantly miserable, I write to her. After all, she was the one who put Elmira on my list.

Mrs. Hiatt writes back with characteristic bluntness and caring. I know she cares because she calls me Lynnie, my childhood nickname that sometimes makes me feel loved.

First of all, dear heart, I understand what you are going through because, even way back yonder, I went through the same thing. It is frightening and painful, but I am terribly proud of you. You have grown immensely, Lynnie. Your perspective has shifted, and you see this extension-of-prep school is utterly ridiculous. The spy-fink-set-up and loyalty-oath-pledge bit that constitute the student government are insulting and abhorrent. When I was there, the vice-president of the student government got suspended and removed from office because she'd been caught spending the weekend in New Haven when she'd signed out for home.

I think part of your unhappiness is your total opposition to this kind of fascism, but what you are going through is also what is euphemistically called "normal." I don't know of a single person who doesn't feel isolated and strange during a first college year. The locale is different, the people are unfamiliar, there is no one who is a friend, and you have to go your lonely way until you make contact with other people who feel the same way.

Lynnie dear, I don't think you are nutty in the slightest degree, but you do sound depressed and anxious, even though some depression and anxiety is part of the game. You are, after all, thrown almost totally on your own inner resources, and trying to cope with external pressures and internal stress is exhausting. No wonder you feel desperate. At home you had a method for dealing with what you didn't like, but the same method does not work at college, particularly a conservative one, which, in a funny way, seems to me to reflect your family.

Maybe this is the beginning of an all-out rebellion against a rigid authority. But cutting loose can be frightening because you don't feel you belong *there*, and you obviously don't feel you belong at home. So there you are, not belonging anywhere.

Dear one, this is the toughest struggle anyone has to face. If you were sailing on at Elmira, I would have thought, "Good product, good stuff, but, essentially passive and accepting of handed values." Now I don't think that at all, even though it is pure hell for you. But pure hell has its values, Lynnie.

Please try not to panic. Please know you'd never know how to be happy if you hadn't first known how to be unhappy.

Relieved I'm not crazy, I'm so grateful for Mrs. Hiatt. But then she invites me to visit her over Thanksgiving vacation and gives me her phone number.

| I mean it, lovey. Don't hesitate to scream if you feel like it.

I feel so uncharacteristically seen and understood, I never contact Mrs. Hiatt again. Not for forty years. Not until she has Alzheimer's and can't come to the phone.

## OFF BOOK

YOU WOULD THINK I'd be happy being away from home, but I'm too troubled to enjoy my freedom. Mrs. Hiatt nailed it. Whatever coping mechanisms I rely on at home do not work at college. Though I pretend otherwise, I feel like a total misfit.

But I do find friendship. Because as much as I fear women, I need them. I make friends with Cyndi from the Bronx, Sally from Spring Valley, Flo from Bayonne, the town next to Jersey City, and Jeanie from Maine. I also have an advisor, Dr. Baird Whitlock, who knows the name of every Elmira student.

Dr. Whitlock knows how to make young women feel more important than they are. A dead ringer for Danny Kaye, he quickly becomes my understanding father figure and does his best to help me. During our office chats I talk honestly, though I never tell him I sometimes sit by the pond in front of Mark Twain's study trying to imagine Virginia Woolf's suicide.

But because I am a funny mix of despondent victim and hopeful warrior, I decide to transfer. I apply to Carnegie Institute of Technology's theater program because Carnegie Tech was the school Miss Jowitt said I should go to if I am serious about being an actress. Carnegie Tech was also the first place my mother said no to. But my mother isn't here now. I will deal with her when I get in.

## REHEARSAL

TRANSFER TO CARNEGIE Tech requires an audition of two monologues, comedy and drama. Because I never ask for help—doing things by myself makes me feel self-sufficient and smart—I don't ask anyone to listen or do much to prepare.

I go to the library and find a monologue in the comedy section of an obscure audition book. I memorize two paragraphs called "The Church Mouse," not knowing where the monologue comes from or if it even comes from a play. I choose it because it's short and because I'm not comfortable with comedy. I'm more at ease in the darkness of drama. For that, I choose mightily. Blanche DuBois from *A Streetcar Named Desire*, a play I know because my mother has instilled in me an early love for melancholy and all things Tennessee.

I memorize the pieces, but never do them in front of anyone. Maybe I'm too ashamed about going after what I want. But I only whisper the words in the darkness of my room. I never say them out loud so I can fully hear them until the big audition.

# WALK-ON

BY THE TIME the Greyhound bus pulls out of Elmira's station at midnight and pulls into Pittsburgh's, two hundred and sixty-eight miles later, it is daybreak and snowing. I have barely slept, but the sight of falling snow makes me as awake as an energized child on Christmas morning. When the driver tells me Carnegie Tech is just up the hill, I can't believe my good fortune.

I walk onto the campus feeling brave and empowered. But the moment I walk into the Drama Department, I am immediately thrown off balance. There are too many young men and women sitting outside the audition room wanting the same thing as me. Suddenly, I'm terrified. I fly better solo. In the company of others, I pale by comparison. As fear rears its hideous head, I do my best to fight it.

"Stop!" I remind myself. "You just rode all night on a bus! Mommy doesn't even know you're here!"

It's not enough.

"Lynn Lobban!" a voice calls out too soon.

As I walk distractedly into a dimly lit, oak-paneled room, I see men and a few women sitting behind a long wooden table. My judge and jury—saviors or executioners—are poised with pads and pens. A woman asks me where I'm from and why I'm here.

"I love the theater and I want to act," I say.

They tell me to begin and I dive in like a brain-dead Esther Williams into an empty pool.

I rush through the comic piece because no one is laughing. It could be because I don't know what I'm talking about. I just want it to be over. I want to get to Blanche. So as soon as the church mouse runs into her hole and without a moment of transition, I launch into the land of Tennessee.

"He was a boy, just a boy, when I was a very young girl," Blanche and I say together.

I forget the Southern accent and act my heart out. And no one interrupts. Maybe they all feel bad I traveled all night on a bus, but they let me finish the entire monologue. All the way to the suicide of my young husband who kills himself because I told him he disgusted me when I saw him with a man. Personally, I have no idea what men do with other men, but I know about sex and shame and what it's like to be the cause of someone's misery. I know how Blanche feels.

Maybe Carnegie Tech wants to teach me a dramatic lesson, but the pause that follows my performance is worthy of Harold Pinter. I look at the faces behind the table. Some stare in disbelief. A woman half-smiles with a look of sorry kindness. One man looks confused, another concerned. Maybe because Blanche is looking back to when she was seventeen and I'm barely seventeen myself. But how could they know my misguided choice of material is my familiarity with the land of high stakes and alcoholism?

Safe behind their table, they thank me for coming. I rush out of the room and don't stay to look at the campus. I walk down the hill and board the next bus back to Elmira.

Though hope will spring for months, Carnegie Institute of Technology's renowned theater program wants me as much as Mitch wants Blanche after he finds out she's a whore.

# SPEED

AS UNHAPPY AS I am at Elmira, I dread going home for winter break. With good reason. The moment I walk in, I am confronted by in-house fighting.

The sound of my family is like a needle stuck in the groove of a broken record. I can't bear to listen to the saga of my mother's miserable life, or why I'm such a failed human being, or how my father is having affairs with other women and maybe the men at his golf club. Home for fifteen minutes, I cannot process the dissolving limits of my mother's paranoia. I have to get out. But before I even make a conscious decision, I am running down the boulevard with my suitcase.

"Lynn! Come back!" voices call out from behind.

My brother and sister chase after me. I don't know why. It's not like we have anything to do with each other except riding bikes and swimming together in the summer. My siblings and I are as close as prisoners in adjoining cells. Probably because my mother labeled us early on. I'm the evil, mean, and ugly one; my sister is the good one; and my brother is the stupid one. My mother's maternal skills nurture rifts, not alliances. But I am touched by my siblings' attempt to stop me. A wave of guilt about leaving them behind washes in, and quickly washes out. But as our family drama plays out in public view, I hope no one is watching. I may act like I don't care what other people think, but I am like my mother and care far too much.

When the weight of my suitcase starts to slow me down, I drop it, trusting my sister will pick it up. As I turn to see, the 99S, the red and tan bus that goes into New York's Port Authority, is barreling towards me. I throw out my arm to stop it, and breathlessly get on board. As I walk down the aisle to take a seat, I look out the window. My sister is standing on the sidewalk, holding my suitcase, staring at me in despair and disbelief.

## CLOSED CAPTIONED

EVERY PRISON BREAK needs a middle and an end. With alcoholic insanity behind me, I am in the Lincoln Tunnel scrambling for a plan. I have thirty dollars in my wallet. Not enough for a room at the Plaza, the only hotel I know. I find a phone booth and call Bobby Edwards, a boy I have dated once or twice.

Bobby goes to college in New Haven, Connecticut. I know him because his sister goes to Elmira, but I'm not that interested, even though his father is the first news anchor on network television. But I like Bobby because he is a gentleman, which is really important if I'm going to spend a few nights in his bed. I'm still a virgin and need to stay that way.

I walk to Grand Central Station and take a train to New Haven to find the apartment Bobby shares with his friends. Wanting to make the most of New Haven, I walk over to Yale to find its drama school since nothing else has been working out. When I run into a building with a sign that says *We Bombed in New Haven*, a play directed by Robert Brustein, the head of the school, I can't believe my good fortune. I'm grateful I can buy a ticket.

Because I forgot my coat when I ran away, I find a thrift store so I can buy something that won't cost a million dollars like the rest of my clothes. I proudly pay twelve dollars for my first and only fur coat. It reminds me of a dog.

"It's early cocker spaniel," I tell Bobby's friends.

As I sit down in my third-row center seat, I breathe in my good fortune. Not only am I in Yale's prestigious theater where I hope to act someday, the play agrees with my political views. I *despise* the war in Vietnam.

I glance over at the well-dressed woman sitting next to me. She's wearing mink like my mother. When she looks down at my furry arm with disgust, as if fleas are going to leap from my coat onto hers, I am paralyzed by her judgment. Barely able to watch the play, I run out of the theater the moment it ends. But when I get back to Bobby's, things get worse.

"You have to call home right away," Bobby says.

But how did they find me? Did the friend I called for encouragement succumb to my mother's interrogation?

My father answers on the first ring. "You have to come home. Right now," he says, giving rare direction. "Your mother is about to call the FBI. I've had to sedate her."

Not wanting the FBI or my mother on my tail, I thank Bobby for his kindness, and travel home when the sun rises. Though I hate being discovered, I take comfort knowing my mother is upset. She must care about me, after all.

When the 99S drops me on the corner, I look across the street. My house looks like a whale ready to swallow anyone who passes by. I don't want to go back in, but I have to ease my mother's pain. I open the unlocked door and see my mother sitting in the gold brocade chair by the fireplace.

"What are *you* doing here?" she sneers.

## EXPLOITATION

ONE OF THE benefits of having a doctor in the family is the availability of immediate medical attention. My father practices on everyone in our family. Cousins, grandparents, aunts and uncles all benefit from his surgical skills. My aunt gets a hysterectomy, her father-in-law some kind of bowel operation, and my sister gets his perfect suture after his colleague takes out her appendix. I am my father's patient only once.

In the spring of my freshman year, I'm making my bed in the room I now share with Ann. Because Ann's first roommate had a nervous breakdown and had to go home, I was able to get out of the basement. I glance at the poster hanging over my bed—a smiling Frank Sinatra wearing a hat like my father's—and randomly put my hand on my breast because we've just been told our breasts need examining. Though I'm self-conscious about touching myself, I check the left one and then move to the right.

Uh-oh. This breast feels different. Thicker somehow. Oh my God. Is that a *lump*? I think there's a lump on the side of my right breast! I leave my pillow on the floor and run to the infirmary, conveniently located right outside my door and up a flight of stairs.

"You have to call home," the nurse says, not disguising her alarm as she hands me the phone.

"Come home now," my father says.

Within the hour, I'm on the Phoebe Snow, the Erie Lackawanna train that travels from Elmira to Hoboken where my father meets me and my breast. We drive to his colleague's office. The doctor puts me in a barren room to lie half-naked on a cold metallic slab. He squashes my bare breast so he can take an X-ray. As *Dr. Kildare* wanders into *The Twilight Zone*, I think I may die of embarrassment before anything else.

When the X-ray is immediately developed because doctors take care of their own, it is inconclusive. No one knows what's going on with my breast. In medical purgatory, my anxiety mounts. When my father sees my distress, he rides in to take my breast into his own hands.

Though everyone knows my father is a master surgeon, they don't always know he is a brilliant diagnostician. When he puts me in one of his examining rooms and tells me to take off my blouse and bra and to lie down on his clean white table, I do exactly what he says.

Stripping in front of my father feels a little creepy. I turn my back, which is kind of stupid because he's going to see me anyway. I don't want this to happen, but there's no better doctor than my father and I have to know what's wrong.

Lying on my back, I stare at the ceiling as my father palpates my breasts. He checks the left one to see if it's okay, then moves to the problematic right. He moves his fingers with gentle then stronger fingers. Back and forth, back and forth, rocking my breasts like a baby.

It takes forever.

While my father gets to know every millimeter of my larger than average breasts, I sneak a look at his face. He is also gazing at the ceiling. I wonder if we see the same things. When he finally takes his hands off my seventeen-year-old breasts, he steps back and pronounces with equal amounts of medical authority and parental assurance.

"There's nothing wrong, Lynn," my doctor-father says. "You have cystic breasts."

"Cystic breasts?" I say, relieved I'm not going to die.

He starts to explain, but I can't hear because my mother is at the door.

"*What are you doing with your daughter?*" she screams.

Covering my chest, I grab my blouse and bra and run out of the room. If only I could stop upsetting her.

# BLACKLISTING

DURING SPRING BREAK, I invite my friend Jeanie to spend a night in Jersey City. Usually, I'm petrified to invite anyone to our house for fear of hell and my mother breaking loose. But my best friend from Maine is the friendliest person I know. Jeanie has this way of making whoever she is talking to feel like the most important person in the world. If anyone can charm my mother, it's Jeanie.

Before we sit down for our formal family dinner, Jeanie follows me around. She watches as I go through closets and look under beds to find bottles. When I find a bottle of Seagram's lying at the bottom of the bathroom hamper in my father's office, I think how clever he is to hide it under the soiled gowns where no one else but me would think to look.

Jeanie watches as I pour the poison down the drain. It feels good to be doing something about the mess we're all in, but it never really helps. My mother is drunk when she comes to the table. But I was right about one thing. With Jeanie there, my mother is on her better behavior.

"Maine is a beautiful state," my mother says. "Where exactly does your family live?"

"Falmouth Foreside," Jeanie says.

My mother smiles. Dinner feels good for a change. But the pleasantry doesn't last long. Somewhere between the shrimp cocktail and the leg of lamb, my mother discovers Jeanie's Irish-Catholic roots.

"You're *Catholic?*" my mother says.

I never understand why my mother hates Catholics so much. Why she says she'd rather I marry a black man than date a Catholic boy. Maybe she learned it from her father who is Lutheran. Or maybe it's all about Mary. Maybe she thinks Mary is getting attention she doesn't deserve. After all, Mary isn't hanging on the cross. Giving birth to the son of God wasn't even her idea.

As the insults fly across the table at my no longer smiling friend, I want to disappear. I listen to my mother's excoriation of a whole religion—and my closest friend—and am mortified.

Years later, Jeanie remembers that night.

"Lobban, no one in my life, before or since, has ever been as mean and rude to me as your mother was that night," she says.

My cheeks flush with shame.

# RISING ACTION

# ROAD TO DARTMOUTH

IN THE SPRING of 1968, as I'm nearing the end of my sophomore year at Elmira, I am finally involved in its theater department. Getting unexpected encouragement as a director, I am almost happy here. But then a chance encounter changes the direction of my education and my life.

Since I'm still screwing up my acting auditions, I never get cast. So tonight, I'm running lights for *Brecht on Brecht*. Insanely anxious about making a mistake, I make one. I bring up a light on a drum sitting on a chair while Irene is singing *Song of a German Mother* in the dark. Already intimidated by confident Irene and terrified of confrontation, I run out of the theater as soon as the play ends. As I am passing though the shop, I see a theater magazine lying on a table. With the turned-on guilt of a boy with his father's *Playboy*, I take it.

Cut to eleven-years-old.

I'm sitting on the toilet in the upstairs bathroom at the lake house when I see a magazine stuck between the toilet and the wall. I know I shouldn't be in the province of men and their sexual desires, but I am a curious child. As the magazine opens to a big colorful picture, I am almost knocked off the seat.

The pretty woman with long dark hair has breasts even bigger than the ones that won't stop growing on me. They look like someone zipped a bowling ball into each one. They look like they're going to explode. But what's really scary is the way she's staring at me. Like she wants something I don't know how to give her. And she isn't wearing any clothes. Naked women are still a mystery to me. I've seen my mother a few times and that was awful. She had weird red lines on her stomach and down the sides of her legs that looked like train tracks. As for my body, I never look. The magazine makes me feel so yucky, I drop it, wipe myself, and go outside to play.

Cut back to eighteen.

Flipping to the back of the magazine where there are announcements for summer theater programs, I see a small rectangular ad in the lower corner of the page for a summer theater program at Dartmouth College.

A buzz goes up my spine. Saliva drips onto the page. I quickly calculate Dartmouth's pedigree, wondering if its Ivy League magic can cast a spell on my mother.

Dartmouth delivers like Houdini.

"That's a wonderful idea, Lynn!" my mother says, eager to shell out my father's money.

"Lynn has done so well at Elmira," I hear her tell her friends, "that we have decided to send her to Dartmouth for the summer. Yes, Dartmouth *is* a men's school, but they let girls in for the summer. She'll be taking theater courses, but only for the summer."

For the first time, my mother and I are in sync. Her blood will touch the ground of Ivy League achievement and I will spend a summer doing what I love.

I throw my suitcase into my new Pontiac Grand Prix and head north to Hanover. Free at last.

## MAGIC HOUR

IN THE SUMMER of 1968—just months after twenty-six soldiers rape and slaughter unarmed South Vietnamese men, women, and children in the massacre at My Lai—Dartmouth College is welcoming young men and women for a summer immersion in the safer world of theater.

As I cross the Connecticut River and drive up the hill for the Dartmouth reveal, I feel like I'm landing on the moon. Not only because Dartmouth is uncharted territory, but because this discovery is wholly mine. No parent or well-meaning high school advisor has pointed me here. I have found Dartmouth all by myself.

The moment I see the Dartmouth campus, I am soothed by its New England beauty. The air smells clean and sweet. Thick-leaved trees burst green into a clear blue Hanover sky. I immediately feel safe. Dartmouth, a natural oasis, reminds me of Lake Mohawk, my favorite part of childhood.

I jump into Dartmouth's theater offerings like a bulimic before her final purge. I ace my courses and get college credit I don't even need. Best of all, I move into Hopkins Center where theater, art, music, and film live happily together.

Nicknamed "The Hop," Hopkins Center is the first academic arts center of its kind. Designed by Wallace K. Harrison—the chief architect for Lincoln Center—the Hop's facade is the early model for the Metropolitan Opera House. My mother would be impressed.

I descend into the basement and park myself on the rehearsal room's cold linoleum floor. I watch The Dartmouth Repertory Company rehearse its summer season and am transfixed. Watching members of Actor's Equity practice their craft, getting paid to spill their guts for other people, falling back on nothing but themselves and their talent, is an undeniable thrill.

I am strengthened by *Antigone* as she rails against her fate. I am encouraged by *Mother Courage* and her appalling ability to survive; excited by *Twelfth Night* when Viola pretends to be a boy; and find love in *The Fantasticks* where just graduated and future famous Jerry Zaks enthusiastically plays Matt.

Because I'm so inspired, I make myself indispensable. I become the quintessential gofer, running out to get whatever the company members want and need. For the first time in my life, I have value. And with a noble focus outside my pain-centered self, I am happy.

When my dedication is noticed, I am given a title. No longer a mere Dartmouth summer student taking theater courses, I am "Assistant to the Stage Managers."

When I walk into the lobby and see my picture hanging with the Equity company, I am thrilled. Not even my visiting father's derisive dismissal after he sees my short-haired picture hanging with the rest—"Oh, I thought that was a boy"—can diminish my joy.

## FILM NOIR

WHEN WILLIAM O. Douglas Jr., actor, mime, and valued Dartmouth Repertory Company member walks into the rehearsal room, he radiates light. When he sees me sitting on the floor and smiles into my eyes, I am ready for his close-up.

I love Bill's face. The lines on his face are chiseled like a movie star's. But Bill's eyes are best. Bill's eyes are a mix of kindness and soulful suffering. I see that in my father's eyes, too. And what a coincidence. Like my father is to my mother, Bill is almost twenty years older than me. Bill is thirty-six and I am eighteen.

Monkey see.

I am sure Bill and I connect because we both love Dartmouth in the summer and we both have important fathers. Of course, Bill's father is more important than mine. His father is the longest serving Justice on the Supreme Court of the United States of America. And because Bill is his father's junior, Bill is important, and in a trickle-down effect, I must be, too.

"You are a very special girl," Bill keeps telling me.

I know. I'm a virgin. With botanic reference, a virgin is green like Dartmouth and flourishing like me. Whenever Bill reminds me, I feel like I'm hoarding gold. But I don't want to give my virginity to Bill. Even though his father is a very important man, I don't think I want to give him anything.

Bill takes me to a company party across the river in Vermont and I go because I like Bill and I love Vermont. Vermont is like a warm leafy incubator which is a good thing because I feel bad at the party. The actors grin at Bill and me a lot, but the actresses look at me funny. When Antigone and Mother Courage look at me, then at Bill, then back at me again, I feel dirty inside. Guilty for something I'm not even doing. Thank goodness I can drink. Alcohol always makes things easier. I think it does for Bill, too.

As soon as the party ends, Bill takes me to his apartment. Because I'm so tired, we lie down on his bed.

"I hope it's okay," I tell Bill, because I don't want to lose my virginity yet, "but I'm not ready to go all the way."

I wonder if half-way is Kansas.

"It's all right," Bill says. "We'll just lie here like friends and I'll behave myself."

That's just what my mother always says. Behave yourself!

"Thank you, Bill," I say, because I'm relieved. "Sweet dreams. See you in the morn—"

I am asleep in seconds. In the dreamy space of forgetting.

*What?*

Go away.

*What is that?*

Be quiet.

*Something heavy.*

I hear faraway groans that sound like pushing.

*Like being buried alive.*

Oh no. Bill is climbing the tree of my virginity. I would tell him to stop, but whatever it is, I think it's already over. Yes, Bill is rolling off of me, and everything is quiet. But I don't know what happened. I know. I'll ask him.

"Bill?" I whisper. "How much farther do you have to go before you've, I mean, how much farther do you have to go, before—"

"My dear, you have just been unfairly screwed," Bill says, staring at the ceiling.

"But I didn't feel anything," I say, because I didn't.

When Bill doesn't answer, I race to find an explanation that will help me survive. It takes only seconds. When it comes to finding apologies for people and for life, I am an expert.

Of course, Bill didn't mean it. Bill is handsome, kind, and extremely talented. He's the son of a very important man. Bill's father is the longest serving Justice on the Supreme Court of the United States of America.

Case closed.

## DOLLY SHOTS

TOWARDS THE END of the summer program, word
gets out that Dartmouth wants to experiment with women.
For one whole academic year, a handful of vaginas will be let in
as regular students. And because they will be in the theater department, I know I have a shot. I have proven myself at Dartmouth, my SAT scores notwithstanding. I rush to find Rod
Alexander, Director of the Repertory Company and head of
Dartmouth's recently formed Drama Department, and throw
myself at his feet.

"Can I please be one of the women, Rod? Please?" I ask,
feeling as if my life may be beginning.

"Absolutely," Rod answers.

Overjoyed, I can't wait to hurl myself into Dartmouth's Ivy
League test tube and be a part of Big Green research. And how
smart of Dartmouth to make practical use of its first women.
Casting their plays will be easier now. Townswomen and faculty wives won't have to play all the female roles.

As for my mother who wouldn't let me transfer to a coed
university, she agrees to Dartmouth. Though she continues to
say, "Make sure you're a virgin when you marry," she doesn't
think twice about letting me attend a college full of men.

# TRAILER

WHEN I RETURN home after my mostly magical summer, I tell my parents about Bill. They are thrilled the son of a Supreme Court Justice is interested in their daughter. As for the age difference, they don't care. All they want is to know is when I will see him again.

I don't mention he "unfairly screwed" me in my sleep because I don't see it that way. I bury that night alongside the other secrets my psyche has to hold until I am strong enough to know them.

But being home after resting in the Dartmouth womb, I am sickened by family. I withdraw into my room. Lying on a bedspread of fragrant-free lilacs and staring at my overhead light, I can't breathe. The air suffocates. Even the furniture is against me. The chair at my vanity table rounds my back into a shape of female futility. If not for the letter lying next to me, the formal invitation to return to Hanover for my junior year as one of Dartmouth College's first women, despair would swallow me whole.

# BACKSTORY

DARTMOUTH COLLEGE WAS founded in 1769 by Eleazar Wheelock, a minister determined to inflict his religious beliefs on Native Americans, referred to then as Indians.

Wheelock believed the savages needed saving. He reasoned a good education would prepare the best among them to spread the Christian Gospel to their misguided tribes.

As time passed, the Indian would become the Dartmouth College mascot. Because the reality was, a Dartmouth education was for white males who could afford it. And give or take momentary impulses toward diversity and change, Dartmouth would stay that way for two hundred years.

## AERIAL SHOT

A STEEPLE PIERCES a bright September sky. Baker Library, filled with the books of powerful men, rises majestic and tall. Its tower fashioned after Independence Hall in Philadelphia, where white men adopted the Declaration of Independence and the U.S. Constitution, a document that wouldn't give women the vote for another one hundred and thirty-one years, even after Australia, New Zealand, Finland, Norway, Denmark, Netherlands, Canada, Austria, Germany, Poland and Russia gave the vote to theirs.

As Dartmouth men cross the Green, traversing one of seven paths converging to the center like planets to the sun, inside a Dartmouth snow globe, a buxom blue-eyed blonde, well-clothed and clueless to herself, arrives for Dartmouth's 1968-69 academic year. Shake her and nothing moves.

## METRO-GOLDWYN-MEN

MEN ARE *EVERYWHERE.*

Big men, small men, short men, tall men, fat men, thin men, fast men, slow men, cute men, hirsute men, muscle-men, bony men.

I *love* men.

Men are not like women. They're not disgusting and scary like my mother. Men are like my father. Accomplished and not really there, except when he is.

The 3,142 almost all-white men of Dartmouth are a boon to my adolescent self. No more suffering through idiot college mixers. No more boarding an Elmira College bus to travel with an estrogen load of enhanced faces and tamed hair to a campus full of men. No more competing for a glance of male approval and an hour of dry humping in a strange man's bed.

I'm at Dartmouth College now. Someone is sure to watch over me.

## SUPPORTING CHARACTERS

THERE ARE SIX other women in the fall of 1968, but I am too male-centric to fully see them. Our contact is in class, the rehearsal room, onstage, and behind. I would never think of relying on women. Women aren't reliable.

Dartmouth doesn't help. There are no welcoming teas or committees, no formal housing to bring us all together. I don't even know where the other six live. If they choose to be close to each other so they can talk about how it feels to be a woman among so many men.

Isolation is what I know. I rent a tiny attic apartment in a house owned by a darkly-dressed woman who bears a strong resemblance to Ichabod Crane. I come and go from her badly-lit side entrance, praying she won't stop and talk to me.

But I am highly aware of the other women. Nanalee, with her friendly and sarcastic edge, who tells it like she sees it, whatever it might be. Binky, who also has an edge, but one brimming with confidence and bravado that always leaves me feeling Dartmouth green. Binky's wild mane of reddish hair sometimes sweeps me off the floor. And Ginny, who's even more wholesome than my external self and someone I know as much about.

Carol is the tough one who doesn't suffer fools, so I am sure she doesn't like me. How I was brave enough to direct her in a summer production of Sartre's *No Exit*—a play I love because there's no exit for me either—I will never know.

Geri is the one I fear the least because Geri's from New Jersey and went to a second-rate college like me. And Kammy, my personal favorite, who is smart, soft-spoken, and kind. But Kammy comes from Smith, a Seven Sister school, so I always feel less smart. After all, I'm the one who would have died at Wellesley.

SURVIVING DARTMOUTH, FAMILY, AND THE WILDERNESS OF MEN

## SIDES

THOUGH I MOSTLY take theater courses, I'm curious about Dartmouth's other offerings. I sign up for 20th Century Art with John Wilmerding, a teacher so brilliant he makes a large survey class exciting. I love studying painting and sculpture with men. It makes up for never seeing my father in a museum.

I also take Human Relations I because I am forever perplexed by human beings. When Nanalee and I get in a heated discussion about which is stronger, nature or nurture, our professor fears we are at odds. Maybe Dartmouth men aren't used to seeing women in vigorous debate. As Nanalee makes her case for nature, she cannot know my insistence on nurture's influence is my need to dispel my mother's theory. That from my beginning, something is inherently wrong with me.

## ANIMATION

THERE'S A LOT of drinking on the Dartmouth campus. A *lot*. Though I drink during my two years at Elmira—what college student doesn't—Dartmouth is another matter.

Kegs are everywhere. Tapped for men like bottles for babies, they provide young men welcome relief from parental and societal expectations, release from fears they don't like to admit, escape from feelings they dare not express.

Dartmouth men are my people.

But Dartmouth drinkers are different from the ones back home, dying of themselves and each other. Dartmouth drinkers are just boys being boys. Virile young men enjoying a carefree weekend after an arduous week of Ivy League striving.

Steady anesthetic drip of forgetting, drinking is expected here.

## PIPELINE

ALCOHOL FLOWS THROUGH my family home like contaminated water. Before I am ten-years-old, I lift the cork from my mother's crystal decanter and pour its creme de menthe contents over my vanilla ice cream. I do this because I can. Because they let me. The creme de menthe burns my throat and tastes like candy. Its bright green color feels like spring.

My father drives us through the Holland Tunnel—I hold my breath because I am sure it will spring a leak and drown us—so we can have dinner in Little Italy. As I walk into the Grotto Azurra, the curly wood shavings scattered all over the floor crunch beneath my feet. My mother orders fried zucchini and spaghetti, but what I'm waiting for are the sangria-soaked apples and pears at the bottom of their plastic pitcher. I can't wait to devour the fruit while my siblings eat their spumoni.

I have my first official drink when I'm fourteen. A screwdriver. Its rocket-fueled breakfast juice lifts me off the ground, and I am blasted out of my body into a more tolerable realm. I don't care what anyone thinks of me. I finally fit in.

Throughout my teenage years, my concoctions for connection grow more sophisticated. There are Whiskey Sours, Gin and Tonics, Bloody Marys, Seven and Sevens, and Rum and Cokes. Though more than a few make me vomit through the night, I am always happy for a chance to drink again.

# OLD BOYS NETWORK

MY DARTMOUTH STUDENT ID says "Non-Matriculated Special Student." I never notice "Non-Matriculated" because I'm too busy reveling in "Special."

Special is something I am used to and always need. It's a voice I can't hear, but always know is there. Feeling singular and unique is everything to me.

Most Dartmouth men are in fraternities, places where men huddle together on a cold New England night with a book, brew, and sometimes random babe. They're staging grounds for male shenanigans sanctioned by the tribe, watering holes where men can practice losing control in the safety of their home.

Though I despise the sound of sorority—a place for silly and inconsequential female agendas—I love the sound of fraternity. Fraternities are where men join hands to run the world. When I get a chance to join one, I jump higher than a kangaroo rat.

## CALL TO ADVENTURE

MY ELMIRA FRIEND, Jeanie, not only has a father who is a Dartmouth alum, she has a childhood friend she says I must meet.

"Lobban, you have to meet Allan McLean," Jeanie says.

Allan lives in Chi Phi Heorot, a fraternity just a few doors away from where I live. When I go over, it's rush night, a night when eager underclassmen, desperate for acceptance into a higher male order, visit different fraternities, hoping to be invited in. The sight of men checking each other out makes me smile.

A few women—pretty girlfriends strategically positioned to make the house look more enticing—are handing out name tags to prospective pledges. I instantly feel superior to these women tossed out as sexual bait. Though I am also most likely being looked at for the way my cashmere sweater clings to my ample breasts, I pretend not to notice. I am a full-fledged Dartmouth student, not some Dartmouth man's girlfriend.

When someone tells me Allan and the keg are downstairs, I spiral down to the basement where I find Allan at the bar. I introduce myself as Jeanie's friend and tell him—because he does not know—that there are women at Dartmouth now and I am one of them. Allan stares past what I'm trying to prove and quickly moves away.

His rejection stings. About to slink up the stairs to get the hell out of there, I am stopped by a cute, boyish-looking man named Denis. As he sits down on the stool beside me, I am as attracted as relieved.

"Hi," Denis says, smiling.

"Hi," I say, smiling back.

Though it's hard keeping up with his smart and clever banter, especially with his Smith College girlfriend lurking nearby, ready to pounce should either one of us cross some fast-dissolving line, I do my best. When he hands me a beer, I gulp it down, gaining confidence with each swallow.

"I'm a student here now, just like you," I inform him.

"Really?" Denis says. "I didn't know Dartmouth was accepting women."

"There are seven of us in the Drama Department. We're here for the whole year."

"I think that's great," Denis says, giving me the correct response. "I think it's a good thing."

Happy my call for equal rights and my right to be at Dartmouth is being well-received, I am thrilled that Denis is so taken with my crusade. But maybe he likes what's in my sweater because he keeps glancing down at my chest.

But because Denis pays attention to me, his brothers start to, too. One suggests I come back the next night and the next, and I do because I love to be included. In fact, I am so enthusiastic about being in Heorot that when sink night—the night when brothers hand out invisible crowns to the winning contestants—arrives, Frank Reynolds, Heorot's Vice President, gets an idea. Whether it's to assuage me or to shut me up, I neither know nor care.

"Let's pledge Lynn! Let's make Lynn a shitbird!" Frank says, to a basement full of men.

As my future Heorot brothers cheer, they give me a jumpsuit and pour beer on my head. I am in heaven. Soaked and smelling of yeast, I have just become the first woman to pledge a Dartmouth fraternity. As for being called a shitbird, it is music to my ears.

## MASTER SHOT

ALL DARTMOUTH STUDENTS are called to Webster Hall for Convocation, the official launch into the academic year. An explorer about to see the shores of her imagined land, I am propelled up the stairs into an enormous room filled with men. Sitting on a hard wooden seat, I watch men stream in from every direction. Hundreds of advantaged white men who already know they run the world.

I am acutely aware I am not like all the rest. I am the one with tits. Tits, that dismissive and angry-sounding word men like to say.

As John Sloan Dickey, Dartmouth's president, steps up to the podium to give his hearty welcome, my spine straightens. My ears perk up like a dog about to be tossed a bone. Dickey's mouth opens with mine.

"Men of Dartmouth," Dickey says.

I'm sorry, *what* did he just say? Did he say *Men* of Dartmouth?

Slipping into a sinkhole as wide as the Green, I look over at my fellow guinea pigs. It's easy to spot them. They're the ones with eyes as wide as mine. We exchange a worried look, but I quickly look away. I have a whole school year in front of me. I have to find some explanation.

Oh, I know why he didn't include us. Dartmouth is probably going to announce its first women at some other time and in some better place.

But what if Dartmouth's first women are supposed to be more secret than fact? What if Dartmouth doesn't want anyone to know we're here?

Pushing past the men, I go up to Thaddeus Seymour, the Dean of Students. I have to tell him I'm not only here, but I have just pledged a fraternity.

## REACTION SHOT

*DATING PROBLEM SOLVED FOR ONE ELMIRA GIRL*

"I knew it would happen," said Dean Thaddeus Seymour in a tone laced with enough astonishment to suggest he really didn't know it would happen. "They told me if we took girls this could happen."

Seymour was speaking to Lynn Lobban from Elmira College and one of the seven female drama students that Dartmouth's administration is allowing to surreptitiously herald the possibility of co-education in Eleazar's preserve.

She had accosted him Monday morning as he descended from the convocation platform and nervously announced that she had sunk Chi Phi Fraternity the night before.

"Of course, you're not eligible," Seymour continued. "But maybe we can work out some kind of honorary membership for you." The prospect could only have been disappointing for the girl, who had invested her last four evenings rushing Chi Phi.

"She was around all the time, pouring punch and so forth," James G. Janney '69, Chi Phi's president, said. "She seemed pretty solid on the house, so we didn't bother to send her any visitations. We could see she was ready fourth night, so we sunk her." L. Marcuse Shay '70, a brother, gave a capsule analysis of the affair: "There's a tendency on the part of the brothers and any outsiders who hear about this to regard the whole thing as a joke.

That's easy enough to do until you confront Lynn, who's completely serious about the matter."

"I had to squirm every time John Sloan Dickey said 'men of Dartmouth' or 'gentlemen' in his convocation address. Are they going to recognize that we're here?"

Miss Lobban participated to the full in her fraternity's traditionally rambunctious sink night, with only a borrowed jump suit between her and a group of pledges who were numbly oblivious to common decorum. But she survived, and was the first to arrive at clean-up the next day.

- *The Dartmouth*

## MEDIUM SHOT

WITH ONE FOOT in Hopkins Center, I put the other squarely in Heorot. I report to the house to do various chores and tasks. I'm happy to comply. I will do whatever is necessary to earn the right to be the only member without one.

When I arrive, the first thing I must do is go to the bottom of the spiral staircase, get down on my knees, and recite the required litany that lets them all know I am here. It is a speech too obscure to remember, except for one word. *Concupiscent.* I say the word mechanically, not knowing its meaning. I have no desire to find out. My encounter with *prodigious* made me once and forever dictionary shy where men are concerned.

When I finish the proscribed recitation, my soon-to-be brothers on the floors above dump buckets of water, beer, and whatever other liquid they can find. Soaking wet, I don't mind the chill, but wonder if they take the same pleasure from the wet shirts of my fellows.

As for *concupiscent*, I don't look up its meaning for forty years. It's a good thing because I'm shocked to learn its meaning. *Filled with sexual desire.* I would have been mortified. Being a brother is supposed to stop me from being a sex object.

## PRODUCTION ASSISTANT

THOUGH I'M HAPPY to be at Dartmouth, I'm not so stupid as to be navigating the experience alone. Sometimes I need guidance. But it doesn't come from anyone at Dartmouth. It comes from Dr. Whitlock, my Elmira advisor. For reasons I don't understand, Dr. Whitlock still cares about my well-being. When I struggle on my Dartmouth journey, I write to the man who always writes back.

> Dear Lynn,
>
> I knew you were going to run up against the problem, but I honestly thought it would take a little longer for the male superiority syndrome to hit. There is a reason, though. You've pushed it pretty

hard from your side as well, and the reaction was bound to set in faster as a result.

What is he talking about? I haven't pushed anything. I'm only trying to find my place in a world of men.

You say you are joining the fraternity in order to assert your equality. Equality is not something you assert if you are to get it the way you want it. You want to be regarded as equal, which is only natural (in some ways); but by asserting that equality, you almost made it impossible to be treated as equal. Assertion really asks for more than equality.

I can't believe he doesn't understand what a big deal joining a fraternity is. I love Dr. Whitlock's letters, but he does go on about things I don't want to understand.

For example, if you want to get into a fraternity (something which it would never cross my mind to want, incidentally, as I think they are the worst vestiges of a snob attitude to college and to society itself) as an equal, you've started in the wrong place. Every pledge system is designed to show the initiate he isn't equal. Moreover, equals come into the system by a series of clearly defined barriers. You walked over all the barriers by being a woman. To ask whether you are being treated as an equal, first ask the question as to whether if you were a boy, you would have been asked to join Chi Phi in the first place.

God, he just doesn't get it.

I suspect you wouldn't have been, for social, political, etc. reasons. If you had been a boy, you asked for your own comedown. Equality is a very difficult thing at best.

No shit, Sherlock.

For some reason I do believe that you would like to be a boy, but we haven't talked about that, so I can't figure out what is behind it. I'm glad you're not, and you aren't, in any way. It is very possible that you are more a girl than you are comfortable with, and that too is very understandable. But you're not going to get equality by denying you're a woman. You're only going to get it—if, indeed, at a place like Dartmouth it is possible for you to get it (most men don't)—when you first admit to being a woman. But what is this business of equality really? Isn't it something to do with being treated fully as yourself? Is there really anything more to it than that?

My head is spinning. I don't really want to finish the letter, but he took so long to type it and I have to be polite.

> I would guess your main problem at this point is not the necessity of being treated like a man, but finding out who you are so that you can expect to be treated like you. But if there is a doubt in your own mind about your identity, it is not so strange that others treat you in ways that you don't consider being really you. Seriously, why should you be treated more of an equal than any pledge coming into a fraternity?

I have a vague feeling if I could understand any of what Dr. Whitlock is saying, I might have to abort my mission and that is not going to happen. Not until hell freezes over.

> Once you have found out who the real Lynn Lobban is, then you can see whether you are being treated as you should be or not. I suspect if you were treated as you say you want to be treated, you'd be a very unhappy girl. You're being given extra treatment because you are a girl; don't be surprised when you are being treated as a girl at other times. You can't have it both ways. If you were a homely creature, built like a rake, you'd probably get all of the equality you could stand, and you'd probably be as miserable as any young

freshman coming in with a social background that
didn't match up to the private schools and rich
families which make up much of Dartmouth.

Now Dr. Whitlock sounds like the worst part of being a
parent. He's trying to get in my way.

But assertion remains the wrong attitude, Lynn.
You're too good a person to have to assert anything. Just be. Don't try to play their game - you'll
always lose. Be yourself with all the drive, beauty,
mentality that you have. That's what they will respect and react to. It does no good to be treated
as a symbol. What doth it profit a woman if she be
the first to graduate from Dartmouth and lose her
own soul?

Dr. Whitlock's words float over my head like the Hinden-
burg about to catch fire.

## DREAM SEQUENCE

I DON'T USUALLY remember dreams, but this time I
do.

Curled up in the corner of a fraternity's leather couch,
beer-stained by men seeking sedation, a dead girl sleeps. The
loud and unmistakable sound of male voices. Men demanding
what they know they deserve.

The girl, blue-eyed and blond, is dressed in hot pink, baby-doll pajamas. Her lips are painted red with Cherries in the Snow, her mother's favorite lipstick, spiraling black and gold with a twist of tiny fingers.

A man enters and sits down. In the sound of crinkling leather, he slides the girl into his lap. The dead girl stirs.

# DAMSEL IN DISTRESS

I HAVE ALWAYS wanted a big brother. An older male who will look after me in the scary world of outside where anything can happen and usually does.

A big brother provides security and protection. He won't let anyone make fun of me or hurt me. And if anyone does, a big brother will tell them to stop. And if they don't, he will hit them until they do.

A big brother will introduce me to his cool and handsome friends. One of whom I will marry so I can live happily ever after.

But most of all, a big brother won't do sexual things even though he could.

I tell my soon-to-be brothers I am equal to any one of them, but what I don't admit—especially to myself—is how much I need protection in this place of oh, so many men.

## CUTAWAY

HEOROT'S PRESIDENT AND Vice President, positioned for perks, claim me as their little brother. So I get not one, but *two* Big Brothers. Ordinarily, this would be good news. But not when I find out I have to make each one a paddle.

I don't know what the paddles are for, and don't want to imagine they could ever be used on me. The thought of spankings makes me cringe. I pour my apprehension into making them. I've never even held a piece of wood much less made something out of it. And the pressure is on. I'm making paddles for the guys at the top.

I grab a phone book, look up Hanover's lumber yard, and drive to the place where men go to get what they need to build their buildings. But I am lost in the alien land of wood, overwhelmed by the volume and variety, hardwoods and softwoods of different grades and grains.

When I start to panic, a middle-aged man in a green apron, gallops in on his horse. Twenty minutes later, I leave the yard with two pieces of pine, a saw, a screwdriver, sandpaper, a paintbrush, white antiquing paint, and a can of shellac.

Working like an overzealous elf on Christmas Eve, I haven't asked anyone for help because I don't want anyone to think I don't know what I'm doing. I saw the pine into two misshapen rectangles, then clumsily use a screwdriver to carve my Big Brothers' names, Frank and James.

I hate working with wood. I stink at it. I can't wait to paint the paddles. Painting may hide their flaws. Antiquing paint might even camouflage the pathos of my execution.

After I finish with shellac, I look at my work. Though I have a profound sense of accomplishment to have done something so far out of my female abilities, I feel a frantic dismay. The paddles look ridiculous and ragged. When I present them to my Big Brothers, I am as self-conscious as a child at summer camp presenting her mother with her first pot holder. Proud of her effort, but ashamed of its loose and gaping holes.

My Big Brothers are kind, but seem a bit patronizing. Their smiles feel like smirks. I hear the paranoid and unvoiced question hanging in the air.

*What can you expect from a girl?*

Years later, I ask Denis what the paddles were for.

"Oh, it was some traditional thing," Denis casually informs me. "Most guys just handed in a baseball bat or some nothing piece of wood and tossed-off the requirement."

## PUBLICITY DEPARTMENT

*MADEMOISELLE*, A MAGAZINE for girls and young women, hears a female has pledged a fraternity. The editor calls Dartmouth and arranges an interview over the phone.

"What's it like to be the only girl in a fraternity?" the soft-spoken journalist asks.

"The only *woman* you mean?" I say, rolling my eyes.

As *Mademoiselle* listens, I tell her about my life as a shit-bird. I talk about my pledge duties and how I am keeping up with the men. When she's doesn't respond, I imagine she's taking notes. I start to wonder if she's bored. Then I mention the paddles.

"Oh! Tell me about the paddles!" she says.

"Well, they were really hard to make," I explain. "I didn't have any help, so I went to the lumber yard and got some wood. Then I used a saw, and carved my brothers' names with a screwdriver, and before I shellacked them, I painted them with white antiquing paint."

"You *antiqued* them?" *Mademoiselle* says, as if I found the cure for cancer.

Oh my God. Is this what she wants to know about? *Antiquing* paint?

"Yes, I did," I reply.

*Mademoiselle* presses me for more details, but I have none to give. Picking out antiquing paint was random. It just sounded good. Like it might make the paddles look interesting instead of shitty. The truth is, I don't care about antiques *or* antiquing paint.

After an long and awkward pause, *Mademoiselle* tells me the thrust of her article.

"How a young woman brings a feminine touch to her fraternity."

"What?" I say, because I am appalled. "But I don't think that's important. I don't think I want to be in an article if all you're going to talk about is antiquing paint."

*Mademoiselle's* voice grows so cold I think I need to put on another sweater.

"Well, I'm sorry you feel that way," she says. "If you change your mind, let me know."

But before I can say I'm not going to, *Mademoiselle* hangs up, pulling the plug on my chance at feminist fame.

Though I have spent hours combing through *Mademoiselle* magazine—looking for ways to wear my hair, lusting after a dress, trying the magic diet to get rid of the fifteen pounds that are ruining my life—I am at Dartmouth now. I have more important things to think about than fucking antiquing paint.

## TALKIE

AFTER INITIATION INTO Heorot, I write to Dr. Whitlock to tell him about my singular accomplishment. Since his voice is the most important one after Frank Sinatra's, I'm glad he answers back.

> You have me very much wrong if you think I be-
> lieve that ceremonies which make people aware of
> their weaknesses are a good thing. I think they are
> the height of cruelty, and like most cruelty, they
> come as a result of the need for feeling superior

on the part of other people. No, the only good part of feeling weak on a given issue is when it comes from within, when you have set a goal farther than you can reach. Then you have gained some genuine self-knowledge. If at that point you want to fight to reach that goal, so much the better. Blake is probably right in a great many of his polarities, and I suspect the only way we ever find our own strengths is when we find our own weaknesses. But weakness imposed from without are not real discoveries.

Dr. Whitlock sounds so wise I sometimes wonder if I'd be smarter had I stayed at Elmira.

## DOUBLE EXPOSURE

WHEN THE DRAMA Department announces its first play, *The Miser* by Moliere, I want a leading role. But ever since my trip to Carnegie Tech, auditioning fills me with dread. Terrified of being badly judged, I can never fully focus with one eye outside myself.

I'm cast as the maid.

With barely a line of dialogue, I feel inferior and inconsequential. Achingly envious of Nanalee and Binky with their lines and fancy clothes, I take some small comfort in my costume. Though not silky and extravagant like the others, it's lovingly constructed and a lovely shade of green. I'm not so sure about the corset.

The tightness of the contraption is unexpected misery. When Alica, our costume designer, turns me around to lace me up, I'm glad I'm not living in a time when women are so constricted. At least not by their undergarments.

Alicia takes a hook and pulls the sides together. She yanks it tight and tighter still. Each tug brings an involuntary gasp. I feel like an accordion squeezed in one direction.

Suddenly, I'm eight years old and my father is kneeling before me on the ground. He's using the same hook to tighten my bright white ice skates.

"Ow," I whine. "They're too tight."

"Your ankles have to be supported," my father says like someone who knows.

When Alicia's last tug snaps me back into the present, I am afraid it will be as hard to move across the stage so corseted and bound as it was to skate across the ice, gripping my father's leather-gloved hand.

"All done!" Alicia says.

I take a shallow breath and look down. Oh my God. My breasts look bigger than they ever have. They're bulging, popping out. They're pushed so high I can almost taste them.

The women look, then look away. The men try not to stare, but cannot help themselves. When Rod takes a too long and interested look, he comes up with stage—more monkey to me—business.

But it's not in the script. Moliere doesn't say a well-intentioned maid has to walk across the stage just so the Miser can peer hungrily at her bulging breasts. Just so he can drool onto her cascading cleavage. Just so the audience can laugh at the sight of a dirty old man wanting to devour a young maid's breasts.

> Lynn, in the cameo role of the maid, made a smash hit, especially to Harpagon's wandering glance in the second act inspection.
> - *The Dartmouth Aegis*

But I never hear the laughter. I abandon myself at every performance. I am dead inside.

## LEADING MAN

FINDING A DATE at an all-male college is harder than expected. There are way too many possibilities. At first, it's easier not to engage at all. Though a few fraternity brothers make an early move, I tell them I cannot date my brothers.

"I don't do incest," I explain.

Until Denis.

Denis is the brother who breaks through. Denis doesn't care if I'm uncomfortable dating within my Heorot family. And because Denis persists, and is as cute and charming as ever, he is impossible to resist. His wavy, black hair and athletic, hockey strong body whip my nineteen-year-old hormones into a non-fraternal frenzy.

I trust Denis because I know he's liked me ever since I first wandered into Heorot. I know he likes my breasts and for once that doesn't scare me.

Denis makes me smile. His light breezy manner blows away the heartache lurking beneath my sunny surface. Denis is sweet relief, and cuter than a man has any right to be.

## FAST MOTION

ONE NIGHT, DENIS and I drive across the river to White River Junction to get donuts. It's not my first trip to White River. I came a month ago when a brother said I could get some Dex, aka Dexedrine, there. The doctor's office was near the railroad tracks and up a dirty flight of stairs. The creepy doctor took my ten-dollar bill and put the little green pill in a brown paper bag. Its emerald green color reminded me of Oz. Dex was supposed to help me stay up all night so I could study for a test, but it didn't work. My hypervigilant-self short-circuited and I couldn't concentrate at all. It's a good thing Denis and I are only going for donuts.

When we walk into the Dunkin' Donuts store, I'm amazed. I have never seen so many donuts displayed in sloping rows, just waiting for me to pick them out of their choreographed line-up. There are plain ones, powdered ones, sprinkled ones, long and short ones, vanilla and chocolate ones. Donuts filled with fruits, creams, and jellies. On a mutual wave of sugar arousal, Denis gets an idea.

"Let's see who can eat the most donuts the fastest!" he says.

"Okay!" I yell, always ready to compete with a man. Even one I'm having sex with.

We pick out a dozen donuts and Denis yells "Go!"

I grab a fruit-filled donut and shove it into my mouth. Denis does the same. But when a smile forms around his white-powdered mouth, I start to laugh which is not good because laughing makes me choke.

As Denis moves onto his second donut, I want to do the same, but I can't. I can't catch my breath. The donut is lodged up inside my head. Panicking, I run outside to the parking lot and imagine the morning headline: *Dartmouth Special Student Chokes on Donut and Dies in White River Junction Parking Lot.*

"Are you okay?" Denis asks, running out.

"I don't know," I gasp. "The donut went up my nose when I laughed and now it's stuck."

Denis goes to get water, but water doesn't help. I have inhaled a fruit-filled donut and now I'll have to go through life with it lodged inside my head. That is, if I don't die first.

"You win!" I shout because every contest needs closure.

"What can I do?" Denis asks.

I can think of only one thing.

"Can you take me home to your mother?" I ask, like a five-year-old afraid of the dark.

Though I have never met Denis's mother, I know how much he loves her. I think I may survive if his mother can tell me I'm not going to die.

After we arrive in Greens Farms, Connecticut, I spend three hours blowing blueberries and residue donut out of my nose. Denis's mother puts me to bed, tucks me in, and sits by my side until I fall asleep. "It's okay, Lynn," she says. "Everything is going to be all right."

# SCORE

WHEN DENIS AND I go to the movies, we could be seeing *Barbarella*, *Rosemary's Baby*, *Funny Girl*, or even *The Odd Couple*. We could be holding hands on a crisp October night as we walk out of the Nugget Theater on South Main Street, referring to each other as Barbarella and Dildano, Rosemary and Guy, Fanny and Nicky, or maybe even Felix and Oscar. But Denis and I have just seen Franco Zeffirelli's *Romeo and Juliet*. So as soon as our feet hit the pavement, Denis, an incurable romantic, nicknames us forever: Roams and Jewels.

The nicknaming is prescient for we are as doomed as our namesakes. Not because of family discord though, but because I cannot tolerate intimacy for long. Whether Denis can or not, I don't wait around to find out. In just a few months, I will abandon my Romeo, and in a later gesture of his own, he will stab me with his hockey blade of betrayal, evening the score and ending the game.

## SET DECORATION

AFTER A REHEARSAL of Gilbert and Sullivan's *Patience* where I am only singing in the chorus, I am passing by The Hopkins Center Art Gallery. I have never gone into the gallery, but there's an opening tonight. Bright lights and cheese beckon me in.

When I first lay eyes on Ed Bonaventure, Dartmouth's visiting teaching artist, I am struck blind. A perfect mix of Greek god and Hollywood heartthrob, Ed stands beside his sculpted rainbow rising red, blue, and yellow to the ceiling sky. When Ed sees me, he stares with equal, though more subtle, interest. It is immediately clear. I am Ed's pot of gold and he is mine.

While Ed talks to enthusiastic students and faculty members, I move around the gallery, self-consciously panting over every object formed by his strong, virile hands. The lure of this twenty-eight-year-old teaching artist is too much for my impressionable self. Denis doesn't have a chance.

If I harbor any feelings of inferiority or self-doubt, they are blunted by knowing there are only a handful of women at Dartmouth, and I am one of the pretty ones with bigger than average tits.

For Ed, I am an unexpected perk. He had resigned himself to a lonely winter among too many penises. For me, Ed is a lifesaver. Denis is liking me way too much. Our attachment feels claustrophobic, like doors closing.

With Ed lined up on my runway, I tell Denis he doesn't go "deep" enough. He doesn't share his feelings like I think I do. Denis protests, but it doesn't matter. I need Ed now. Only Ed can see how mature I am. And Ed should know. He's an artist *and* a teacher.

In the farthest reaches of my mind where I hide so much of the truth, I sense something not quite right about Ed and I coming together. But secret-keeping is in my DNA. Besides, Dartmouth isn't keeping track of its Non-Matriculated Special Students. The college doesn't seem to really care about what happens to its first women.

## CROSS FADE

DENIS DOES NOT go gentle into my proscribed good night. In a last-ditch effort to keep us together, he hands me a yellow-lined letter, a legal brief of his heart. I go into the snack bar to read it, hoping no one sees me.

I'm shocked by Denis's letter. The surface banter of Dartmouth's soon-to-be hockey captain is replaced by an uncharacteristic outpouring of feeling. The man who skates on frozen surfaces spills his love like knocked-over beer. But his words come too late. Besides, they scare me. The woman he writes about is no one I know. I am not a person anyone should love for too long. I have done terrible things, though I can't tell you what they are. You would have to ask my mother and maybe my father.

Sadly, the more Denis pleads, the more I want to run away. I brush away a descending cloud of guilt and do the only thing I can. I tear up the letter and throw it into the nearest trash can.

## STAND-IN

IT'S TRUE. WHENEVER a tall, good-looking, smart, and funny enough man appears, I hop onto his horse and toss him the keys to my kingdom.

My intimate relationships last a blissful and predictably short time. At the end of three months, an invisible switch is thrown by a hand I cannot see. I go from feeling undying love for my perfect prince to feeling absolutely nothing. I can't even recall the thrill of infatuation.

Tossed off his pedestal, the man of my moment is left fumbling in the dark, banging into the broken furniture of my psyche. I do not waste one second caring. When I dump Denis for Ed, I tell myself Denis will be the captain of the hockey team. Denis can have any woman he wants.

## INSERT

SINCE I AM a master at adjusting reality for what needs to happen in my life, I convince myself my affair with Ed is more or less acceptable. I'm not really a Dartmouth student even though I really am.

I decide to take Ed's art class, but drop out after the first session because I hate having him tell me what to do. Not to mention how hard it is to draw. I figure he can teach me other things. After all, Ed's my first wide-awake sexual encounter with an older man.

One night, Ed and I are doing the usual warm-up kissing and touching. But tonight, Ed seems to have a new lesson plan. Just when I think he's about to put his penis in, he puts his hand on the top of my head and pushes me down towards the end of the bed. I try to look up, but Ed won't let me. I could ask where I'm going, but I don't want him to think I don't already know. Besides, Ed is a man. He's in charge. I'll just have to go on this fast-moving ride and see where it takes me.

*Holy shit. Ed's penis.*

Coming face to face with Adonis's appendage, I am ready to excel. As Ed guides his penis into my mouth, I try not to choke. He thrusts himself in and out and tells me to watch my teeth.

I don't know what to make of all this. Having the world's most powerful weapon in my mouth seems as much a privilege as some terrible joke. How strange to have so much control even as I've lost it.

## TEST SCREENING

WHEN I TELL Dr. Whitlock about my relationship with Ed, he doesn't mince words.

> You wanted me to agree with you that your private lives were no one else's business. Sorry about that, but I don't. You are the one that constantly wants things to be seen in totality and not artificially broken up. In that respect you are often very right. But if you then think that a person's private life and his life as a teacher and student are separate, then you are simply not even living up to your own goal.

I hate when Dr. Whitlock sounds as if I'm doing something wrong. Maybe I should stop writing him.

> You want to be thought of as a person, not as a girl, at a men's college. O.K. Then why do you expect anyone to make a separation of you as a girl and as a student at Dartmouth when it concerns your love life? You are a student at Dartmouth, and he is a faculty member at Dartmouth. This is part of the total reality of both of you, not something separate. You seem to agree that if you were a boy, or if he was married, that people would have a valid gripe, but not under the present circumstances. What's the difference, except perhaps in your own moral values?

Dr. Whitlock really should have been a minister. But how dare he imply I'm immoral! Doesn't he know I spend my waking life trying to be good?

> The situation is basicaly the same - what are the standards of behavior which a given social entity enforces for its own survival? As a part of that entity, you have to judge your own actions in relation to that entity. You want to do that when it favors your position, but not when it goes against it. This is usually known as selfishness - or at its philosophical extension, solipsism.

Solipsism? Now he's showing off. Or has he been talking to my mother?

> The world is not going to adjust to your own personal positions and has no particular need to. You have a perfectly free hand to make your decisions in relation to that world, but you can't ask that the world change so that your decisions do not incur reactions. You have a perfectly free choice to go ahead with your relationship, whatever it may be, and the Dartmouth "world" has a perfect right to read it in its own terns and act accordingly. If your personal relationship is such that you feel that it is so right that Ed's job, your own standing as a student at Dartmouth, and the future of women stu-

> dents at Dartmouth are relatively unimportant,
> then go right ahead and thumb your nose at the
> rest. But don't ever let me hear your letters claim
> that all you want is equality, not to be treated as a
> woman but as a person, and that Dartmouth is ter-
> ribly wrong in not admitting women on the same
> basis as men. This sounds more like an attack than
> I mean it. But I did want to put it forcefully.

Before his words have a chance to sink in, they're moot. My relationship with Ed is over by the time I get his letter. But I don't write to Dr. Whitlock for months. Life is challenging enough.

## DIRECTOR'S CUT

I DON'T APPRECIATE Elmira's theater department until I've left Elmira. Robert Engstrom, in particular. A dynamic teacher who thinks outside the box, Mr. Engstrom tells me to inhabit a painting. I choose Van Gogh's *The Night Café*.

Lying on my back, half-drowned at the bottom of the billiard table, I look up at wooly green water. I see a cue stick, floating-colored balls, a green ceiling, red walls, blazing yellow lamps, and a man in a white suit lurking nearby. I start to cry because I think the man is going to hurt me.

When Mr. Engstrom introduces me to The Theater of the Absurd, it quickly becomes my favorite form of theater. Discovering Beckett, Ionesco, and Sartre is thrilling because life finally makes sense. It's not supposed to.

When Mr. Engstrom tells me to direct a short play, I find a nonsensical piece by Gertrude Stein and create a scenario about power and sex. Though I'm embarrassed by the lesbian suggestion, I am happy when he praises my work. Falling in love with *Waiting for Godot*, I direct an all-female production under a dead tree outside and Lucky a slave with a noose around her neck.

It's because of Robert Engstrom that when my Heorot brothers ask me to direct our entry in the Inter-Fraternity Play Contest, I choose Ionesco's *The Future is in Eggs or It Takes All Sorts to Make a World* because of course it does.

My brothers hate my choice of play. They say it's ill-advised at best. But I am confident my theatre savvy outweighs theirs. So, like Saint Joan, I ignore the naysayers and assemble my troops. I cast the brothers who are willing to trust me— including Heorot's kind resident thespian, John Myers—and Geri, Kammy, and Binky because they always want to act. I also cast two Heorot girlfriends who don't mind me bossing them around.

Every rehearsal brings unexpected joy. Sitting in testosterone's seat, I move my brothers around like puppets in service to my vision. When they struggle with Ionesco's text, I give them dictatorial line readings. I costume them in the black and white of my mind and turn their faces into masks like the ones I'm used to wearing. I highlight Ionesco's ridicule of the status quo by projecting photos of anti-war demonstrators, Martin Luther King Jr., and Robert Kennedy Jr. whose body is still warm. The multi-media life I create onstage is more dynamic than my own.

Oh my God, I love running the show.

## FIXED COST

ON THE NIGHT of the contest, my anxiety is higher than a kite in a hurricane. Pacing back and forth in the back of the Warner Bentley Theater, I cannot let go. Standing helplessly by while actors are free to do whatever they want feels almost life-threatening. I recite a foxhole prayer that Heorot can sing its absurd song without me.

Miraculously, Heorot comes through. The play, directed within an inch of its life, runs like a well-oiled machine. Beer-drinkers, jocks, thespians, non-matriculated special students, and girlfriends deliver for Ionesco, Heorot, and me.

When the winners are announced, Foley House, with most of Dartmouth's theatrical talent, wins Best Acting, Best Directing, Best Costumes, and Best Lighting. By the time Best Play comes around, I'm barely listening.

"Chi Phi Heorot!" a man announces.

The room gasps.

Wait a minute. Was *Heorot's* name just called?

As the audience erupts, I am catapulted into joyous vindication. I run up to accept the trophy but am so flustered after thanking the cast, I leave it behind. Someone calls me back and I grab it like a baton at the end of a relay race.

I run to Heorot to shout the news. Few brothers have bothered to come to a contest they are sure they will lose. I burst through the door expecting coronation, but am smacked back by a wall of silence. If I didn't know better, I would think the house was empty.

"We won the play contest!" I yell up the staircase.

My words hang in the air.

"We won the play contest!" I yell, more loudly.

Again, no answer. Where *is* everybody? Studying? Sleeping? Out somewhere without me?

Finally, a brother pokes his head out of his room. He walks to the banister and looks down.

"We won the play contest," I say.

"That's nice," he says, and walks away.

Heorot has won the play contest for the very first time, but my brothers don't seem to care. Oh, a few think the trophy is nice—another feather in Heorot's cap—but most are not that interested. And no one ever admits he may have misjudged me and my choice of play. Future governors, publishers, and financial giants, they seem to dislike admitting a mistake, especially to a girl.

I leave the trophy and my feelings on the table and run to share the news with Denis who is still my friend in spite of how I've treated him. But when I open the door to his room and see him fucking his loyal Smithie on his couch, I back out like a reprimanded puppy.

Fuck these Dartmouth men who can't be pleased.

## DIVERSITY IN CASTING

1968 IS A boon year for equal rights at Dartmouth College. The same year its first women arrive, the first tenured African-American faculty member does, too.

Errol Hill, a Trinidadian-born actor, playwright, historian, and educator, earned his Bachelor of Arts, his Master of Fine Arts in Playwriting, and his Doctor of Fine Arts in Theater History from Yale University. All in a record four years.

A brilliant and reserved man, Dr. Hill exudes more passion for the theater than anyone I know. I can't wait to take his playwriting class. Dr. Hill makes me want to write for the theater because he makes me think I have something to say.

Though I sorely lack craft, dramatic story comes easily. The operatic nature of my childhood makes the requisite life and death stakes of drama easy to understand. When Dr. Hill tells us to write about something we know, I write about my family. I include my mother's word-for-word rants and remembered scenes I am still trying to survive. My only imaginative leap is making the oldest daughter pregnant so she can die at the hands of her doctor-father who's giving her an abortion in his office. As she hemorrhages and dies, her drunken mother barges in. The daughter is the sacrificial catalyst for change in a family stuck in a cycle of alcoholism and abuse.

It is my hopeful play.

"No one will believe such a story," Dr. Hill says. "It's pure melodrama."

I don't tell Dr. Hill my mother still says my father killed her first baby, and if my father could have given my mother an abortion, why couldn't he give one to his daughter?

I don't tell Dr. Hill my mother continues to call me evil, mean, and ugly, and I have come to believe her. And I certainly don't tell Dr. Hill the death of the daughter *would* make everything better because if everything is all her fault, then everything can only get better when she dies.

I say nothing to Dr. Hill. I just stop writing plays.

## SPECIAL EFFECTS

SATURDAY NIGHT IS party time at Heorot. Floating free in an eye-blinking break between Denis and Ed, tonight I am without a man. I don't like being without a man. I feel more untethered than usual.

I look around at my brothers so at home in themselves—laughing, dancing, getting cozy with their dates—and feel out of place.

I need a drink.

I cross the room to get punch. The pale pink liquid sloshes gaily against the plastic sides of a fake crystal bowl. I quickly down three already-ladled Dixie cups full of party fluid and am instantly buzzed. I love rounding off my edges. It's feels so good to hover above myself and everyone else.

*Whoa.*

What?

*Holy shit.*

No kidding.

*I don't know what is—*

Me either.

*Something's not right.*

I know.

*All of my edges are melting.*

I can't speak or even form words. I know. I'll go outside and get some air. Maybe the cold air can shock me into a life I recognize. As I stumble onto the front lawn, I feel the reverberations of magnified music spilling from the window. I run over to a tree.

*When did they put a tree here?*

Wrapping my arms around the tree, I embrace it like a friend. I lean against its trunk. Reassured by its solidity, I slide against it to the ground.

*I love this tree.*

The tree feels kind. I stroke its trunk with uncharacteristic reverence and rip off a piece of bark. I'm sure I hear it scream. As the bark rests peacefully in the palm of my hand, I stare at the sliver, the size of a misshapen quarter. My eyes bore past its jagged surface to see a pulsating universe. There's a connection between the quivering threads of the tree and the shredding threads of myself. I cannot describe the feeling, but nothing separates me from this piece of violated bark.

*The tree and I are one.*

Whether I am sitting there for six seconds, six months, or six centuries, I do not know. How the night ends and how I get home remain a mystery.

The next morning, news spreads throughout Heorot. The punch was laced with LSD by a brother seeking thrills at the expense of others. I should be outraged, but am only grateful my first and last acid trip was a positive one. Common sense says I should have climbed onto Heorot's rooftop and taken flight.

## MOTION CAPTURE

I NEVER THOUGHT I could benefit from football, but when Dartmouth's coach decides ballet and modern dance might improve the team's performance on the field, the college—sparing nothing for its men—hires Ray Cook, a prominent Australian dancer and teacher.

I am thrilled. I have a vague memory of ballet slippers at four and love dancing at parties. I don a leotard and take my place at the bar behind Dartmouth's wide receivers and tighter ends.

Ray teaches us ballet's five positions. He watches as we fall in and out of piqué turns. He shouts as we leap unbounded across a concrete floor. Shin splints are a small price to pay for learning how to fly. He teaches Martha Graham contractions that feel like getting punched in the stomach. When he tells me to make up a dance, I choreograph a solo for myself and a chair and call it "Alone."

The physical freedom I experience while dancing is both relief and revelation. Out of my muddled head, I almost feel my body. I extend my arms and feel life's energy moving past my fingertips. I lift my head and rise to new heights. I move my pelvis in a rhythm that feels even better than sex. Probably because I am more present dancing than in bed.

"Dance your heart out so people can join souls with you," I write in my diary, knowing it's safer to join with people's souls than their bodies.

In the Spring, Dartmouth invites Alvin Ailey's American Dance Theater to the Hop and I am finally taken hostage. Watching Ailey dancers move to jazz, blues, and gospel music is life-changing. When the night ends with *Revelations,* a dance I will see throughout my life, I love being alive.

## CUTTING ROOM FLOOR

AFTER HEOROT'S RESPONSE to our play contest win, I sense I may not be as equal as I think. It takes a sledge-hammer wallop to the side of my head to shock me into the truth. It comes with the unveiling of the composite, Heorot's collective picture of 1969 brotherhood.

"No smiling. Keep your mouth closed," the not-so-friendly photographer says when it's my turn to pose for the individual picture.

Darn it. My smile is one of my best attributes. Though there are rebellious brothers who bare their teeth, most are like me and do not.

When the tiny portraits are assembled into neat and predictable rows, Heorot 1969 is a collection of sixty manly—and me—profiles looking left and right.

I look at the finished composite and see my somber face rising out of a silk-ruffled blouse. My eyes glance glazed to the right. But something feels off. I step back and look again.

Oh, I know what it is. I have not been graced with alphabetized, or even random, placement like my brothers. I am dead center. Well, I am almost dead center. Tukka, Heorot's dog, is dead center.

Tukka, beloved Winter Carnival, sledding in the snow dog. Tukka, handsome husky with eyes a woman would kill for. Tukka, male canine worthy of fine breeding. Tukka, the dog, is dead center, and I, the only woman in a fraternity of men, am directly below him.

I would bark if I wasn't so afraid.

## MUTE PRINT

THE DARKEST DAY in Hanover is still better than the brightest one in Jersey City. Having to return to the turreted house on the corner for Christmas break fills me with dread. I don't want to leave my Dartmouth tower. I would imprison myself there forever if I could.

As I pull my car into the carport, I remind myself I am a Dartmouth man now. I can handle anything. I ring the doorbell because I don't have a key. Hester, kind, long-suffering woman who continues to work for our family, opens the door. She gives me a warm and sad hello and hurries into the safety of her kitchen.

I see my mother. She's wearing a stained, blue nylon nightgown and sitting on the third step of the living room's grand staircase. I think she must not know it is the middle of the afternoon. I wonder why she doesn't say hello. I move closer to see.

My mother has clearly changed. She's lost a lot of weight which would be a good thing, but somehow, it's not. And her skin isn't white anymore. It's an odd yellow color. When I see a bottle of White Label Dewar's Scotch Whisky sitting by her side, I think drinking must be the only thing she knows how to do now. She finally looks up and says a disembodied hello that sounds as if it's coming from some other person in some other room.

"Oh, someone you your father not me where that brings to me nothing," my mother babbles.

Wondering where even my bad mother has gone, I pick up my suitcase and walk up to my room, not realizing that alcoholism has begun to kill her. Though she has longed to breathe

the rarified air of her daughter's Ivy League achievement, my mother never finds her way to Hanover.

# CREW

THROUGHOUT MY CHILDHOOD, my mother never ever asks how I am—come to think of it neither does my father—but when she starts to disappear, I grow desperate for female connection.

Enter Jane.

Jane Hastings, a junior from Mount Holyoke, arrives in January to spend one semester at Dartmouth because that's all she wants. One semester as a broad. Though Jane would never put it that way. Jane is much too gentle and genteel.

Jane is also smart and self-assured. When Jane smiles, her voice, pitched high like a delicate soprano's, is sweet and soothing. But Jane gets angry and speaks the truth when she needs to.

I feel safe with Jane.

So, when Jane needs a roommate, and I weary of living alone in an old woman's attic, I volunteer. I never tell Jane about my mother because to tell anyone might make it true. But I depend on Jane's empathic presence. Her loving heart helps me survive my fear of what might be coming next.

# LIP SYNC

MASTURBATION NEVER OCCURS to me. I don't remember anyone telling me not to do it, or that I could go blind. It's simply not on my radar screen. I can't imagine giving myself pleasure.

One night in the spring of 1969, Denis and I are walking back to the apartment I share with Jane. Our place is in back of the Hop and right above the pizza parlor. The proximity of the theater and the smell of baking dough and melting mozzarella is sometimes too much goodness to bear.

Though Denis and I are no longer dating—he knows better than to trust me with his heart—Ed has returned to New York, Denis's girlfriend is in Northampton, and Denis and I remain turned onto each other. He still loves my breasts, and I still covet his hair.

As we cross the street, I move closer because I love the smell of Denis. He smells like soap and what I think might be his father's aftershave. He pulls me in to smell the Shalimar I wear because some hippie girl once told me to. Denis knows he's one of the lucky ones. He doesn't have to leave campus to have sex on a weekday night or import it in like other Dartmouth men.

When we walk in, Jane is studying in the living room. We say a quick hello, go into my room, take off our clothes, and lie down on the bed. I'm ready for him to shoot his puck into me as always, but tonight Denis has another idea because he's still kissing me. And not just on my lips. He's kissing my neck and shoulders like a priest with an alabaster statue of Mary.

I like Denis's kisses because they're sweet and gentle and don't scare me. Unless there are too many. And now there are too many. The score I keep is falling to one side. I try to volley back, but Denis doesn't let me. He's on some unexplained mission and will not be deterred.

Oh no. Now he's kissing my fat stomach. I try to pull him up, but again he doesn't let me. I don't know what he thinks he's doing, but I'm getting really scared. I like to know what's going on. I like to know what is coming next. I like sex to be predictable.

Oh shit. Now he's kissing my hips. I squirm like a worm dumped into a truckload of dirt. As he moves down my body to the bottom of my bed, I'm sure he will fall off.

But then, Denis does a magic trick. He transforms his tongue into a rattlesnake's protrusion that tickles the insides of my thighs, right where my usually dissociated legs attach. I take a worried breath as the snake slithers over the border to a place I didn't know was there.

No! Don't! There's danger there! Foreign language and dysentery! I hope Denis has been vaccinated. I want to ask him if his mother knows he does this, but I don't think he can hear me.

Oh. My. God. What was that?

Oh, yes. Yes, that feels good. Do that. Please keep doing that. Suddenly, I'm a radio with all its stations turned on and tuned in. I haven't felt this much down there since my mother licked my neck. But I'm not thinking about that now. I'm thinking about this. *This* is everything. *This* is a reason to live.

*Oh God! Oh God! Oh God!*

My buttocks tighten as a strange and pulsating sensation ripples out. I think Denis must have put an electrical charge inside me.

*God! Oh God! Oh God!*

Stung by a swarm of bees whose stingers have been soaked in holy water, I think this must be orgasm. But really it is more like dying into God because His is the only name I can think of or say. As my body arches, then quickly drops into the softness of my bed, Denis, sweet Cheshire Cat, lifts his head. If I could speak, I know what I would say. "Go ahead and fuck me. Do whatever you want. Just promise you'll do this to me again."

The next morning, Denis goes off to his class. I linger behind, wondering if I can touch myself where Denis had his tongue and scream for God again. It takes less than a minute.

## GREEN SCREEN

EXCEPT FOR THE obligatory call home so my parents know I'm still alive, I don't talk much to them. My calls to my father's office to tell his secretary about my financial needs are few and far between. My father never questions me about the money I spend. He knows I'm not a spendthrift like my mother.

Having such easy access to money is as confusing as it is reassuring. Though I count on money always being there, I am embarrassed by its supply. My less affluent relatives and the women who cook and clean up our messes make me shamefully aware most people suffer from money's lack.

But I am always grateful because money is the one thing my father gives me. The one thing in life I can depend on. So as guilty as I feel when he replenishes my account, I am also incredibly relieved.

At least at Dartmouth there are those way more privileged than me. At least at Dartmouth I never have to deal with the fallout of envy.

## PLOT POINT

MY FERVOR FOR fraternity fades when my brothers, hoping I might pull off another win, ask me to direct them in the Hums singing contest.

I politely refuse. Not just because I have zero skills as a musical director and will surely fail them, but I also feel slightly used. My brothers seem to be more interested in what I can do for them than with them. They never invite me on road trips, and no one ever asks my help in dissecting the nearest female and whether she is worthy of pursuit. I remain the outsider.

Ignoring my own disappointment, I shift to a more important cause. I will end the Vietnam War. After all, I was teargassed at the Pentagon a little more than a year ago. Moving from fraternity to Dartmouth's anti-war movement is just me getting back to what matters.

And there is a perk in this as well. Since it's not safe to express my rage at home—smashing my own belongings in a child's helpless hysteria is always met with threats of the looney bin—I can focus my wrath on evil Richard Nixon, a Republican like my father.

## ANTAGONISTS

ROTC, RESERVE OFFICER Training Corps, is the organizational training ground for Dartmouth men aspiring to positions of military power. It is also Dartmouth's most direct link to the war. Those of us fighting American aggression want ROTC removed from campus and we want it removed now.

Anti-war protests begin peacefully as students, faculty, and Hanover residents stand side by side at candlelit vigils on the Green. As we honor lives lost, we send out vibes for peace. But the passivity of peaceful protest feels too tame for my adrenaline-junkie self. I grow tired of singing another chorus of *Kumbaya*.

## ENTER SDS

I'M NOT REALLY a member of Students for a Democratic Society. I would join them, but they seem too dark and unpredictable. Their willingness to explode the envelope feels like the fanaticism I'm filled with and can't cop to. Mirror gazing does not interest me. It's not something I can survive right now.

But I am happy to do whatever SDS asks. When they call for a strike, I wrap a white cloth around my bicep and boycott my classes, even rejecting the only acting role offered to me all year, the opportunity I have been waiting for. But who cares about acting now? Ending the war is more important than playing the lead in The Marriage Proposal. Besides, now I won't have to prove I can act, in case I can't.

## RESTRICTED

WHEN SDS CALLS for a fast, I am thrilled to kill the two birds of weight and war. If the fast doesn't get rid of ROTC, at least I'll be thinner. At least I'll have the body I have always wanted.

Like most women, I've been taught that thin is divine. After all, Jesus is not some fat guy hanging on the cross. He's a thin man who's suffered. Even Buddha starved himself before he got enlightened. And Gandhi who almost changed the world. As for girls and women, they just look better when they're thin. Ask any man.

I did my first fast at Elmira when I needed to lose a quick twenty pounds. More than a few of us liked to go to the snack bar after a healthy binge at dinner. Dinner was a balanced meal with extra helpings, several pieces of pecan pie, and as many Ritz crackers slathered with peanut butter and jelly as we could stuff into our bloating bellies.

The snack bar spree was simpler. We scooped out whatever was left at the bottom of the gallon-sized ice cream containers because Jeanie, unlike me, worked for her spending money and could sneak them out at the end of her shift. Pigging out with friends was always fun. I loved knowing I wasn't the only one who couldn't get enough of what was missing.

But my Elmira fast didn't last a day. By five o'clock I was at Moretti's—the best Italian restaurant this side of Horseheads—wolfing down a large butter-soaked sirloin burger that gave me the worst stomachache of my life.

My Dartmouth fast will be easier because it's for a noble cause. I will muscle through like the men. But fasting still doesn't come easily, not even to my protesting self. Though I like not having to think about food—deciding what to eat next or wishing I hadn't eaten what I did—by the fourth day on the picket line, I am woozy with hunger. I'm glad when it ends.

And this time I'll be smarter. I'll break my fast the Dartmouth way. When a bearded friend tells me to break my fast with an apple, I do exactly as he says. I just wish he had told me not to follow it up with a glass of milk and a large bag of chocolate chip cookies.

The consequences are punishing. The concurrent diarrhea and vomiting turn me inside out. When I come close to passing out, I drag myself over to Dick's House, Dartmouth's aptly-named infirmary.

A nurse puts me in a bed and checks my vital signs. A doctor comes in, orders an IV, and says I have to spend the night. When I mention my father is a doctor—it always makes a good impression on another in the club and the extra attention never hurts—he doesn't pause. "I want to speak to your father," he says, handing me the phone.

But I don't want him to talk to my father. It makes me feel like a five-year-old who did a really dumb thing. But I have no choice. I'm in a bed confronted by male authority.

"Yes, she'll be fine," the doctor reassures my father. "She just needs hydration and rest."

Then the doctor hands me the phone. He listens, as I tell my father about my fast to end the war.

"I don't have time to talk about that now, Lynn," my father says. "I have a waiting room full of patients."

## VISUAL EFFECTS

UNTIL SPRING, MY drug of choice is alcohol, Dartmouth's most available fluid. My loyalty to the substance should be questioned. More often than not, I am throwing up and suffering crushing hangovers. My body rejoices when I move from fraternity to anti-war protest and a less punishing escape appears.

Marijuana.

When John Beck, a kind and gentle man who is also passionately against the war, offers me a toke, I take it. He introduces me to his more hippie-than-preppie friends and I do my best to fit in. Being stoned helps. Usually, the hippie love approach scares the shit out of me. I love Ram Dass, but I think being here now is highly overrated.

John invites me on my one and only Dartmouth road trip. We squeeze into a crowded car and drive to a Christmas tree farm in Vermont. As we turn into the farm's entrance, I gasp at the sight of tiny fir trees on their way to growing tall enough to die a holiday death.

Sometimes opens a Tupperware container filled with brownies. Thrilled to discover drugs and dessert mixing together, I devour one and reach for another. Someone says I have to share.

When we get out of the car, John takes me by the hand. Speechless and stoned, we walk to the edge of the arboreal sea.

"Get down on your knees," John says.

Falling to the ground, I am grateful my mother isn't here to yell at me for dirtying my clothes. But who cares about my mother now? Fuck my mother.

As we crawl to the center of the Christmas universe, passing dozens of tiny trees sparkling and shimmering in the sun,

I can't see an entrance or an exit, and for the first time in my life that's okay with me. That's how stoned I am.

When John stops crawling and lies down on his back, I follow along. Looking up past the trees and into the sky, I am flying higher than I have ever flown. I am the red balloon. I am Alice falling down the rabbit hole for a private meeting with Santa Claus.

## INCITING INCIDENT

BY LATE APRIL, the stakes in Dartmouth's anti-war movement are rising higher than a stream in a biblical flood. For all our protest, Dartmouth's power-brokers are not budging. They leave us no choice but to match a desperate time with a desperate measure. We must seize Parkhurst, the administration building, where the men at the top make weighty decisions about the fate of the men and a handful of women below.

It begins on the afternoon of May 6th. We gather on the Green while Dartmouth is in the middle of its workday. Students are in class or studying, and Dartmouth employees are doing jobs both big and small. We will take everyone by surprise. No one will know what hit them.

Though stealing a building is over the top daring for my good girl self, the thought of kicking authority onto the street is more intoxicating than any drink, drug, or handsome man. As SDS leads the way, I enter Parkhurst to topple tyranny itself.

# INTERIOR

TOO COWARDLY AND polite to assist in the physical removal of those working inside, I am happy to watch as Dean Seymour is escorted from his office and ushered out of the building. He looks as surprised as I was at Convocation when President Dickey chose to ignore me.

Inside Parkhurst, men lock doors and nail them shut in sounds of crucifixion. They shove desks against the doors for barricade and good measure. It feels like home. In fact, I haven't felt this galvanized since the last time I tried to stop my mother from killing herself.

Hours pass. People come and go, in and out of the back of the building. The room is crowded and claustrophobic. I hear people gathering outside. I push away the thought there could be some who disapprove of what I'm doing. The people-pleaser swallows hard for revolution.

Hours pass. Men mill about, executing tasks that look and sound important. I, a passive cheerleader, sit on the floor and sing songs of liberation.

Hours pass. Dartmouth's young get hungry. Some sneak in food. Men and women break bread in political communion.

Hours pass. Night falls dark and dangerous. The time past midnight when anything can happen.

Hours pass. Time enough for the weather to change and for Dartmouth to want its building back.

When the patriarchs decide to end their extended time-out for Dartmouth's children, they call in New Hampshire reinforcements.

"Come out of the building now!" a deep-throated man shouts through a bullhorn. "Come out or you will be arrested!"

The ultimatum is terrifying. As desperate as I am to stand with these brave Dartmouth men, my body is in full flight. If Dartmouth is my escape from my familial prison, jail will be my undoing.

Frank, Big Brother from pledge and paddle days, notices my distress. He listens to my struggle, knowing he may be dragged out soon. John, pacifist friend from fir tree marijuana haze, says there's no shame in leaving. I think he says this because he's going to jump ship, too.

While better men than I make themselves a flashpoint for ending Dartmouth's involvement in an unjust war, I am helped out a back window like a woman stepping over a rain puddle.

## EXTERIOR

I RUN TO the front of the building because I have to stay connected to those I've just spent twelve hours with, the men and women I've just deserted. Two men lift me up to stand on the ledge of a front window.

The scene below is surreal. Dartmouth looks more like a brightly lit, rain-drizzled movie set than tranquil Ivy campus. The Green, dark and in shadow, is filled with extras yelling one

way or another. I notice an empty yellow school bus parked in
the street.

My breath quickens as darkly-dressed, riot-geared, ba-
ton-wielding state troopers straight from central casting line
up below in carefully choreographed rows.

"Pigs! Pigs! Pigs!" I shout, because these men don't look
human.

"Pigs! Pigs! Pigs!" I shout again, spilling my guts in triple
time.

But our incantation is futile. Like the enemy back home,
these men don't take insult for long. They move in to free the
building.

When the Parkhurst Takeover wraps on May 7th, the sun
is up. Twenty-nine Dartmouth students are escorted out of
Parkhurst, arrested, and put on the school bus. They will be
sentenced to thirty days in jail.

## GO MOTION

MY LAST DARTMOUTH break comes in the spring.
Home for less than an hour, my mind becomes as clear as a
Windexed window. I have to leave home for good. Not as a
runaway tearing down the boulevard in an adrenaline-fueled
flight, but as an adult making a conscious decision.

My mother is worse and my father is not helping. Maybe
because he's too drunk himself. I try not to think he wants her
dead. All I know is that I have to surrender. Nothing is going

to change, and no one here can help me. It's every man for himself.

I gather my belongings, write a note for the ones I hear fighting in the background, and place it on my mother's Ampex.

> Dear Mommy and Daddy,
>
> I don't know why you keep hurting each other, but it makes me really sad. I'm starting to lose myself and I can't let that happen. I want to have a good life. Please don't worry about me. I will find a way to earn my own money and take care of myself. Thank you for everything. I love you very much.
> Lynn

If not for Mrs. Cangemi, the nosy neighbor around the corner who is married to the doctor who saved my mother the night she overdosed; if not for Mrs. Cangemi, who makes it her business to worry about my family; if not for Mrs. Cangemi, who happens to be walking by as I am backing out of the carport, I would be on the road to a new life.

"Lynn!" Mrs. Cangemi calls out.

I turn my head. Mrs. Cangemi pops up outside my window like a dead dog who fell through the ice in the winter and floats to the surface in the spring.

"Where are you going?" she asks, nailing me with her question.

"Back to Dartmouth, Mrs. Cangemi. I can't live here any-more."

"You can't go anywhere," Mrs. Cangemi replies. "Don't you know your mother is *psychotic*?"

The word sounds big.

"Your brother and sister need you. Your father needs you," she says, opening the trapdoor to a lifetime of guilt. As I topple headlong in, I am dumbfounded by how important I suddenly am to my family's well-being.

Mrs. Cangemi waits until I walk into the house, and the door shuts behind me.

## WIPE

IN THE AFTERMATH of Parkhurst, Dartmouth's President and Board of Trustees invite its students to the Top of the Hop where there is room enough to gather. Dartmouth's aging men in suits and serious faces are going to listen to student concerns. They want to hear from its men—and whether they know it or not—one of its women.

With the end of my Dartmouth year fast approaching, I'm in a panic. I don't want to leave Dartmouth and return to Elmira. I want to stay and get my Dartmouth degree. I see no reason why I shouldn't be allowed to.

Dartmouth's power-brokers, lined up behind a table, look more like judges than friendly father-types. With one exception. Handsome, tanned Tom Braden. When Tom Braden smiles, I feel a familiar attraction. I never question my inclination towards attractive men old enough to be my father, nor their proclivity towards me. It feels natural somehow.

As I listen to students rage about friends still sitting in jail, I sit in estrogen's wings. I don't really want to stand up in front of all these men, but I have no choice. Dartmouth is not inviting me back for another year so I can graduate. Most likely, they simply don't see my value. I will make them understand.

As I walk nervously to the microphone, the pit in my stomach grows as wide as the Green. My legs are rubber. My hands, pins and needles. I exit my body and go into my best Perry Mason.

"Hi, I'm Lynn Lobban," I say. "I'm one of the women students. I've been here all year and I feel like Dartmouth is my school now."

It's true. And I have done well at Dartmouth, give or take joining a fraternity, having an affair with a visiting art teacher, and participating in the takeover of Parkhurst. All of which I hope they might have somehow missed.

"I don't want to leave. I want to stay and get my degree just like everyone else. I don't see why I shouldn't be able to."

My fellow students look like they're enjoying my earnest plea. Some are cheering for coeducation. Or maybe it's all about my breasts again.

When Dartmouth's kingmakers don't respond fast enough, I jump in to fill the gap.

"But what's wrong with us?" I ask, because I truly want to know. "You *marry* us!"

As if the fact men share their lives with women must make them worthy.

As my words reach out to grab their lapels and shake them to their senses, I see a few are amused. One is laughing as if I am just the cutest and most clever thing. Finally, someone says they're studying the issue. But I barely hear him. Devastated, I slink away.

In a few weeks, I get a letter from Tom Braden. When I see his name and address on the envelope, I think he is going to ask me on a date. But Tom Braden surprises me. He is the rare older bird with boundaries.

His letter is kind and sympathetic. He praises my courage and commends my commitment. I'm glad he's so impressed. But then he explains the politics of progress, and I wonder if he wants me to feel better.

> It is unfortunate that the sowers of the seeds of revolution are not always able to reap its benefits.

Sorry, Tom Braden, but that just makes me mad.

## HEAD-ON SHOT

MY QUEST FOR formal admission into Dartmouth is not a solo one, nor is it limited to my verbal plea. Arthur Fergenson, fellow thespian and future law clerk to Chief Justice Warren E. Burger, takes up our cause.

## STUDENTS CLAIM DISCRIMINATION

Several Dartmouth students have filed a letter of complaint with the Equal Employment Opportunity Commission against the College for its discrimination against women.

Arthur F. Fergenson '69, Katherine G. Brooks, Lynn L. Lobban, and Nanalee Raphael sent the letter last week, criticizing the College for "its active discriminatory policies on the admission of women," and calling for an investigation under a provision of the Civil Rights Act of 1964.

The four students went on to urge action by the Federal Government, including the immediate suspension of all federal aid to Dartmouth and projects under Dartmouth sponsorship or supervision, to rid this school of a "morally and sociologically indefensible institution: single-sex education."

Fergenson wrote in a column in The Dartmouth last week that Dartmouth is "its own employment agency. For Dartmouth College to refuse to admit girls on an open basis with men...is to restrict the pool available for filling jobs."

He also noted that with the acceptance of the Afro-American Society's demands, up to eight black "special students" will be admitted to a degree program, while female "special students" are still denied degree candidacy.

A spokesman for the Commission said yesterday that Fergenson must now file an "official charge." He said the Commission would then conduct an investigation and issue a decision "within fifteen months."

The spokesman expressed skepticism toward the charge's success, citing a clause from the Civil Rights Act which specifically states, "Title VII shall not apply to...an educational institution with respect to employment of individuals to perform work connected with the educational activities of that institution."

Speaking of earlier efforts toward coeducation, Fergenson said, "Everything attempted in Dartmouth's incredibly muddled regular channels has failed."

- *The Dartmouth*

We try everything. Nothing works.

# CROSS-CUT

NEWS ABOUT MY mother wipes out all other concerns. I find out when I make an obligatory call home in early June. Hester answers, and asks how I am.

"Fine, Hester," I lie, because if I tell her the truth, I may start crying. "Is Mommy there?"

"No, Lynn," Hester says slowly. "Your mother isn't here."

"Is she in New York?" I ask, imagining her at the Plaza under a palm tree.

"No. Your mother is in the hospital."

"How long has she been there?" I ask, shocked.

"About a week," Hester says.

"A week? But what's wrong with her?" I ask.

When Hester doesn't respond, I think she doesn't want to tell me, or she simply doesn't know.

"Is Daddy there?" I ask.

"No, your father isn't here," Hester answers.

That's right. My father isn't there. But he's not at the hospital with my mother, or with patients in his office. He's not even in Jersey City. He's on a road trip to the University of Virginia so he can show his alma mater to his son. Who knows? Maybe his junior can follow in his southern footsteps.

I say goodbye to Hester and call someone who will speak the brutal truth.

"I just talked to Hester, Mrs. Cangemi, and she said Mommy's in the hospital."

"Yes, Lynn," Mrs. Cangemi says, with uncharacteristic kindness. "Your mother is very sick."

"Could she die?" I ask, because I hope I don't have to come home.

"Yes, Lynn," Mrs. Cangemi says.

Her frankness is a gut punch.

"Thank you for telling me."

As my mother's life flashes before me, all I can think of are the times I've yelled *I wish you were dead!* in a helpless adolescent rage.

# TREATMENT

THE NEWS OF my mother's possible demise at the end of what I still need to believe is my first, and not last, Dartmouth year is devastating. I have no skills for this. I swallow my macho-sized embarrassment about needing anything from anybody and seek out Dartmouth's shrink.

Dartmouth's doctor for more fragile beings is in his office. As I peek through his half-open door, I think of *Dragnet* and downtown questioning. When the shrink sees me, he invites me in. My timing is perfect. Not many Dartmouth men are seeking help today.

I sit down and tell him my mother is very sick, but that is not the real reason I'm here.

"Something happened with my mother three years ago," I confess, because I have to. The secret is so heavy I can't lift it anymore.

"I'm glad you're here," the shrink says, and I think he is because he looks interested.

He waits for me to say more.

"One night my mother got really drunk."

Big surprise, though it is to him.

"It was the middle of the night and she wouldn't stop yelling and I couldn't sleep."

The only reason I'm telling him this is because my mother might be dying. Otherwise, I'd keep the secret to myself. Probably forever.

"Go on," the shrink encourages.

"So I went into her room and told her to be quiet."

I'm shocked the shrink doesn't mind I'm still talking. I don't think anyone has ever listened to me before.

"I told her I had to get up in the morning. I had to go to school. She said she'd be quiet if I'd sleep in my father's bed."

The shrink looks confused.

"My mother and father have two single beds pushed together," I explain.

"Where was your father?" the shrink asks.

I wonder what my father has to do with any of this, but I answer because the shrink is a man, a doctor, and older than me.

"My father drinks a lot, too," I explain. "He fights with my mother so he doesn't sleep in their room anymore."

"Where does he sleep?" the shrink asks.

"Sometimes he sleeps in my brother's room, sometimes in his office under his desk, sometimes on a couch in his waiting room, and sometimes under the piano."

No way am I telling the shrink my father used to sleep in my bed until I was twelve when my mother finally threw him out. The last thing I need is for Dartmouth's shrink to blame me, too. Besides, I don't need to get more confused.

"My mother and father fight a lot," I say, giving him something else.

"I see," the shrink says, and I think he does. In fact, he looks a little like Wendell Corey in *The Eleventh Hour,* the show where people have nervous breakdowns and get normal at the end.

The shrink tells me to go on, but it's getting harder because the bad part is coming. I take a breath and my words ride out on an anxious exhalation.

"I told her I'd sleep with her, but only if she'd be quiet and let me sleep. Then she said I had to kiss her good night, so I rolled over and kissed her on the cheek, and then she started to—"

The shrink leans in. I feel like a paperback potboiler and he needs to turn my page.

"She started licking my neck. She licked me all over my face and then I felt this throbbing."

I wonder if the shrink knows it was a little like Denis's trip south of my border. I think he might because he's looking at me in a way I don't recognize. I rush to finish the story because I have to get the hell out of here.

"So I ran out of her room and went back to my bed and cried all night long."

The shrink takes an agonizing moment to think all this over. But because I can't bear silence, I keep talking because if I don't, I will go crazy.

"Sometimes I tell boys there's something about me they don't know. When I was at Elmira, I thought maybe I was a lesbian, but I'm really not."

Sometimes I wish I could be. I think it might be easier.

Finally, the shrink takes pity on me. He speaks with Ivy League assurance and says something that might be helpful if it wasn't so stupid.

"Family members are often sexually attracted to each other, Lynn. It's only society that puts taboos on it."

"Oh," I say, as if I understand. But what does that even mean?

"I think it would be a good idea if you went home and talked to your mother," he advises.

"Okay," I say, because he seems so proud of himself.

I don't tell him I already talked to my mother and she just laughed it off. So now I think the shrink must be the crazy one because talking to my mother only made me feel worse. Because if my mother could think I was my father, then something is really wrong with me.

Thank God, I didn't tell him my father used to sleep in my bed because I'm confused enough by what he said about taboos. That things that don't seem good are normal. I thank him for the help he hasn't given me and exit his office.

## EXTREME CLOSE UP

I TURN NEXT to one of Dartmouth's chaplains. Having attended Sunday school for most of my childhood, I've been led to believe a man of God will throw me the collar around his neck. He will toss me Jesus' life-preserver so I can be saved.

When the chaplain opens his door, he is happy to see me. His oak-paneled office, bathed in the ambient light of the Lord, is instantly soothing. Since I've been trained to feel safe with God's messengers, I get down to business.

"My mother is very sick," I say, with tears brimming.

I leave out the licking story. The shrink is one thing, but even I know you don't talk about sex in front of God.

The chaplain smiles with sympathetic concern. He clearly wants to help.

"A neighbor said she could die," I say. "I know I should go home, but I'm scared."

It's true. I'm scared about my mother, but what really scares me is leaving Dartmouth. I'm afraid if I leave Hanover now, Dartmouth won't let me back in. Dartmouth will forget all about me, and for reasons I can't explain, to be forgotten about by Dartmouth feels like death itself.

I tell the chaplain how much my mother drinks. He looks fatherly and kind. I think his plaid shirt and sweater vest are what Jesus would wear if he were a man of Dartmouth.

"I'm so glad you're here, Lynn," the chaplain says.

"I am, too," I reply, because I feel protected.

But then the chaplain says something pre-recorded and straight out of God's tired playbook. It is the last thing I want to hear.

"Your mother is in God's hands now," he says.

I grow as cold as the ice in my mother's glass of scotch. But I hide my disappointment. I don't tell him I think God is washing his hands of my mother like Dartmouth is trying to wash its hands of me. Instead, I take his outstretched hand, bow my head, and go along with his meaningless prayer.

But just as I am about to say a well-mannered goodbye to all Dartmouth authority, the chaplain pushes back from his chair and stands up. I feel instantly diminished. I want to stand up, too, but he's coming towards me. His plaid shirt and sweater vest, so Ivy safe and smart, flood me with foreboding. His corduroy pants, too close to my face, remind me of the ones my father wears when he's raking autumn leaves at the Lake.

The chaplain is talking, but I cannot hear him because his hand is pressing down on my shoulder. I close my eyes and pray for the help that will not come. I flinch as he puts his other hand on my chest, so cashmere soft it must feel good to his open palm. He braces himself against me and pushes down.

I open my eyes. God's closed-eyed emissary is gazing into heaven while he rubs and fondles my breasts, these too big breasts that have attracted so much attention here. A familiar despair swoops in.

"I have to go! My mother is dying!" I yell, so loudly I can even hear.

When the chaplain drops his hand, I grab the doorknob mercifully near and make an exit my mother would not only think impolite, but unforgivably rude. As I run across the Green, I already know I will not tell anyone about my visit to the chaplain. No one—not even Denis or Jane—can know how bad I am.

## UNIT DRIVER

I HAVE TO go home, but I can barely function. I run to Denis who is still the most loyal man in my life. When I find him studying for his final exams, I hate to interrupt him, but I have run out of ideas and everything else.

"My mother is really, really sick," I say. "I think she might be dying."

"I'm so sorry, Jewels," Denis replies, with immediate and genuine concern.

He must think my mother is as wonderful as his.

"Do you want me to drive you home?" he offers.

I don't know why Denis would want to do this, especially before his exams. But I accept his offer because the end of my rope has already slipped from my hands. Overwhelmed by his kindness, I hand him the keys to my car.

For the five-hour ride home, I can't even fake a conversation. Usually afraid in the unknown space of silence, I don't know what to say. I am suspended in a reality I can barely acknowledge. I lean my head against the window and gaze into a cloudy sky, looking for answers.

## GHOST LIGHT

I TELL MYSELF Dartmouth is only momentarily behind me. As soon as whatever this is with my mother is over, I'll return to Hanover and resume my Dartmouth fight to stay.

"Here comes Lynnie!" Aunt Pauline says, as I step off the hospital elevator.

My aunt and uncle scramble to intercept me. As Denis hangs back, I think he doesn't like this part of life. I tell myself he can't handle it. I tell myself I can. As I walk to my mother's private room at the end of the hall, my aunt and uncle walk on either side in case they need to catch me should I fall.

When I walk into my mother's room, the smell is putrid and antiseptic, all at once. My mother is lying still in a bed. Her skin is a sickly orange color because poison is filling every cell. Her belly is so big she looks pregnant, but she's incredibly skinny. A steady stream of nurses flow in and out of her private room, giving top of the line though pointless treatment to the once head nurse and wife of Christ Hospital's Chief of Surgery.

I think my mother has drunk herself to the doorway of her death. No prince can wake her from her cirrhotic sleep

I move to the side of her bed, holding back tears because if I let go, I will be lost forever. I lean down and whisper into her shoulder.

"I love you, Mommy," I say, because I do.

Barely conscious, my mother cannot open her eyes.

"I love you too, Lynn," she whispers.

It is our final exchange.

But it can't be. I can't let my mother die. Surely, I can keep her alive. If her life has always been my fault, then I am the only one who can save her.

I walk onto the balcony outside the visitors' room and look up into a star-filled Jersey City sky. I haven't spoken to God since my visit to the chaplain, but it's not like I have somewhere else to turn. "Please don't let Mommy die," I pray. "Please let Mommy live. I promise I won't eat anything until she gets better."

Sadly, my sacrificial starving is as effective as my fast to end the war. In two days, my mother slips into an irreversible coma and I eat a pint of ice cream.

For the next two weeks, I visit my mother to keep her company. I sit in a high-backed chair in the corner of her room and watch her breathe. Every inhalation and exhalation, saturated with the possibility of life's end. But being with my mother in her last days is existential agony. Watching her breath quicken, slow down, then quicken again, is more frightening than any drunken attack. As our lives hang in the balance, my mother and I are one in matching mother-daughter gasps.

# MARTINI SHOT

MY MOTHER EXHALES her final breath on June 21, 1969. It is the summer solstice, the longest day of the year. My mother dies alone, a few minutes before my father goes into her room after seeing his other patients, and just as I am turning off Saturday morning cartoons.

When my father calls to tell me of her death, I sob so loudly I can barely hear what he says next.

"How would you feel if I gave away your mother's organs?" My father asks, as if he needs my permission.

"What?" I say, because I don't understand.

"Your mother has a strong heart," he says, as if he installed it.

He explains how her liver has failed, but her body is not without value. I am horrified. I don't know about organ donation, or how my mother might save someone else. I only know I don't want her cut up. I don't want her to suffer anymore, alive or dead.

"No! Don't do that!" I yell, trying to save her one more time.

When my father hears my distress, he drops the subject and never mentions it again. All these years, I have never imagined it might have actually happened. That someone got to live because of my mother's strong and beating heart.

## OUT-TAKES

Curled up in the cellar freezer
Peeing on the fruit bowl
Wielding a kitchen knife
Double stingers
Triple martinis
Her drunken hands clasped behind her back
Her intelligence
Her wit
Her deafening voice
Her love of opera, art, books, and Broadway
Her pretty face
Her bloated face
Her youth straining to be old
Her smell of alcohol and Arpege
Her rubber girdle gouging her body
Her clothes all navy blue and black
Her criticism
Her meanness
Her words cutting me in half
Her unending pain
Her unending sorrow
Her shame, then mine

Her pearls
Her diamonds
Her rage
Her outrage
Yellow with jaundice
Dying then dead.

## POETIC LICENSE

AFTER MY MOTHER'S death, I find a poem written on the back of my 1957 fourth grade report card. On one side are six beautifully handwritten A's for Class Assignments, Home Study, Citizenship, Health, Courtesy, and Self-Control. On the other side is my mother's written-in-pencil poem.

The Croesus of misgiving,
Lurking from the depths
Of infinite darkness.
Infinite because never looked for.
Infinite because never thought of.
Misgiving - cruel and unreal
But yet devastating
Like the locust of old.
Thought of but not expected.
Learned of but beyond reality.
Yet here.
Still cruel lustful angels

> Ugly as unkind thoughts
> Waiting, watchful—deviltry.

I read the poem, not understanding. I look up Croesus and wonder if my mother knew she had overestimated the importance of wealth, if she knew money was not worth her life. Or maybe what she took from Croesus was that his wife committed suicide.

I look up misgiving—*a feeling of doubt or apprehension, especially concerning a future event*—and wonder if my mother knew what was coming.

As for "still cruel lustful angels," that sounds too scary to contemplate. I don't want to think the beings of virtue and light use humans for their sexual pleasure. But maybe my mother knew evil was lurking and she would never get away.

Overwhelmed by the obtuseness of poetry and my mother, I push away her despair and turn the report card over, shocked to see a C in math.

## ACADEMY AWARD

TWO WEEKS AFTER the end of my Dartmouth year—and without having to audition—I play the gracious eldest daughter hosting three nights of casket viewing, a morning funeral, and an early afternoon burial. I don the black dress, black patent leather heels, neutral stockings, and short white gloves. If my mother could sit up and see me, she would heartily approve.

In an open casket, my mother is wearing more makeup than she's worn in all her life put together. She'd be appalled by her tawdry appearance. Her head, shoulders, and a portion of her chest are her only visible parts. The lower half of her fancy mahogany coffin is covered with yellow roses, her favorite flower. Unlike the empty box of fraternal initiation, my mother's casket is filled with a forty-five-year-old alcoholic who never went to college.

Like a friendly and competent tour guide, I walk family and friends up to her body, explaining her light blue dress. "She would only wear dark colors, and my sister and I always wanted her to wear light ones," I say, remembering the moment in Macy's when my sister and I, in a rare sibling conspiracy, realized we could pick whatever dress we wanted.

As for the funeral, it remains true to the spirit of alcoholism. It ignores how and why my mother died, and what it cost the rest of us. I stoically endure the charade, anxious to get to the cemetery at my beloved Lake, fifty miles away.

# IT'S A LOCK

AS I STEP into the lead limousine with my father and siblings, I am aware how even in tragedy I like feeling special. I slide into the limo and lean my head against the tinted window. Gazing up into the sky, I search again for an answer. This time I get one. It's raining. The sky is crying. The very atmosphere grieves.

Roll sound.

As our car leads the head-lighted procession into the cemetery behind the First Presbyterian Church, I remain courageous and contained. But the moment I see the hole in the ground awaiting my mother's body and the giant pile of dirt that will entomb her forever, the reality of her death drops down like an atomic bomb. My body slips from its fragile mooring and I collapse into my father's lap.

Drowning in a sea of grief, I hear my brother and sister get out of the car and quickly move away. My father offers the only support his World War II self knows. "Chin up!" he says, grabbing me by the shoulders and lifting me up.

I pull myself together and return to being the man I forgot to be. But as soon as the last person leaves the obligatory post-burial social, I run upstairs to my room and sob uncontrollably and uncomforted for six straight hours.

## HORROR FLICK

TWO WEEKS AFTER my mother's death, I'm at the Lake doing what I can to mitigate intolerable pain. Fighting a daily battle with my feelings is exhausting.

Drugs help.

I walk down the hill to stand on the point, a protruding piece of land where I once caught a fish so big it set a lake record. Tonight though, I'm only angling for relief. And I'm not alone. I'm with Timmy, the boy I just let fuck me on the itchy carpet in the den while my father slept in the room above.

When anyone offers me a drug, I always take it. So far, it's been marijuana, LSD-laced punch, and hash brownies. Smoking hashish is something new. As Timmy lights the pipe, I remember how nice my father looked when he smoked one. My mother always nagged him to smoke a pipe, but he never liked it. Now he never has to smoke a pipe again. My father's free like me.

Timmy passes me the pipe and I inhale its magic potion. I stare up at the full moon, so big and bright it makes the night look like day. I draw in the resinous fumes like a Native American desperate for peace. I cannot get enough.

But then I get too much and everything reverses. I start falling into an invisible abyss. Falling, falling, falling in a nonstop tumble into hell. I drop the pipe and run up the hill though it's hard to lift my feet. Propelling myself into the kitchen, I try to solidify myself with food. I eat ice cream, cookies, frosted flakes, and peanut butter, but no childhood remedy can stop my tortuous descent. If only I could pass out. But if I do, I know I'll be buried alongside my mother.

I need help. But Timmy ran away, my father drank himself into oblivion, my sister is asleep, and my brother is out with friends. Not that my siblings would help me. Ever since Mommy caught Daddy in my bed, I'm pretty sure they hate me.

As the world spins too fast for me to stop it, I stagger into the living room and sit in my mother's yellow chair at the table where she and Besta used to play canasta. But it only makes things worse. There is nothing left to do but to pray another foxhole prayer. I just hope it works better than the last one. Toppling to the floor, I land on my over-worked knees.

"Please God, please. Don't let me die. If you let me live, I promise I will never take another drug again. Not for the rest of my life."

Within minutes, the falling ends. But because my terror this night is so great, I keep my promise to God. To this day, I rarely take a Tylenol. And it's a good thing too, because if I had not fallen into the fullness of the drug, the moon, and my mother's death, I am sure I would have ended up in a gutter somewhere, dying from heroin and an overdose of pain.

## CONTINUITY OF MOTION

BEFORE I'M FINISHED with Dartmouth and Dartmouth is finished with me, I have to go back and take my final exams. Dartmouth is not letting me return as a senior in the fall—I have lost that battle as surely as my mother has lost hers—but the college needs closure. I wonder if anyone knows my mother is dead.

It's probably a good idea to finish my junior year. After all, my father paid a lot of money to send me to the Ivy League. And I will finish. But only after I spend six weeks at the American Dance Festival in New London, Connecticut because that's where Ray Cook said I should go if I want to be a dancer. That's what I'm going to do now. I'm going to dance because if I stand still, grief will swallow me whole.

Anyway, the timing doesn't matter. I can do whatever I want now because my mother is dead and my father only says, "Do what makes you happy, Lynn."

Thank God, I still have my good parent.

# LEGS

THE AMERICAN DANCE Festival lifts me out of self and sadness. I hurl myself into as many classes as my body can endure. I inhale Twyla Tharp and Yvonne Rainer who teaches me *Trio A*. I take an early morning class with Jamie Cunningham and another with Al Huang who makes me feel whole for an hour at a time. When I see Talley Beatty's company, I watch Debbie Allen dance and am sure I see her fly.

I love being at the festival. Except when Jamie teaches yoga's sun worship with its slowed-down, breath-coordinated movements and I have a debilitating panic attack that feels like dying. Ever since I watched my mother die, I can't stop watching myself breathe. I'm convinced if I don't make myself breathe, I'll end up dead like her.

As for my Dartmouth exams, I neither study nor prepare. It's only when the dancing stops do I realize I have to go back to Hanover and take them.

## MIT OUT SOUND

AS I DRIVE up the hill to Hanover, the trees have a hazy white glow. They look like they're covered with snow. But it's August. Shit. I'm on the verge of another panic attack. I park my car and run into the Hop.

My hands push against the revolving door and deposit me in the lobby. I immediately relax when I see a banner for *The Royal Hunt of the Sun*, the Peter Shaffer play about Atahualpa, the Inca King, and Pissarro, the conquering explorer who destroys him. I head to the box office and buy a quick ticket out of myself.

With hours to kill, I drink a Tab in the snack bar. I visit the bookstore and buy another Dartmouth shirt. I walk around the campus, but skip going to Heorot because in my unsteadiness I dare not risk rejection. I should let someone know I'm here. I have been a good girl. I've come back to take my final exams, just like I've been told. The only problem is, I no longer see a reason to take them.

It's not that I'm unfocused, unprepared, and will most likely fail every single one. It's because Dartmouth won't let me stay for my senior year. And since I refuse to return to a campus of disempowered women on an ugly washed-out campus in upstate New York, and because neither dancers nor actors need college degrees, I see no reason to put myself through the ordeal of taking them. Fuck academia. After *The Royal Hunt of the Sun*, I am out of here.

# PLOT TWIST

I ENTER MOORE Theater and take my seat on the aisle. I love the aisle. Being able to make a quick getaway is always a good idea. As people sit down around me, I look out at the stage. My chest aches remembering the mocking of my breasts nearly a year before. I open the program to escape my shame and feel a familiar pang of exclusion. *The Royal Hunt of the Sun*, a play about men, was written by a man, and directed by a man. Every actor onstage—with two exceptions—will be men, including Rod Alexander, the man who used my breasts to his theatrical advantage. Once again, I am roiling in a vat of testosterone.

As houselights dim, I consider fleeing. But I don't, because the theater remains my refuge. Not to mention the man playing Atahualpa, whose name happens to be Bill, is looking into the audience and I swear he's staring straight at me. Bronzed and golden tan, the gorgeous Dartmouth man towers over everyone. His naked chest glistens in the heat of the blazing sun. When Atahualpa speaks, his deep Sun King voice resonates in a place I haven't felt since my mother died.

"Atahualpa wants! Atahualpa gets!" Dartmouth's Sun King proclaims.

"Oh yes! Yes!" my body screams with hormonal longing. "Whatever you want, Atahualpa! Whatever you need!"

But wait just a minute, Lynn. Not so fast. Let's reason this out. Okay. Since I am not taking my exams, I'm not technically finishing my Dartmouth year. And since I'm not finishing, I am and always will be, a Dartmouth man. After all, I am still a member of Heorot. Anyone can see my picture in the composite. So, I don't think so, Atahualpa.

*Lynn wants! Lynn gets!*

I can't wait for the play to end so I can rush backstage and claim what's mine.

## DOUBLE BILL

I KNOCK AND slowly push open his dressing room door. Atahualpa Bill is wiping body makeup from his chest.

"Hi," I say, trying to contain my excitement.

"Hi," Bill smiles. «Come in."

I tell him I am one of Dartmouth's first women.

"I heard you were on campus," he grins.

I shower him with flirtatious praise, telling him how much I loved his work because actors love to hear this.

"How long are you here for?" Bill asks, writing his address on a slip of paper.

Well, I *was* going to drive back to Jersey City, but I take the scrap without making a commitment. I wait a cool hour before I head across the river to fuck my last Dartmouth man.

When Bill opens the door, he's sleepy and surprised. I drop any hint of coyness, take off my clothes, and throw myself onto Bill's mattress on the floor. After a wild strangers' kind of sex, I dress as quickly as I haven't come.

"Why don't you leave in the morning?" Bill asks.

Ugh. He sounds like a needy girl. I hate seeing this in a Dartmouth man. I can't leave fast enough.

"It's been nice meeting you, Bill. Take care!" I say, trying to reassure him because he looks so confused.

Without looking back, I open the door and exit like a Dartmouth man with the whole world in front of him.

# CLIMAX

# TWO-SHOT

AFTER BLOWING OFF my exams, I return to Jersey City and a life without my mother. Though I am profoundly grateful I no longer have to contend with an insane drunk whose hatred of me increased with every passing day, I feel lost.

61 Gifford Ave. is as quiet as an empty tomb. My brother and sister are at their respective colleges doing what is expected, while I, the college dropout, am living at home with my father before a permanent move into New York.

My father's drinking has progressed. He passes out every night and sometimes during dinner. I don't know why his passing out makes me feel so safe, even while it makes me feel so orphaned. As his bald head lowers into his plate, I wonder if he misses his wife. If he's sad, glad, or indifferent.

I've only seen my father cry once. The time he told me about his infant brother dying of peritonitis because the doctor didn't sterilize his instruments. It's why he became a doctor. I suppose as his mother's favorite son, he had to do something. As for the loss of his wife, I don't know if he cares enough to cry.

But tonight, I cannot bear my feelings. The friends in my TV are unable to soothe or distract me, and there's not enough sugar in the world because I have eaten everything I could find. I hate to admit it, but I need someone to talk to. I have to tell someone my mother is dead.

I decide to use the phone in my father's office because even though my mother is gone, it still feels like she could listen in. She would not approve of my calling my Catholic friend. But Jeanie always makes me feel better. When I pick up the rotary receiver, I feel thirteen. I'm helping my father in the summer when his secretary is on vacation.

"Dr. Lobban's office," I sing, because I love having a job.

Filing patient charts, I rest in the safety of the alphabet. I tear off yellow-stained paper on the examining table, crunch it in my hands, and toss the sickness into a silver can. I pull down clean white paper and tear it off a few inches past the silver stirrups. I walk down the hall to the waiting room filled with the people my father will fix and call out, "Next patient!" Yes, this office phone will keep my call to Jeanie from feeling too intimate and close.

After a few rings, Mr. Vallely answers. "Jeanie! It's Lobban!" he yells.

That's funny. Mr. Vallely usually asks how I am.

When Jeanie picks up the phone, her voice sounds strangely laden. It's unsettling, but I'm too afraid to ask what's wrong so I blurt out my news.

"My mother died," I say, because there's just no way around it.

"Oh Lobbs," Jeanie cries. "I'm so sorry."

But before I can say more, Jeanie blurts out her own despair. Her brother Timmy, the oldest son who skipped college to join the Marines so he could fight in a war I'm still fighting against, stepped on a mine.

"Oh no!" I say, not knowing what that means.

"Both of his legs were blown off," Jeanie says, with the heaviest heart I have ever heard.

## FEMME FATALE

I HAVEN'T THOUGHT about Ed Bonaventure since he finished his Dartmouth stint and returned to New York. But a few months after my mother's death, he calls. The moment I hear his sexy voice I remember being madly in love with him though I can't recall the feeling. When he asks me to have dinner, I say yes because I'm sure I must owe him something.

I take the 99S into New York and meet Ed at a Greek restaurant on West 47th Street. I'm wearing a dress, which is unusual for me because since my mother died, I only wear jeans. But I want Ed to want me, even though I don't want him. The dress must work because as we're finishing a bottle of Retsina, and with dessert on the table, Ed proposes.

"What?" I say, because I cannot fathom why he would ask such a thing.

"I want to marry you," Ed says, again.

But I haven't seen Ed in months. Why on earth would he want to marry me? His request feels like winning the lottery and being hooded for the guillotine.

"Thank you for asking," I say, dying for more wine, "but I'm never getting married."

I'm not. I saw what it did to my mother.

Ed stares at me. I can't tell whether he's angry or disappointed. Excruciatingly awkward in the face of my first marriage proposal, I don't know what to say.

"I'm sorry," I mumble, "but I have to catch my bus."

Leaving oozing baklava on the table, I run out of the restaurant and never hear from Ed Bonaventure again.

## FINANCING

WHEN I CROSS the Hudson River and move into New York, the distance feels like a million miles and not the actual ten. But I'm not moving into Manhattan like most people. I'm moving in with the full force of a stock portfolio. My father hands it to me—no strings attached—after my mother dies. Maybe he feels guilty. But whatever the motivation, I get to devour the shiny Big Apple because I can afford to.

For the next seven years, I live off the money that comes from the selling of my father's wisely invested stocks. I need to dump them anyway. When I discover the blue-chip companies have defense contracts with the U.S. government—including

Dow Chemical which makes napalm so I have been melting the flesh off of innocent Vietnamese—I am horrified.

But the blood money is well spent. It pays for dance classes, acting classes, and singing lessons with the finest teachers in New York. It also pays for much needed twice-a-week therapy because if I don't get help, I will not survive. I avoid analysis because I'm not lying down for anyone. I find a female psychologist I can look in the eye. A woman who listens. A woman who seems to care.

The money also pays for rent, utilities, phone, food, restaurants, clothing, plays, movies, haircuts, subway tokens, and the rare vacation. I live off my father's money from the time I'm twenty until I'm twenty-seven. I should be grateful, but I'm not.

It will be years before I see how my father's money subsidized my survival. How blessed I really was. Living beyond a traumatic childhood is easier when you can afford the help you need. One of the lucky ones, I no longer take the privilege lightly.

## BUDDY MOVIE

BECAUSE ALVIN AILEY studied with Lester Horton, I study the Horton technique with James Truitte, an important Ailey dancer. Jimmy's class is where I meet Barbara Ellmann, my first and only roommate. I think Barbara and I hit it off because we're both so serious about dance and we really love to laugh.

We find a small apartment on the Upper East Side because it's supposed to be safer there, though after living in Manhattan for forty-two years, it is the only place that's ever been robbed.

Our landlady, Mrs. Fred, a short, pudgy, middle-aged, heavily made up, bleached blonde from Eastern Europe, lives on Park Avenue. When I drop off my rent check, her bordello-red, dimly lit apartment reminds me of a whorehouse.

# CAMEO

THOUGH BARBARA HAS a longtime boyfriend, I'm always on a date. I have to keep them coming and going, going and coming. I have to find the right one.

Tonight, I'm having dinner with Joe who is tall, handsome, and five years older than me. Joe's not like the dancers I know. Joe makes a lot of money in construction. I wonder if he has a horse.

As we sit at a corner table in Trader Vic's, a restaurant that feels like a dark, faraway Polynesian island, I remember my mother used to come here. She said she liked drinking from a skull. I agree. Though the skull is pretty scary-looking, what's inside sets me on fire in a really good way.

Oh, look. Joe is grinning. I think he likes me.

*Uh-oh.*

What?

*I can't feel my legs.*

What are you talking about?

*My legs are numb.*

Eat a wonton.

*I can't! They're pulsating!*

Pick up the skull!

*But my hand is weak!*

Jesus Christ.

*I'm having a stroke!*

No! You're not!

*Maybe it's a heart attack!*

You're going to ruin everything!

*Or MS!*

Quick! Smile before he notices!

*But Mommy and Daddy are here. They're getting drunk and I know what that means.*

Pull yourself together!

*I'm trying.*

Look around! See where you are! You're at Trader Vic's in the Plaza Hotel. You're on a date with Joe, a handsome man who likes you.

*Right. I'm at Trader Vic's with Joe who really likes me. I know. I'll have another drink, eat dessert, and later we can have sex.*

Good girl.

# "A" LIST

I HAVE ANOTHER good friend in New York. Sylvia. I didn't know her at Elmira, but when we bump into each other at Clark Center when she's coming out of an African-Caribbean dance class and I'm coming out of jazz, we become instant friends. Probably because we both love talking about sex. Talking about sex in the 1970s is empowering and fun.

"I have an idea!" I say one night when we're on the phone. "Let's make a list of all the men we've had sex with!"

Sylvia loves my idea. Probably because her list will be longer than mine. I take out a pint of ice cream, and pick up a pen.

1. Bill Douglas.

I'm not sure I should include him because I didn't really know we were having sex until it was over, but Sylvia says technically, he counts. But she refuses to list the man who raped her because it was at knifepoint.

Sylvia will always remain at least ten men ahead of me. I think it's because she travels so much. Some of the men on her list don't even have names, like "the Israeli," or "the Greek guy on the beach." Most of the men I let fuck me live in Manhattan and I usually get their names though not much else.

As Sylvia and I laugh together, I think how nice it is to put men down on paper where I can see them.

## DOCUMENTARY

AT THE END of 1969, Barbara gives me a present. A 1970 appointment book, lovingly collaged with pictures and wise sayings. Because of the beauty of her work and because it's shellacked for posterity, I save it, which turns out to be a good thing.

I open to January 29, 1970 and am shocked to see the day's notation.

> The crazy chaplain from Dartmouth calls Lobban
> for yet another try. No comments for once.

Wow. I forgot the chaplain followed me to New York. Probably for another whack at my chest. I vaguely remember his calls, and how I swatted him away like a mosquito.

I turn to February 10, 1970. Bill Douglas hasn't given up on me either. He must have told me to "Walk into the Light" because I have written it all over the page in big purple and blue letters. And he invited me to San Francisco because I asked my father for his opinion.

My father is a beautiful man. He says "If you have a yen for him, I say go to San Francisco." Wow. My father will let me go! But in the end, I decide not to.

Seeing the handwriting of my twenty-year-old self is reassuring. I'm not crazy, after all.

## TOP BILLING

IN 1971, TWO years after my mother's passing, I want to find out why she said I wasn't her first baby. Now that she's dead and I've had a year of therapy, it feels safer to ask. I figure my father knows.

Standing side by side in the sunporch, my father and I are facing my mother's floor-to-ceiling bookcases, filled with her beautifully bound and cherished books. Oh how I wish I had been a book. How carefully I would have been broken in by her beautiful hands. How lovingly respected and read. I look over at my father who still only reads newspapers, unsure he will remember.

"When Mommy was drunk, she always said I wasn't her first baby," I say. "I never understood."

My father's silence speaks volumes. But I don't wait for his response because if this conversation is to continue, I have to move it along.

"So *was* Mommy pregnant before me?" I say, trying a direct approach because my father usually answers a question.

"Yes, she was," he says, quietly.

Oh God. I'm in for it now.

"So *did* Mommy have an abortion?" I ask, shocked I said the word.

"Yes, she did," my father says.

I still don't understand.

"But if Mommy had an abortion," I say, with my existence hanging in the balance, "why did she have *me*?"

"Your mother didn't want to go through that again," my father says, as a matter of fact.

"Oh," I say, and the conversation ends.

I don't have the guts to ask if he performed the abortion himself because I've always imagined this other baby was a full-fledged sibling. I don't want to know if he was capable of stopping his own child, potential or not.

Many years later, I come up with a theory. My mother was most likely pregnant with some *other* man's nondescript fetus. Some *half*-sibling my surgeon father probably aborted as a favor to the pretty young nurse who took such good care of him. And then, when my mother had sex with my father to return the favor—didn't women have sex with powerful men because they had to—my mother got pregnant *again*, but this time with *his* baby, as in, voilà, *me!*

Sometimes I wonder if my mother ever used birth control. If there even was birth control. In any event, my mother was throwing me a drunken and repetitive truth. I *was* her first baby, but only her first *born*, as in the first to show up. Kind of like me at Dartmouth.

# PERFORMANCE

BY 1972, I am sick of looking at myself in mirrors, struggling to get thin after crazy food binges, and searching for the perfect leg warmers so I can look as cool as other dancers. Though my teachers are all saying I'm ready to dance professionally, I don't care. I jettison my dream of Alvin Ailey and go back to acting. It's not because I'm terrified to leap into the world and risk rejection. It's because I love to talk too much to just be dancing.

Nina Fonaroff, my ballet teacher and mother-figure who says, "People can never want to *be* something, they must want to *know* something," recommends her friend and colleague, Sandy Meisner. Sandy is a brilliant teacher, Nina says, but can sometimes be unkind. That's all I need. More verbal abuse.

I decide to study with his protege, Bill Esper, a comparatively gentler soul. When Bill gives me permission to feel all my feelings—including anger—my work garners high praise. He calls me as "a young Geraldine Paige." But it's easy going the distance in the womb of class. After two years of training, I'm not so happy when Bill says it's time to go out and find work.

## POSITIVE PRINT

THOUGH I LOVE to act, sing, and dance, I always wonder if it's enough. Maybe it's postmortem mother-guilt about finally getting to do what I want, or because I told God I would save the world if he'd let me survive Jersey City. But whatever the reason, I'm not convinced a life in the arts is a good enough way of helping other people.

I write to Dr. Whitlock who rides in, if not to rescue, at least to guide. Not that I am ever willing to listen if it's not what I want to hear.

> I can only tell you the way I saw my way out of the problem you face. During my last two years in college, I was in the Rutgers theater group. By my senior year, I was offered a place in the Columbia Workshop, which, at the time, was the hottest thing in experimental theater and training. I was also doing Danny Kaye routines in the college night club, and got several New York offers for that. Now you and I know the greatest pleasure you can get from all that is the reaction from an audience when you've moved them in the way you want, whatever the way may be.
>
> Actually, I don't think I have ever moved *anyone* the way I wanted. Onstage or off.
>
> My chief memory was playing Lachie in *The Hasty Heart*. I had a two-and-a half-minute change onstage behind a screen after a pretty emotional encounter, and not a sound came out of the audience for that whole time. It was great, and anyone who pretends it isn't, hasn't experienced it. But I went into teaching. Why? Who really knows the answer to that kind of thing? I know my father, who died

> when I was eleven, inculcated into all of us the
> idea that the only life worth living is one where
> you try to do things for others.
>
> When you get down to it—if you're honest with
> yourself—you have to admit the pleasure you get
> from what I've been describing is basically a self-
> ish pleasure. Because it honestly isn't what you're
> doing for them. It's what you're doing to them,
> and that's a very different thing.

I don't really know what he means. Though I volunteer on
Friday mornings at the Foundling Hospital, and on Monday
afternoons at Lenox Hill Hospital, I don't do it for long. I'm
too in need of self-expression, too beholden to the artists who
have helped me survive. I have to put all my energy into chas-
ing my dream.

But reading Baird's letter after many decades in the arts, I
finally understand. Though I'm certain his performance might
have done something *for* me, I cannot imagine my life without
his letters.

## SPOTLIGHT

AFTER DARTMOUTH, I continue to be sized up as
a cute, sometimes pretty woman with larger than average
breasts. Some men call me hot, though I dare not take that
in. In fact, I make a point of never wearing dresses and skirts

when I audition because my genetically well-shaped legs would show like my breasts do. I face a strange conundrum. As desperate as I am to be seen, I am terrified of exposure.

But I am aware that the way I look is an advantage as I venture into the wilderness of show biz. Since men make the decisions, they need to like what they see. Within days of sending out my first headshot, I get calls from twelve agents. All men.

Fast-talking Peter promises me the moon. He puts me in a limo and whisks me over to CBS and ABC to meet their casting departments. But a week later, he puts his hand on my thigh and asks me to have dinner. When I decline, I never hear from him again.

The next agent is kinder. Monty, seventeen-years older and newly-separated from his wife, says I have talent and sends me on high-end auditions.

"You're going to do very well in film, Lynn," Juliet Taylor, a casting director, says.

I'm so grateful to Monty for giving me so many chances, after four months of friendly in-office conversations, I surrender to a three-month affair and a lifelong friendship.

As for my auditions, they are uneven at best. I do well when encouraged and usually get called back. But when I get close to landing a high-profile job, a voice inside reminds me I am inherently unworthy. I don't deserve success. It's a miracle I ever get to Broadway.

When I'm cast in *Quilters*, a musical about pioneering women forging their way across the frontier, I think it's because I spent a year at Dartmouth and know what obstacles are. But maybe some unseen force is steering me to the comfort of women. Because the experience of *Quilters* remains one of the highlights of my life.

## COMING OF AGE

WHEN I MOVE into New York, I put a river between my father and me. I have to. His drinking is so bad now, I can only bear to call him in the mornings. If I call him at night, his slurring speech sends me into despair. But my father and I have our distanced moments.

Before I run out of the stock money and have to start earning my own, I take my first trip to Europe. I fly to Paris with my best friend, Murray Moss. Murray and I met in the 1968 Dartmouth summer when he was an acting apprentice. We had a three-month romance and I still think he is my soulmate. But Murray turns out to be gay. Sometimes I wish he'd change back so we could live happily ever after, but his being gay turns out to be a good thing. Now I can love him forever.

When I get to Paris, I do what my mother did. I write to her husband.

> April 20th - early morning 1 AM
> Dear Dad,
>
> It's not often I get a chance to write you. It's actually easier for me to communicate on paper. I

tried calling from the airport, but got no answer. I felt badly not saying goodbye, but trusted you understood.

The flight scared me at first, but I love 747s. You're so well taken care of, it's hard to worry for long. The food was even good.

Murray and I arrived in the morning, and I cried when I saw the Eiffel Tower. You can't imagine how thrilling all this is for me. Every time I come to a new place—the Louvre and especially Notre Dame today—I burst into tears. I am overwhelmed by the existence of these things. The world has opened up to me, or rather I have opened up the world to myself. I love Paris and everything about it. If I could think of something to do here, I would live here someday. It's such a beautiful, proud, spacious, and civilized city. Never have I felt a city so much in my blood. And I like the French people, too.

Murray and I have done miles of walking, and I'm exhausted at the end of the day. But it's all so glorious, even the fatigue is satisfying. To live so fully is wonderful. After five long years of struggling with the past, the past seems dead to me now. One must live in the world and enjoy it as much as possible.

Take care of yourself. Don't worry about me, and thank you for your generosity towards your children.

Much love,
Now your friend, too,
Lynn

# TRANSITION

THOUGH I SAY goodbye to Jersey City in 1969, my father doesn't until 1975 when he moves permanently to the Lake. Our house sits empty for five years. Drug addicts break in, shoot up, and squat. No one wants it until 1980. Once again, we are a *Jersey Journal* story.

> *AGUDATH SHOLOM BUYS GIFFORD AVENUE BUILDING*
> Congregation Agudath Sholom of Jersey City has sold its building at 472 Bergen Ave. and bought a new structure at 61 Gifford Ave. at the corner of Kennedy Blvd. Orthodox Jewish services will continue to be conducted at the Bergen Avenue building until the congregation is ready to move to its new synagogue. The Gifford Avenue building is a large house, formerly a doctor's residence, that

has been vacant for years. Area residents said they are glad to see it put it back into use.

Seeing my childhood home turned into an orthodox synagogue is surreal. Though a necessary purging, all I can think of is how glad my mother would be a rabbi will live there instead of a priest.

When the entrance where I walked in and out of alcoholic insanity is turned into the Holy Ark which holds the Torah, Judaism's most sacred text, I joke that God is moving into our house. And as far as I'm concerned, He can have it.

## COMMERCIAL BREAK

WHEN IT COMES to my career, I don't know how to live with success. I understand when Freddie Prinze puts a bullet through his head because he can't handle the discrepancy between being told how great you are and knowing you're not. The discrepancy would kill me, too. I may not have a Dartmouth degree, but I am smart enough to let self-sabotage protect me for as long as it is needed.

When Tex Beha, the kindest of agents, suggests I audition for television commercials, I balk. I'm a serious actress who wants to do theater and film. But actually, commercials are the perfect fit. How safe to succeed in thirty and sixty-second increments. And commercials don't cost anything. There's nothing I have to feel or lose in front of other people. Best of all though, after a day's work, I can walk away. Though I test for a role on *The Doctors*, one on *The Edge of Night*, two on *One Life to Live*, and five on *The Guiding Light*, I'm happy not to get them. I don't want anyone telling me I have to show up day, after day, after day. I don't want to feel trapped by anything.

TV commercials are good for other reasons, too. Just as I'm getting to the end of the blood money, I'm beginning to make my own small fortune. My wholesome, blond, blue-eyed, mid-western white-bread look is the rage now. I'm making a killing in the United States of Advertising because I'm so good at playing the sincere wife, mother, and spokesperson. In fact, I am so practiced at presenting, I can convince anyone—including myself—of almost anything.

I love seeing myself walking and talking in the television itself. Watching myself in the happy playground of childhood, I feel safe and content. And my family is thrilled. They love seeing me in a box, talking about things that don't matter.

## ON SET

BY 1975, AUDITIONS, callbacks, and commercial shoots are a regular part of my life. I love being on a set, staring into the deep black well of a lens while grips and gaffers light me to look good. Just knowing a camera is focused on me makes me feel happy. And earning my own money gives me an incredible sense of well-being.

Because my mother left a big empty ledger behind, I record every audition, callback, and job. Too bad she's not around to see how successful I am.

I open to an entry. One of three principals in a Hardee's "Big Twin" commercial, I have spent my day touting the virtues of a double cheeseburger with lettuce and Thousand Island dressing.

> It's such hard work...you always have to be on and ready to go...I love the camera and may even give up the theatre because it feels so right...I somehow ended up in the center spot and received quite a bit of attention—even more so than Candy who's the lead in *Grease* or Gary who's also in a show. They pretended to hit me out of jealousy. I started to apologize until I realized I was damn glad to be getting extra exposure, so I just shut up. The handsome director, Sid Meyers, appreciated my hard work and enthusiasm, but my best moment came after, when Candy and I were asked to stick out our chests for a Big Twin gag shot for the clients and agency men. Candy started getting ready to do it, but something went off in me and I almost started crying. I walked around the set and turned to several people. I told them it felt humiliating & did I have to do it. No, I said to myself. I don't have to do that. "No," someone else

said, too. Then I told them there was a limit and I didn't want to be exploited. So they stopped and turned the lights back on. And you know what? Candy thanked me for stopping it. Leslie the producer thanked me, and no less than five men, including Sid, came over to say I was right. I earned respect only because I respected myself not to be exploited. A cameraman who was ready to shoot the "gag" looked at me & said, "Right on." I'm really proud of that moment. I followed my instincts and believe I am mostly on my side, more often than not.

Baby steps as I begin to stand my female ground.

## MELODRAMA

IN 1975, BILL Douglas, Jr. calls out of the blue. He's in New York taking his father to see his doctors because Justice Douglas is recovering from a stroke. When Bill asks me to have lunch with them at The Drake Hotel, I say yes because I want to meet a Supreme Court Justice.

Sitting next to William O. Douglas makes me feel special, especially when he leans in and whispers, "I've just had a waterfall named after me."

Bill smiles from across the table, pleased his father likes me. I'm not so sure about the Justice's much younger wife.

Though I smile at her, hoping she doesn't think I'm flirting with her husband, she doesn't smile back.

As for Bill, I've already told him I'm moving in with my boyfriend, but he doesn't seem to care. He walks me out to Park Avenue, puts a letter in my hand, and tells me to read it when I get home. I read it on the bus.

> July 7, 1975
> Dear Lynn,
>
> I love you and want to be with you and I want to marry you. I feel like Om. I feel like I am one with you. I also feel crazy irrational stupid to leave this city without you or not to stay here with you. The flat-footed fact is that I must be six years old or less, dressed up in adult disguise to leave you like this. I DON'T BELIEVE THIS HAPPENS TO GROWNUPS IN THIS WAY! I'm in love with you and you are about to go make a life with someone else. Whoa. Wait. I feel like I've been waiting all my life to be with you. Your soul is inside me. I love you. Help. Something is really dumb in life if we don't live together forever; not long distance, but face to face, side by side. Say something. Anything. Yell it, write it, touch me, scratch me. Kiss me. I love you, Lynn.
>
> Bill

The effusiveness of his feelings scares me, though it *is* nice getting a second marriage proposal.

I'm just glad I'm moving in with Sam, the actor I met a month ago on an audition for Maxwell House Coffee. Otherwise, I would feel like I have to do something for Bill who needs me so much.

I put the letter in a box of mementos so I can prove a man with a famous father wanted me. A few days later, I get another letter. This time it's in a Supreme Court of the United States envelope which is reason alone to save it.

> July 9, 1975
>
> WHAT I WOULD LIKE LYNN TO REMEMBER: I hope you will be so happy the world will smile. I wish you peace deep down inside. In my upstairs, in my downstairs, and on my mezzanine, I love you very much. Inside me and outside me, too. There's no repayment expected for that love. No obligation. Since I first knew you seven years ago, I have said, "I love you" to two people. One person was you. I wrote it in a letter sent from San Francisco, and the other person was a girl in California I met three years ago. I love you, Lynn. I cannot tell you how much.
>
> Bill

I would like to believe I'm this incredible person Bill can't live without, but I wonder if his declarations of love are guilt about screwing me in my sleep that summer night. Or maybe he wants to lock in acceptable sex. Anyway, it doesn't matter. I'm just relieved he's moving on.

Years later, when I google Bill Douglas, Jr. and find out he died of alcoholism in 1989 at the age of fifty-six, I'm not surprised. But I feel overwhelming grief. Like all the alcoholics in my life, William O. Douglas Jr. got way too deep inside me.

## CASTING NOTICE

WANTED: ONE MAN. Minimum intimacy requirements. Both parents abandoned you or died by the time you were eight. Residence in another country, or occupation with lots of travel.

Highly stubborn, set in your ways, requiring the relationship to be strictly on your terms. Experience with addiction—drugs, alcohol, or sex—desired. Ideally currently active.

One man tall enough to tower over a smaller woman. No absolute religious preference, but uptight WASP type most appealing.

One man disdainful of other people's feelings and completely shut-off from your own.

One man willing to allow a woman to do her dance of trying to fix you while giving her as hard a time as possible so she can hone her skills of fighting lost causes. One man willing to provide a familiar pain to a woman too fearful to feel her own.

# GRIP

IF ONLY I liked my body a tenth as much as men do. But at twenty-six, I am still fifteen pounds overweight. Haunted by my mother's Metrecal, the gross-smelling liquid she drank to get thin, I am determined to find my own way.

I drink a cup of black coffee for breakfast, eat an apple for lunch, and have cottage cheese and zucchini for dinner. This diet works for a few days, but is not sustainable. I feel so deprived—especially when life gets too hard—I swing to the other side and binge. What else can I do when food is still my comfort and escape?

Sam, the first man I love for more than three months and the first man I live with, comforts himself with marijuana and beer. I don't mind because I'm used to that. What's hard about living with Sam is that he's more successful than me.

When I get an audition for the leading role in Tabitha, a spin-off of Bewitched, Sam auditions for Tabitha's boyfriend. I nail my first audition and get called back to meet the producers and director, but I don't get the part. Maybe I'm too nervous, or not blonde enough, or weigh 120 pounds instead of 105, but the rejection stings. Especially when Sam is flown out to LA for a screen test.

As his cab drives away, I run to the corner deli to get a Sara Lee Banana Cake, a pint of Haagan-Daz vanilla ice cream, and a jar of Golden Blossom honey. I throw the ice cream on the cake, dump the jar of honey over the ice cream, and eat the whole thing while watching *Days of our Lives*, my father's favorite soap opera. Filled with shame and sugar, I am only vaguely aware I'm upset about being left behind. Bleary and bloated, I crawl to the phone and dial 411.

"Can I have the number of Overeaters Anonymous please?" I ask the operator, forgetting how I know it exists.

Six months later, I am fifteen pounds lighter. I leave Sam, who never did get the *Tabitha* part, and never do a crazy food binge again.

## ROM-COM

WITH DARTMOUTH AND its men ten years behind me, I suddenly want to get married. Though I was determined to be the man who no one could tie down, when I turn twenty-seven, a voice goes off inside. *It's time to get married!*

John is the next man I meet. Tall, talented, and Texan, John is a fashion photographer. We meet when he's shooting a print ad for Singer Sewing Machine where I play a bride.

*Walk down our aisle first*, the ad says.

Dressed in a white lace wedding gown, I am heavily made up with baby's breath woven through my upswept hair. But

I forgot to bring the right shoes. John says my red sneakers won't show.

"You're so cute! You're so pretty!" he yells, from behind his camera as disco music blares in the background and strobe lights flash in my eyes.

Completely turned on because I love being loved through a lens, I write him a note as soon as I get home.

> Dear John,
>
> Thanks so much for the shoot. I really enjoyed it. I know I'm going out on a limb, but if you're not married or living with someone, and want to get together for coffee or anything, let me know.
> Sincerely,
> Lynn

As if I want coffee. What I want is to throw him on the floor and fuck his brains out. After all, it's 1977. Women's Lib tells me I don't have to be a man to go after what I want. So when John invites me over, I buy red tulips, two Jon Vie croissants, and put my diaphragm in, hoping the spermicidal cream will last.

But John surprises me. As we're rolling around on the floor, he laughs and calls me greedy. I'll have to wait, he says, because he has an appointment at GQ. But he invites me back for Sunday brunch, and after a ratatouille omelet, we not only have sex, but the beginning of a romance.

In a month, I move into his studio, and twelve months after that—since he hasn't mentioned it and it's something I must do—I propose. I don't mind making another bold move. I like playing a man, calling the shots and going after what I want. It makes me feel powerful, and in control.

Fairly confident John will say yes, I order a dozen red, long-stemmed roses with *Will you marry me?* on a small rectangular card. But when I walk into the studio after a long day of auditioning, I see the unopened box. Even worse, John is shooting Apollonia Van Ravenstein, a ridiculously sexy model with legs as tall as me. Sprawled half-naked on a beanbag chair for *Cosmopolitan,* Apollonia makes me feel ugly and small.

Suddenly, I'm scared. I almost feel sorry for guys and the risks they have to take. With the direction of my life—not to mention my desirability—hanging in the balance, I go upstairs to wait.

It feels like forever. But the shoot finally ends, Apollonia leaves, and John comes up to find me. As he walks towards me, I hold my breath. He sits down on the bed, takes my hand, and with tears in his eyes, says yes.

## REAR PROJECTION

WHEN A MAN'S work is in his home, there's nothing more important and it never seems to end. I hated our Jersey City house with my father's office just steps away from the living room. I'm not so happy living in John's workplace.

After months of listening to my complaints, he finally agrees to move to an apartment on West 21st Street across the street from The General Theological Seminary of the Episcopal Church. I love living across the street from God, especially when He's gated in.

One morning, after John goes off to shoot supermodels, I'm making the bed. As I pull up the sheet, I look down. Wow. I'm wearing boxer shorts. White boxer shorts like men wear, in a size that fits me.

All of a sudden it feels really weird. But it didn't when I bought them. When I was passing the wall of boxer shorts in Bloomingdales on my way to see *Autumn Sonata*, a movie about a woman desperate for her mother's love, it made total sense.

I need shorts to wear around the house. I need shorts to exercise and stretch in. Boxer shorts are perfect. They're cool, cotton, and light. I can sleep in them, too. And I don't need fancy prints or stripes. White ones are just fine.

But now I'm not so sure. Staring down at my legs falling from the whiteness of the shorts, I feel lightheaded and dizzy. Oh wait. I know what it is. Daddy wore white boxer shorts. That's right. Daddy wore white boxer shorts, and now I'm wearing them, too.

## DAY-FOR-NIGHT

In the night I am special
In the day nothing much

In the night I am too loved

In the day never touched

In the night he consumes me

In the day he isn't there

In the night there's too much passion

In the day he doesn't care

In the night there are no boundaries

In the day the fragments fly

In the night I have my Daddy

In the day I wonder why

## SCRIPT ANALYSIS

AFTER I FIND myself in my father's shorts, I call my therapist and make an emergency appointment. I haven't seen her in two years because I thought I was finished.

"I always knew my father slept in my bed," I say, sitting in her office, "but I think something might have happened. I think my father might have done something to me."

When my therapist sees my distress, she does her best to help in a time when no one is really talking about these things.

"Lynn, it doesn't really matter if anything happened to you or not," she says. "It's what you think about it that matters."

Though this therapist has helped me a lot—I have come to understand, intellectually at least, that I didn't kill my mother—now she reminds me of the Dartmouth shrink. All she's done is confuse me. But I pretend to understand. I take "it doesn't really matter" as an out. But just in case, I check in with Dr. Whitlock.

> Lynn, I'm not sure what to say about your memory. You say now you *know* something, but it's obvious you don't *know* anything happened. I assure you that the fact you're wearing shorts to bed is no proof of anything at all. I'd say that everything I know about you argues *against* anything having happened.

I guess he doesn't take it seriously either.

> If you want a typical Elmira graduate situation, it would run like this: in cases of parental or close family (uncle, for example) rape or forcing, the girl is typically sexually frigid and has never had an orgasm. She can't establish any lasting relationships and usually she goes through an unending series of being rejected by older men she tries to live with. I make these generalizations from far too many cases, as such parental attacks are anything but uncommon.

First of all, I am not frigid. Second, I have had at least three orgasms from other people. Denis, maybe my mother, and John the night I turned thirty and we both got drunk on champagne. And third, Monty, my agent, was my last older man, thank you very much.

As for your doctor's statement that your current state is a result of your fear of coming out as a woman, all I can say is that kind of trendy nonsense isn't worth talking about. Coming out as a woman indeed. I would have thought you had been doing that rather successfully ever since I knew you. Oh, by the way, if your father had fooled around, you would probably have been throwing yourself into my arms for the past fifteen years—and don't fantasize that you have been—you haven't.

Yuck. Why would I ever do that? I hate Dr. Whitlock even said that.

If I'm a father figure, as we both know I am, just remember that this one never attempted to take any advantage. Maybe that is a clue to the other situation. Let's hope so. I don't know whether your father touched you or not—and neither do you. Let's worry about something specific—like how am I going to get to see you in November.

## NEGATIVE PICKUP DEAL

SKILLED AT ON-CAMERA commercials, I'm always glad when a client wants me back. When Sears hires me as its spokesperson for women's underwear, I'm excited to get a guarantee, a sum of money I'm paid no matter how many times the commercial runs. It almost makes ignoring my serious acting aspirations worthwhile.

And you never know what might come from a commercial. When my agent calls to tell me Joe Brooks, who wrote, directed, and produced *You Light Up My Life*, a film that gave him an Oscar and a Grammy, saw me in a Sears commercial and wants to meet me because he's casting his next movie, I am overjoyed.

"Yes! Please! Give him my number!" I say, marveling at my good fortune.

He must have seen the spot where I'm wearing a pink leotard and tights, the one where I move from bra-covered mannequin to pantie-covered mannequin, then look up at the camera high above me, throw up my arms, and say with a great big smile, "Sears! Where America shops for value!"

Personally, I'm not so crazy about the commercial. I look like a busty. overly-zealous Peter Pan. But I'm thrilled Joe Brooks wants to meet me.

When I'm told to go to his Upper East Side townhouse, I wonder why it has to be at night. But I don't ask questions because this could be my break, my chance to prove how talented I am. Joe Brooks may not be Woody Allen, but he still makes movies.

Joe Brooks ushers me into his office. Gold records, an Oscar which makes me feel important in its presence, and other random awards decorate the room. As soon as I sit down, I notice the quiet.

Joe Brooks opens his mouth and stutters. I try not to notice. I dare not embarrass the man who may hold the key to my future.

"I'm w-w-riting my next movie," Joe Brooks says, "and I'm l-l-l-ooking for the lead. I can tell you have a very sp-sp-special quality."

Music to my ears.

"In fact, I think you m-m-m-ight have the m-m-makings of a star."

The star thing makes me cringe, but I'm ecstatic he thinks I might qualify for the lead in his movie. And how great would it be not to have to go to LA, New York's bastard cousin? But then he asks a question I'm not prepared for.

"Do you have a b-b-boyfriend?"

It's a strange question, but I have to be polite. I'm on the verge of a breakthrough.

"Yes," I say. "We live together."

"You know," he says, "m-m-making a film is a very intense experience. People get v-v-very involved with each other, especially if the script is a r-r-r-omantic one."

I don't understand.

"I need to know, if you and I were to f-f-fall in love, if you would be wi-wi-willing to leave your boyfriend."

Whoa. That feels scary. It's getting harder to separate fantasy from fact.

"But why?" I ask. "Why would I have to do that?"

"Don't you want to be a st-st-star?" Joe Brooks says.

"I want to do film, but I can't say I would leave my boy-friend."

"I'm t-t-telling you. That's what ha-ha-happens," Joe Brooks insists. "It ha-ha-happened with Shelley Hack and me on my last f-f-film."

"But I can't tell you I would leave my boyfriend," I say, trying to find my balance on his shifting ground.

"Well," Joe Brooks says, "then I ha-ha-have to question what you wa-wa-want for yourself."

The house suddenly feels empty. I'm scared. He must notice because his voice softens.

"All I'm asking, is if y-y-you and I were to f-f-fall in love, if you would leave your-b-b-boyfriend."

"Why do you stutter?" I say, attempting to take control.

"I've st-st-stuttered since I was child. It's not important," he says, dismissing me. "Would you like a glass of w-w-wine?"

For sure I need to relax, but my survival self knows better than to drink with this man.

"No, thank you," I say, "but I would like some water."

As Joe Brooks leaves the room, I wonder what starring in a movie is worth. Maybe I should leave, but making a movie is still too seductive. I don't want to blow what little chance I have. I'll just have to get through to him. I'll have to find a way to have my cake without having to eat his.

In the end, I am alone with Joe Brooks, awarded composer and filmmaker, for two long hours. While he dangles fame and fortune, I try to star in his next movie without having to leave John. The back-and-forth is exhausting. I feel worn down. Sensing I'm in danger, I look at the clock.

"I have to go," I lie. "My boyfriend is meeting me outside."

"Oh. Okay," Joe Brooks says, standing up. "B-b-but I want you to t-t-think about everything I've said. This is your career we're t-t-talking about."

He shuts his door. I step onto his dark street and run to the nearest pay phone.

"I just met with Joe Brooks and I think he really mind-fucked me," I cry to John. "I feel crazy inside."

John tells me to get in a cab and come home.

Three days later, Joe Brooks calls again. This time I'm smart enough to meet him in the brightness of day, at a Broadway coffee shop near his recording studio. And I'm ready. When he pitches film and fame, I respond with practiced resolve.

"I love my boyfriend," I say, risking the truth, "and I don't want to be in your movie if I have to promise to leave him."

"You surprise m-m-me, Lynn," Joe Brooks says, shaking his head. "I thought you were serious about your c-c-career." He stands up, throws a five-dollar bill on the table, and walks out the door.

## SNUFF FILM

FORTY YEARS LATER, in the time of Harvey Wein-
stein, I google Joe Brooks to see if he's alive. As I read his Wiki-
pedia entry, I am gasping for air.

> In June 2009 Brooks was arrested on charges of
> raping or sexually assaulting eleven women lured
> to his East Side apartment from 2005 to 2008...He
> allegedly lured the women to his apartment to au-
> dition for movie roles... Brooks committed suicide
> on May 22, 2011, before he could be tried.

It feels like discovering a dead body. How lucky I was
that Joe Brooks only mind-fucked me that night. That he
only ridiculed me for rebuffing him and fame that midtown
afternoon. I remember calling my agent so she could warn
others, and Sylvia who remembers to this day.

Grateful to have dodged the Joe Brooks bullet thirty years
before his arrest, I feel sad and angry for the women who did
not. When I read how he abused his daughter, and how his son
went to prison for murdering his own girlfriend, I think it is
not a bad thing Joe Brooks tied a plastic bag around his head
and attached himself to a tank of helium.

# NOTICE

BEFORE *QUILTERS* GOES to Broadway to garner five
Tony nominations, I'm in a regional production at Pittsburgh
Public Theater. I haven't been to Pittsburgh since my Carnegie
Tech fiasco. Though it's hard leaving John behind, something
unusual happens. My father writes me a letter.

> My dear Lynn, it looks like "Show Biz" is turning
> down in NYC. Only the rich charge card business
> write off can afford prices like in NY. Only a few
> middle-class can afford it. Anyway, it will contin-
> ue, but poor shows will lose their shirts! A friend
> saw Quilters and thought it was very good, and
> "you were great." So the Lake knows about your
> play, etc. Glad you got a mention in the newspa-
> per. They didn't give the 1st act very much, but
> was high on the second act. By the time you get
> this you will have only 3 wks to go - and that will
> go fast - we are all for you. Our love to you – Dad.
> Sorry about my spelling & English!

# LAY-OUTS

I WORRY WHEN my father shows signs of decline. Four
years after moving to the Lake, he falls down drunk in his car-

peted den and breaks his neck. It's a miracle he isn't paralyzed. As I watch him navigate the weight of a heavy metal halo, I want to help. I sit him at the kitchen sink and wash his bald head with soap and water. I stare at the mercurochrome-soaked screws drilled into his skull and the intimacy makes me weak.

After his neck heals and his halo is removed, my father spends a night in Morristown Memorial Hospital undergoing tests for osteoporosis. Three months pregnant after two miscarriages, I visit him in his private room. As my father reads *The Wall Street Journal,* I am eating a tuna salad sandwich on whole wheat. Suddenly, he slumps down in his chair.

"Daddy?" I say, dropping my lunch.

My father mumbles something. The only word I can make out is "shit," a word I have never heard him say. I run into the hall for help. A nurse comes in, takes one look at my father, and calls a Code Blue.

A team swoops in. A doctor asks my father if he knows who the President is. Woodrow Wilson is not the right answer. As they whisk him to the ICU, a nurse says he's had a stroke. I grab the phone and call my brother, my sister, my husband, and my aunt. Then I call my doctor because what I fear most is losing another pregnancy. I'm afraid the shock of witnessing my father's stroke might cause another miscarriage. But Shelley, my brilliant and easy-going doctor, assures me a viable pregnancy cannot be dislodged. Just in case though, I eat a pint of ice cream.

As my family finds its way to Morristown, an ICU doctor pulls me aside. "If your father lives—and we don't think he will—he will be paralyzed on his left side," he says. "Probably for the rest of his life."

Within the week, my father starts to improve. After a month in the hospital and six months in rehab, he makes a full recovery. Even after being far gone, he says, "I'm the only black man in here." It's a comment I don't correct. Having grown up with the eConfederate flag, I savor the moment.

But even after my father breaks his neck, then suffers a massive stroke, he doesn't stop smoking or drinking. It's not until he diagnoses himself with mouth cancer, caused by years of alcohol and tobacco abuse, does he finally stop.

"I'm only stopping because I know you kids won't leave me alone," he says, as if it's our fault.

But even with my father's uncanny ability to survive, he is clearly moving to his end. As his body weakens, I dream about rape and castration. It's time to ask my father one last unexpected question.

## CONFRONTATION

ON A HOT summer day, my father is sitting in a tattered lawn chair in the front of the lake house. Without a wife to dress him, he wears old and mismatched clothes. His back, rounded after decades of surgery, slumps forward. His arthritically-gnarled fingers, stained yellow from smoking, are hold-ing a newspaper.

I have come to see him because I'm having nightmares and panic attacks. I have this dreamy sense of a hidden reality, a sense that something happened when he was in my bed.

"Daddy?" I say, as if I don't know who he is.

"Yes, Miss Lynn," he says, as if I'm his mistress on a plan-tation in the South.

"I'm having really weird dreams."

I pause because I expect him to be curious. But he only listens. He doesn't move or say a word. I feel like a patient getting his best bedside manner.

"I had a dream about castration. I castrated someone in my dream and it was really upsetting."

It was. It was horrible.

My father stares down at the grass. He does not flinch or register surprise.

"So, I was wondering." I say, slowly, "did anyone ever break into our house and rape me?"

Who knows? Maybe they forgot to tell me.

"No," my father replies. "I don't think so."

## STUNT DOUBLE

NOTWITHSTANDING HIS RESPONSE to my dis-turbing father thoughts, I continue to check in with Dr. Whit-lock for some assurance of myself. I spend so much money on therapy, it's nice when someone cares enough to listen for free. Sometimes we get together when he comes to New York.

It's 1986. I'm living in an 8500 square ft. loft on the corner of 19th St. and Fifth Ave. with John and William, our three-year-old son. Though John's studio takes up most of our ninth floor, our home is also impressive, with windows all around. Embarrassed I continue to live a most privileged life, I can't wait to show Dr. Whitlock how well I'm doing.

When Baird—I'm too old now to call him Dr. Whitlock—steps off the elevator and into our loft, he is as glad to see me as I am to see him. As morning light bounces off the white-pickled floors, we drink tea and eat scones.

Almost forty, I look across at Baird who is sixty-three. Suddenly the gap in our ages seems small. I feel self-conscious and uncomfortable, unsure how this friendship is supposed to work. Though I sometimes feel like one, I can't be the needy child. I have one of my own and another on the way.

Baird listens as I tell him about my happy marriage, my need to keep performing, and anything else I can think of to fill the silence. When he smiles, I don't like being looked at. The absence of our power differential is confusing to my wife and mother-self. I can't pretend I'm his student. I'm a grown woman sitting alone with a grown man who's not my father. I'm relieved when he says he has to go.

As I walk him to the elevator just steps away, I am ready to hug him goodbye. But as I move in, he plants his lips on mine and thrusts his tongue into my mouth.

"Wow," I say, stepping back. "That was a surprise."

It was worse than that. It was one of the biggest shocks of my life.

Baird steps into the elevator, turns around, and gives me a sheepish grin. As the door closes, the world as I've known it comes to an end.

## ADAPTATION

MY BREASTS HAVE caused so much trouble in my life. I've experienced unwelcome touch and endured too much ogling. My breasts remain a threatening part of my body until I give birth to my son and daughter. I finally come to a resting place when my babies do.

From the moment my children latch onto me, lactation is both revelation and redemption. When my breasts have greater purpose than filling out sweaters and turning on men, I finally accept their size.

My body has value, after all. Not to mention how healthy breastfeeding is for children and their mothers. Its short and long-term benefits are well-documented. And the oxytocin coursing through my body instantly calms me down. A human pacifier, I love nursing. I am as happy as my babies gazing up at me as if I am the world.

# FADE TO BLACK

MY FATHER TAKES his last breath on May 26, 1988, two weeks after he moves to Pennsylvania to live with my sister. Of a generation too proud to depend on anyone, he only goes because he knows he's dying. The last time I see him alive is on the day he dies.

When I walk into the room, I see my father lying motionless in my mother's old hospital bed. I am shocked by his decline. His body, filling up with the fluid of a lifetime of unshed tears, is drowning in its own congestion. I hear his liquid breath, the rush of water coming to drown him as I so often have been drowned.

"I love you, Daddy," I say, because there is nothing left to lose.

"I love you, too," my father says, for the first and last time.

The sickness of sex when he was big and I was little hovers somewhere in the room, still lost in my memory.

"I'll see you in a few days," I say, not so sure I will.

I say goodbye to my sister and drive back to New York. Home for all of ten minutes, the phone rings.

"Daddy's near death," my sister says.

Apparently, he spiraled down after my exit. Gee, I think, another two hours in the car. Though I'm not expected to return—my sister says she doesn't need me—for some reason I have to see my father dead.

"You might not get here in time," my sister warns.

It's a chance I have to take.

"If he dies before I get there," I say, "don't let them take his body. Please. I need to see him."

She promises to do what she can.

I don't know why I'm not upset my father is about to die, or why I'm so consumed with seeing his dead body. I feel more like a detective who has to mark and preserve evidence than a soon-to-be bereaved daughter.

As I run up the stairs three hours later because of Friday night traffic, the coroner is unzipping the body bag. He's endured my sister's pleadings long enough. I thank them both and run in to see my father's corpse. He's right where I left him.

"Wow," I say, staring at the body he left behind. "He's really gone."

I have no idea where, but clearly, he no longer exists.

I feel overwhelming relief. Like a long chapter has ended and another is about to begin. But I also feel oddly numb. I don't shed a tear for my father. Not at his deathbed, not at his funeral, not even at his burial alongside my mother. I don't know why, but I don't feel anything at all.

## RULE OF SIX

I CANNOT DESCRIBE the sexual abuse the way I can tell you what I just had for breakfast. A banana, a rice cake with almond butter, a cup of Tazo Awake tea. The abuse occurred in the hazy sleep of nighttime when I was too young to understand. Like Mr. Duffy in *Ulysses* who lived "a short distance from his body," I excised the part of self that couldn't bear the reality.

But with my father's permanent disappearance, it becomes safer to contemplate our connection. Memories start to surface. I want to tell them to John, but he cannot listen. That a father could do such a thing to his child puts him in a rage. It's not something he wants to consider, much less talk about.

I call MJ, a trusted friend.

"I have always known my father slept in my bed," I say, "but I think he did something to me. I feel like my body knows."

MJ suggests The Best Kept Secret: The Sexual Abuse of Children by Florence Rush. But I can only skim it. It scares the shit out of me. To discover children have always been sexually abused, and that it was even once acceptable for fathers to have sex with their daughters, makes it more real than I am ready for.

## SUBTITLES

BY THE TIME I'm forty, my marriage is falling apart. It's possible neither John nor I can tolerate intimacy over the long haul, but with his attention elsewhere, my loneliness feels like childhood. I don't share my profound unhappiness with him, nor am I able to issue an ultimatum. Self-care is not a language

I grew up speaking. But as my marriage becomes intolerable, I grow desperate.

Enter Ken.

Ken and I met several years ago when I sang in his opera, *The Marriage of Heaven and Hell*. Because we were both married, our relationship was purely professional and platonic. But when he calls out of the blue to say he's developing an early childhood music program called Music Together and needs a Mommy voice for the recordings and thinks I might also like to teach—and, by the way, he's divorced—my ears perk up.

"Oh yes, I'd love to be the Mommy voice and do the teacher training," I say, because it's the perfect job for a mother of two. I can bring Music Together to Manhattan, teach when I want, earn money again, and finally do good in the world. What could be better than encouraging parents and caregivers to make music with the children they love?

After the training, Ken becomes my mentor. One month later, we're in love. But because I am incapable of having an affair—I may lie to myself, but lying to someone else is still something I can't consciously do—I ask John for a separation, even though the thought of not being with my children all the time fills me with bone-aching grief.

I am only half-aware that the only reason I can break up my family, especially amidst my children's protest and pain, is because I have the love and reassurance of a man.

# THE BIG REVEAL

ONE SUNDAY, WILLIAM and Lucy are with their father, and Ken and I are making early morning love. As I wrap my arms around his bony shoulders, I think how tall and thin he is. How physically similar he is to my father. In fact, sometimes when I glance down at his arm, I think my father's there.

I feel so good about myself. How brave I was to leave a man who didn't want me for one who does. How wonderful to be sexually present with a man. But as Ken's penis moves in and out, a door in my psyche springs open.

"Get off of me!" I suddenly scream, as if I'm being raped. "Get off! Get off of me!"

My gentle Ken is shocked. He quickly pulls away. Sobbing, I don't understand why I feel attacked by a man who loves me. I pick up the phone and call my new therapist. I tell her voicemail I'm ready to join her incest survivors' group.

For the next year, memories come back with full force. I have terrifying flashbacks and debilitating panic attacks. I keep a journal so I won't go insane.

> I had a massive anxiety attack today. A strange feeling flashed through my body and I thought I was going to faint. I felt unbelievably scared. My heart was racing. I almost threw up. I still feel panicky and dizzy and wonder how I will ever sleep. There's a buzzing in my head, a feeling of being out

of my body. My legs are numb and my shoulders are up around my neck. I hit a pillow, but there's more despair than anger. My father was so present I could almost see him. His t-shirt, boxer shorts with the slit, his smell of alcohol and stale tobacco. His hand over mine. His fingers opening me, trying to put his penis in. My legs went numb and I started to cry. I was aware of enduring it, holding my breath, drawing in all my energy, holding still until it was over, wanting to die. When Sue asked if there was someone I could bring in to help little Lynn, I brought in policemen to pull him off and beat him. I put his spirit aside—I don't want to hurt his spirit—and watched him get dismembered. Then I castrated him and laid his body (and my mother's) on hot coals. I peeled their skin off, and smashed their rotting bones. I am astounded by the magnitude of the wound, the event, the fact of it all.

## FLASH FORWARD

ONE WEST VILLAGE afternoon, as I'm walking down Christopher Street on my way to the Archive, the building where I live with twelve-year-old William and eight-year-old

Lucy, I can't believe my eyes. Miss Jowitt, my beloved Bergen School drama teacher, is walking towards me.

"Miss Jowitt!" I call out, despite the fact I'm forty-four and she is fifty-nine. "It's Lynn! Lynn Lobban!"

"Oh, my goodness! Lynn!" Miss Jowitt says, equally amazed.

Except for her silvery hair, Miss Jowitt is her same smart, statuesque, and gentle self. Though I'm aware of her standing in the dance world as critic, choreographer, teacher, and author, my happiness to see her outweighs any feeling of intimidation. I tell her about my career, my marriage, my divorce, and my children. Then I mention the reality of my childhood.

"I'm so sorry," Miss Jowitt says, with sad, stricken eyes. "I wish I had known."

Because she has to be somewhere, I say I'll write to her because I have a few questions. Like why did she cast me as Martirio, "the evil one," in *The House of Bernarda Alba*? Did she see the same things as my mother? And why was I cast as Lee in *The Young and the Fair*? I remember standing onstage at the principal's desk and confessing, "Miss Cantry, I'm Jewish." Did she know I was good at keeping secrets?

> Dear Lynn,
>
> Your letter moved me very much. It's a tribute to your inner strength, as well as to your talent, that you have achieved so much in your career as an ac-

> tress and singer and that you have a loving family
> who supports you.

I'm not sure which family she means. I hardly ever talk
to my brother and sister, and my children are too young to be
supportive.

> As I told you on the street corner, I wish I had
> known what you were going through in those
> years at Bergen. Could I have helped? I don't
> know. But the moments you remember are tell-
> ing, and I started to think back to my image of you
> then. You were a "good girl"—you know, polite,
> did your homework, etc—but I sensed something
> else in you, some undercurrent of anger, unhap-
> piness with yourself, and some kind of strength.
> That's why I cast you as Lee, and as Martirio. Not
> because I thought you were evil—anyway, Mar-
> tirio isn't evil either.

> It's also interesting that, quiet as you were, I seem
> to have had no doubts that you could come up to
> those roles. And that must have been because of
> the power I felt in you. Your decision to act and
> to dance was probably the most healing thing you
> could have done; as you said in your letter, ex-
> pressing anger and pain became legitimate, even

something you could win praise for. You were lucky.

I wish there'd been theater programs when you were entering college like the one at NYU Tisch. On the other hand, your mother probably wouldn'thave approved. How brave of you to travel to Carnegie on your own to audition!

Miss Jowitt's letter moves me to tears. To know she thought well of me then comforts me in a way I did not anticipate. It's never too late to be mothered in hindsight.

# BACKER

FROM THE AGE of fourteen, I am never without a man. Not until my relationship with Ken ends in 1995 because he won't move into New York and I won't move to New Jersey. Though it could also be I'm looking for a way out.

When my Alanon sponsor—I go to Alanon because our couple therapist said my emotional recovery depends on this program for family and friends of alcoholics—suggests I take a break and date my Higher Power—whatever *that* is—I follow her suggestion for three dateless years.

Well, not exactly. I can't let go of men completely. I have an obsessive fantasy going in my head. An unrequited romance with another Dartmouth man. A Heorot brother, in fact, and Denis's best friend. I just can't help myself. When I run into

Jim on a Chelsea street, I turn into Meryl Steep without the Italian accent in *The Bridges of Madison County.*

I didn't really know Jim when I was at Dartmouth, though I directed his girlfriend in the Ionesco play. Of course, he's a world-renowned and well-awarded war photographer and photojournalist now. But I'm not intimidated by his fame. Though the horrors of my childhood will never compare to the things he's witnessed and recorded, I know he understands. As I turn the pages of *Inferno,* his giant black book of human cruelty and suffering, I weep with him by my side.

Though we sometimes meet for dinner when he returns from *Time* assignments, our romance is all in my head. I dream about how happy we could be, how we could grow old together in Vermont and be free of human despair. If only I was twenty years younger, and he'd stop calling me "Bro."

## FINAL CUT

ON THE BRINK of a new millennium, it's time for another whack at Dartmouth College.

On a college tour with William, I'm trying to be the best mother I can be. Since the mother act I'm following is so dismal, I'm pretty much succeeding. Who knows? Maybe I can make up for my childhood by getting things right with my children.

Having a highly intelligent son, I take William to Princeton first. Not just because the university is close by, but because I spent many an hour there. We used to take Besta to football games because her husband and son were Princeton men. When I step onto the Ivy campus and my Princeton present becomes my Princeton past.

It's 1962. My father parks our station wagon at Palmer Stadium and my mother gets out the tailgate lunch. While I eat fried chicken out of a Hammacher Schlemmer picnic basket, the adults drink martinis. As for the football game, I hate watching men bash into each other. I focus on the cheerleader in the tiger suit because I'm sure he's cute. I hope he sees me.

"It feels like you have to do too much work here," William says, snapping me back to 1999.

He's just finished a rigorous year at Trinity School where he's gotten a better education than I did at any college. He wants a break. Sighing, I move on

We go to Brown, but in the summer the deserted, dirty dorms are an irrational turnoff. We visit sprawling Cornell in bleak upstate New York. We trudge around Wesleyan where a father laments the naked dorm has come too late for him. We visit Middlebury because it's in Vermont, and travel down to Georgetown, though we exit the tour after passing through a room with large religious portraits. Finally, in a nostalgic nod to my father, we visit the University of Virginia which sadly remains in the South.

But it doesn't really matter what other colleges we see. All I want to do is to show William Dartmouth. I want my son to see the place where his mother made history. Lost in a Big

Green delusion, I have worked overtime to convince us both I must be some kind of legacy.

When we walk into the admissions office, I cheerily bounce over to the young woman behind the reception desk. "Hi," I say, "I'm Lynn Lobban, and this is my son, William Lobban-Bean. He's here for his interview."

As she looks down at her appointment book, I am compelled to add important information.

"I was one of the first seven women at Dartmouth in 1968."

She looks up. Her face is as blank as the paper in the nearby Xerox machine.

"We were here for a whole year," I explain, because she's clearly forgotten. "From 1968 to 1969."

"Did *you* ever hear of women in 1968?" she asks a nearby friend.

They look at each other as if I've just told them Mars was once colonized. Because the truth is *no one* knows about the pioneering women of 1968-69. Oh, they know there were women in the fall of 1970 because that's when Meryl Streep left Vassar for a Dartmouth semester. They also know Dartmouth gave Streep her first honorary degree. Though none of us knows that in 2012, when she wins an Oscar for playing Margaret Thatcher, she will credit her Dartmouth semester.

"There were 60 of us and 6,000 men," she will exaggerate in an interview, "and I had a little flashback to that moment, and so a little bit of my emotional work was done for me."

Yes, Meryl Streep they know all about. But the trail I once so boldly blazed is as smooth as Sahara sands.

I look at William who looks away, embarrassed for his mother. When he goes in for his interview, I try to hide my deflation by pretending to read an outdated issue of *Time*.

But wait. I can take William to Heorot. I can show my son my fraternity. He loves my stories about how his mother kept up with the men. He's even written about me in proud grade school stories about his parents.

"If I go here, I'll be in a fraternity for sure," William says, picking up the Dartmouth vibe as we cross the Green.

Unnerved by how much he loves the idea of fraternal bond, I hate the thought of macho-drinking contests, and his knowing fraternal secrets I still know nothing about. I note my hypocrisy.

As we step into Heorot, time stands still. The stench of tapped kegs is as omnipresent as ever. Fermentation seeps from the walls. I glance into the room where I was initiated. Couches are pushed against the walls, evidence of the last bacchanal. I'm disappointed the mighty house of Heorot is a dirty mess in the bright light of summer, but William doesn't seem to care.

A student comes up from the basement. I introduce myself, proudly telling him I am his brother. But he looks confused. As if I might be crazy.

"Do you know where the 1969 Composite is?" I ask, because I clearly have to prove my existence to us all. "It used to hang over the fireplace."

"You're in luck," he answers.

I am, indeed. Heorot 1969 is stacked against the wall with other composites getting ready for a reunion I have not been invited to.

"Here it is!" I say, pulling out Exhibit A. "Heorot 1969. See, William? There are my brothers. There's Denis, there's Tukka, and there's—"

Bullshit. It takes no time to see. Enemy fire takes me down in the blink of an eye. Because I'm not there. My silk-ruffled face is gone. The space where I was once so deliberately placed—right below the dog whose picture still remains—is a blank square. If there was a coffin, I would crawl in and close the lid.

"They took me out! I can't believe they took me out!" I cry out, mortified.

But I dare not share the depth of my disappointment in the presence of these men. I shake my head in disbelief, say a quick goodbye, and lead William out the door.

Whether I have been excised one night by a drunk and angry brother, enraged his girlfriend has dumped him for another man, or by some ancient alum, outraged a woman once dared to invade his sacred Chi, I do not know.

With two colleges left, William's seen enough. He wants to go home. I drive onto Route 91, as silent as my son.

## PULL FOCUS

THOUGH I DON'T really need one, I'll be damned if my children are going to get their college degrees before me. Stricken with a competitive urge to finish what I never wanted to start in the first place, I am happy to hear about Goddard College in Plainfield, Vermont.

A low-residency college whose mission is "to advance cultures of rigorous inquiry, collaboration, and lifelong learning, where individuals take imaginative and responsible action in the world," Goddard College is most appealing. Not just because it's in Vermont, but I can create my own curriculum and study what I love.

Though Goddard's muddy campus is not manicured like Dartmouth's—there are no fancy buildings carrying the weight of the Ivy League—I am a somewhat wiser fifty-one. Goddard's egalitarian beauty suits me just fine.

Returning to college in 2001and learning alongside people of all ages, races, and genders, is inspiring. My advisor, Lucinda Garthwaite, is as brilliant as she is kind. In fact, my Goddard experience is so satisfying that as soon as I get my BA, I roll into the MFA Writing program. Who knew college could be fun?

## OBLIGATORY SCENE

ON SEPTEMBER 10, 2001, I am living on Warren St. in Lower Manhattan with my kids, my soon-to-be second-husband Kenny, and Molly, our five-year-old cairn terrier. Kenny and I met in 1998 when I answered his *New York Magazine* personals ad. Since he was looking for an "emotionally honest" person, I figured he must be emotionally honest, too. Kenny, the only straight man who has ever made me laugh, is a lawyer, which is coming in handy because John and I are fighting in court over money and our children's education.

On September 10th, 2001, William is in California starting his freshman year at Pomona College because he wanted to go west; Lucy is beginning high school at Trinity; Kenny is working in his law office in Queens; and I'm on my way to a nearby Alanon meeting because I still need to hear "You didn't cause it, you can't control it, and you can't cure it." Though I don't really believe it, it does make me feel better.

Taking my usual shortcut through the World Trade Center, I see a bookstore ahead. Pema Chodron, a Buddhist nun whose books sometimes put me in the present moment, has a new book. Pema, nee Deirdre Blomfield-Brown, was raised in New Jersey and went to a private girls' school like me. I walk into Borders and buy *The Places That Scare You.*

On the night of September 10, 2001, Kenny and I are walking Molly along Greenwich Street. I have no idea my second time around will crash and burn in just three years as addiction and betrayal take another marriage down. On the night of September 10, 2001, I am hopeful and happy.

As Molly steps off the curb to pee, I throw my head back and look up. The brightly lit Trade Towers loom high above like giant metal mountains. "Isn't it weird we live right under these things?" I marvel to Kenny and myself.

## SECOND UNIT

THOUGH I LOVE Goddard, some part of me still wants that Dartmouth degree and I am as shameless as my mother in its vicarious pursuit. Hope springs when my daughter is ready for college.

Lucy has different schools on her list. We have to visit Bowdoin and Bates in Maine before heading over to Hanover. Though Lucy hasn't filled out her Dartmouth application yet—a teenage girl, she is skeptical about her mother's enthusiasm for most things—I'm not worried. Dartmouth is beautiful in the fall. Lucy loved her fall semester at the Mountain School so I know she loves this part of New England. I can play this uncharacteristically cool.

As we walk around the campus, I'm stunned by the number of women crossing the Green with a full-fledged right to be there.

"When I left in 1969, Dartmouth was still experimenting," I say, giving her the backstory. "It didn't commit to coeducation until 1972."

I don't tell her it took Dartmouth sixteen years to change the name of its alma mater from "Men of Dartmouth" to "Dear Old Dartmouth." I don't tell her there were men who referred to the women as "co-hogs," a combination of female genitalia and a clam; or that several women received letters demanding they go topless in the dining hall; or that a few were threatened with violence. Instead, I take her to the Hop. Since Lucy loves the arts like her mother and grandmother, I know she'll be impressed. When she is, I am emboldened.

"Do you want to see my fraternity?" I say, as we exit onto Wheelock St. "It's right down there."

"Not really," Lucy says, calmly.

"Really?" I say, because I thought she'd want to.

"Really," Lucy says, not caring I call myself a brother.

Shit. I never should have told her they took me out of the composite. Oh well. I'm disappointed, but I have to let it go. If I say anything to annoy her, she might not want to come here and get that fucking degree.

In the end, it doesn't matter. My final Dartmouth disappointment comes faster than Superman's bullet. Lucy and I are at Dartmouth for all of thirty minutes when she wants to leave.

"You're kidding," I say, stunned again.

"Oh, I like the campus," she says. "It's really pretty here. But something feels weird. I don't know what it is, but something feels off."

Not knowing what to make of my daughter's off-hand comment, I wonder if her instincts might be better than mine. All I know is, I've run out of children.

# THE SET-UP

AS MUCH AS I disparage Jersey City, Jeanie is forever grateful to the place.

"I would be nobody without Jersey City," Jeanie says today.

I'm always startled to hear my old friend credit the direction of her life to her time in Jersey City. I guess in the spring of 1970 it's safe to go there. My mother and her insults are dead.

An Elmira senior, Jeanie is covering the New York Senate race for her thesis and needs a place to stay. Because I'm couch-surfing in New York, and my father never says no, I offer our house in Jersey City. I explain how easy it is to get into New York on the 99S, but warn her about my father's drinking. Jeanie isn't concerned though. She's just grateful.

One morning, she walks into The New York Times building on West 43rd St, not knowing who she wants to see. When a guard asks why she's there, she looks down at the paper and sees an article by Richard Reeves. She boldly says his name. The guard calls up. When his assistant asks for her number, she gives our Jersey City one.

"But you're not from Jersey City!" Richard Reeves says, when he calls and hears her Maine accent.

That's right. Jeanie's not from Jersey City. But her enthusiasm charms the Chief Political Correspondent for *The New*

*York Times,* and by the time their conversation ends, she has an appointment to meet him.

"The only reason I called her back was because I thought she was from Jersey City and that's where I'm from," Reeves says whenever he tells the story of their fifty-year friendship.

But there's more to Jeanie's Jersey City story. After she graduates from Elmira, she asks my father if she can spend another night. She has an interview at *Time.* Timmy, the brother who lost his legs in Vietnam and who will one day die from the war's effects, is driving her down from Maine.

"Timmy had just gotten a car outfitted so he could drive," Jeanie says. "He drove me down and we both spent the night with your father. Dr. Lobban was so wonderful to my brother. He asked him a lot of medical questions. He really extended himself, and I will never forget his gentleness. 'How can I help you? What can I do?' he asked. Lobban, your father was a deeply flawed man, but he had empathy for his patients. Your father wasn't a jerk."

No, not to his patients. In any event, Jeanie got the job and lived with my father for six weeks.

"Hester always served dinner in the dining room," Jeannie remembers, "and your father would ask me questions and give me advice, but by eight o'clock, he was drunk and gone."

Jeanie's memories muddle me with feeling. I'm glad to hear my father took an interest in my long-time friend—that he cared enough to ask her questions—but hearing how he passed out every night makes me feel angry and ashamed.

# STAR POWER

I LIED. BILL of *The Royal Hunt of the Sun* is not the last Dartmouth man I fuck. Freddie, Dartmouth '69—and another childhood friend of Jeanie's—is. I meet Freddie in 2007 at one of Jeanie's dinner parties. Whether they're rich, poor, famous, obscure, accomplished, or struggling, Jeanie loves gathering her friends for dinner.

The most unforgettable dinner is the one when it's Calvin and Alice Trillin, Mike and Mary Wallace, Bill and Rose Styron, Art Buchwald, Jeanie, and me. Sitting at a table with such renowned people, I am oddly relaxed. Not because everyone is so warm and friendly, but because discovering the most accomplished are also human beings takes the sting out of feeling lowly.

While Art, Bill, and Mike discuss their shared depression, I have to blow my nose. I'm in the last days of a cold. I pick up my dinner napkin and blow out the leftover mucus.

"Lobban!" Jeanie whispers. "What are you *doing*?"

Art, a loving friend, also leans in. I wonder what their problem is.

"Don't blow your nose in your napkin!" Jeanie says, as if I have just peed on the floor.

As Art nods sheepishly along, I quickly mount a defense. It's what I do when anyone criticizes me. "What are you talking about?" I whisper. "I was practically raised by Emily Post. I had to stand up when older people came into the room. I never heard that before."

Thanks, Mom.

"It's just not done, not at the dinner table, and never into a cloth napkin," Jeanie admonishes.

I don't understand why I don't already know this. Maybe I never had to blow my nose at the dinner table, or if I did, my mother was upstairs drinking in her bed.

Thankfully, the rest of the evening goes well. Though it bothers me a lot when Mike Wallace looks me up and down, and up and down again, and says, "Such a pretty girl."

I bristle when I hear it, feeling put in some irritatingly lightweight place. But I smile and go along because he's Mike Wallace of *60 Minutes*.

But then I run into him at a book party. He's standing in a circle of adoring fans and friends when I walk over to say hello.

"Such a pretty girl," he says, as if he's never met me.

"I am not a girl. I'm a *woman*," I say, hoping to put an end to it.

And I do. Mike Wallace turns his back and never looks or talks to me again.

## TEASER

I MEET FREDDIE at a less stellar dinner party when he's visiting from Maine. Three years past the debacle and disappointment of my second marriage, I am here with Don, a man who just happens to be another Dartmouth man. Sometimes they seem to be coming out of the woodwork.

Though Don and I have been dating for a few months, he doesn't take my breath away like Freddie who does the moment I see him sitting under Jeanie's Warhol prints of Mick Jagger. Tall and movie-star handsome, Freddie has that soulful suffering quality I love so much in men. And Freddie has never been married, so maybe I can be his first. But what is really great about Freddie, is that he goes to Alcoholics Anonymous, an organization co-founded by yet *another* Dartmouth man. Though I'm a little confused because he just finished his third glass of wine.

"Why are you in AA?" I ask, because I thought people who went to AA stopped drinking forever.

"I go for the community," Freddie says.

"Oh," I say.

But at least he goes to meetings. Who knows? Maybe this handsome Dartmouth frog will get sober and turn into a prince. Maybe I will finally be loved. As for my own croaking, I cannot hear it. Female frogs are almost inaudible among the croaking males.

## ADVENTURE FILM

IN TWO WEEKS, I dump Don and set out to trap my Dartmouth prey. I come up with a reason to travel north so Freddie can invite me to his house. It takes only an hour of conversation to start a weekend of sex and romance. The deal is struck on Sunday when Freddie makes what he calls an "uncharacteristically bold move."

"I'm turning sixty in a few weeks," he says, "and I'm going to Europe to celebrate with friends. I think you'd like them and they'd like you."

Drum roll.

"I have never asked anyone to travel with me before," Freddie says. "Would you like to come?"

"Yes, I would," I say, as the glass slipper blinds my eyes. "I would *love* to come."

Freddie's timing is perfect. John Wallowitch, my eighty-year-old, gay, brother-father-husband figure whose songs I have been singing for thirty years, has prostate cancer that has spread to his bones. I am his healthcare proxy and have been by his side for every doctor appointment, procedure, surgery, and almost every chemotherapy and radiation treatment. I tell people I would rather go to chemo with John Wallowitch than to the Bahamas with anyone else because John is the funniest and most present human being I know. And though he has no intention of dying, he is, and I can't bear it.

I tell myself I need a break. Spending two weeks in Europe with a man I barely know is a wonderful idea. I turn John over to his devoted friends and pack my bags.

In no time, I'm clearly in trouble. Freddie and I are on the plane for all of five minutes when he reaches into his pocket and pulls out a fistful of pills. Tiny pink, blue, and yellow pills. I haven't seen this many pills since my mother.

"What are those for?" I ask, scared shitless.

"This one's for anxiety, this one's for depression, this is a sleeping pill, and this is a muscle relaxant. Would you like one?"

Oh. My. God.

"No, Freddie, no," I say. "I don't do drugs. I rarely take Tylenol."

It's true. Ever since God let me live after my full-moon-hash-freakout, I have kept my end of the bargain.

"But are *you* going to take them?" I ask, wondering if the plane door is shut.

Freddie is silent.

"So you're telling me that you're going to take these pills, pass out, and wake up in Geneva well-rested, and I'm going to be up all night and exhausted when we land?"

The truth is, I don't want him looking better than me in the morning.

Freddie shrugs and throws the pills into his mouth. Unconscious by take-off, he sleeps through the night. Abandoned and alone, I grip the armrests because I have to fly the plane.

But how can this still be happening? I'm doing everything I can to recover from the effects of my childhood. How can I be making the same terrible mistakes?

## PAN

FREDDIE'S BIRTHDAY TRIP is as glorious as it is pure agony. France and Italy are magnificent, of course, as are Freddie's friends. They cheer when I sing Noel Coward's *Why Do the Wrong People Travel* at Freddie's birthday dinner. The lyrics are impossible to remember, but I'm glad I pull it off because even Freddie jumps up and hugs me.

But as Freddie's drinking progresses, mine does, too, though compared to his, I might as well be drinking Shirley Temples like I did when I was five.

Freddie's coldness grows, too. By the time we get to Venice—after my passport is stolen at an Autogrill in Milan—he makes a pronouncement. "I don't want to be in a relationship," he says, as we're lying together in the dark, "*especially* with you."

With alcoholic malice, he turns his back and passes out. I smell the alcohol seeping from his body and think of my father. I push the thought away.

Intellectually, I know I'm not trapped here with Freddie. I even look up trains to Paris in an attempt to take care of myself. But when I tell Freddie I'm leaving, he begs me to stay, and I do. It's still easier for me to blame a man than to take responsibility for myself.

## HOMAGE

THE ROOTS OF alcoholism entangle my family tree.

My mother died of the disease when she was forty-five. Her grandfather died of the disease when he was forty-five. Her uncle did as well. I guess she was just following in her family's drunken footsteps.

I don't know if alcoholism was as pervasive in my father's family. When he left West Virginia, he left his family behind.

But alcoholics are my tribe, the people I am most familiar with. Raised in and by the disease, I have never met an alcoholic I didn't try to love.

## DISTRIBUTION

A MONTH AFTER my trip to Hades, Freddie calls to apologize. "We were getting too close," he says. "I got scared."

As I listen to Freddie cop to his cruelty, and assure me I did not—nor could I ever—deserve such treatment, the orchestra warms up.

"Would you come up this weekend?" he asks, because he wants to make it all up to me.

I don't think a man has ever confessed his flaws before. This symphony is new.

"I'd love to," I say, without thinking.

Freddie's timing is once again perfect. John died three days ago and I cannot bear my grief. Though John nicknamed Freddie "the monster" after I told him about our trip, John's not here to roll his eyes about what I'm still doing with men. Anyway, I'm doing a good thing here. I'm giving a contrite Dartmouth man a second chance.

And this time I'll be smarter. Though the weekend holds promise, I will keep my female wits. I will not drink with him, if he's even still drinking. Anyway, I'm not much of a drinker. Though I like one or two glasses of wine at the end of each and every day to get the necessary buzz and break from life, I probably can do without it.

"I'm not going to drink with Freddie," I vow to a friend, "because if I do, we'll have sex, and if we have sex, then I won't be able to make a rational decision about whether or not to get involved with him again."

Two hours after I arrive, Freddie and I are sitting in a restaurant, looking at menus.

"I've been playing with sobriety," Freddie says. "Do you think we should get a bottle of wine?"

Oh no. I don't want Freddie tossing me his sobriety ball. I don't want the responsibility of what feels like a life and death decision.

"I don't know," I say, throwing it back. "What do *you* want to do?"

Twenty minutes later, as we're finishing a bottle of Cabernet—I call it the health drink because it has resveratrol and is good for my heart—something feels off. I'm not buzzed. But I'm always buzzed after two or three glasses of wine. I was right about one thing though. As soon as we get back to Freddie's house, we have sex.

Game on.

The next morning, Freddie announces he won't drink all day. Since I'm determined to encourage our ever-budding relationship, I tell him I won't either. I will do whatever it takes to get my Dartmouth frog sober.

And Freddie comes through. He doesn't drink all day. Not until eleven o'clock at night when it's too late for me to start my controlled wine-drinking.

As I watch Freddie drink a glass of scotch and pop whatever pill his tortured being needs to get through the night, I notice how clear my mind is and how much better I feel.

## RESCUE FROM WITHOUT

BY WEEKEND'S END, I am once again in Freddie's deep freeze. Resigned and ready to leave this elusive man—no closer to me than he was the night I met him—I feel a familiar sadness. I don't know why I care so deeply for Freddie. Maybe my wounds need the friendship of his.

But before I go, Freddie wants me to go with him to an early AA meeting. What's the point, I think. But hey, you never know. Freddie could get sober. I could be his first and only wife. I could finally mean something to this Dartmouth Class of '69.

"But Freddie, the meeting is a closed one," I say. "It's only for alcoholics. I can't go to a closed meeting."

"It doesn't matter," Freddie says.

Oh, right. Freddie is a Dartmouth man who gets to do whatever he wants. I swallow my compulsion to be my most honest self and get into his car to please him.

When we walk into the large church basement, his friends come over to greet him. But just when I think he's going to introduce me, he shoos me away. Annoyed and hurt, I banish myself to the other side of the room and pretend not to know him.

Sitting in a room filled with alcoholics—even in recovery—is terrifying. These are the people who do bad things. These are the people who hurt me. Steeling myself, I listen to a man share his tale of despair and transformation. As he speaks his truth from what feels like his heart, I almost feel sorry for my mother.

"Now is the time to go around the room and introduce yourself by first name only, stating your disease," the leader of the meeting says.

Holy shit. I'm not supposed to be here. These people are going to be so mad. I know how they can get.

"I'm Freddie and I'm an alcoholic," Freddie says, from across the room.

Yeah, right. From where I'm sitting, I don't see a desire to stop drinking.

As the introductions speed up, I start to panic. If I don't say I'm an alcoholic, they'll throw me out. Or worse, they'll think I'm fooling myself. With the circle closing in like a noose around my neck, I make an executive decision. Okay, I'll tell a once-in-a-blue-moon lie. I'll say I'm an alcoholic, then get the hell out of here. They'll never see me again.

"I'm Lynn and I'm an alcoholic," I say, disembodied.

"Hi, Lynn," the drunks reply, acknowledging my existence.

Gasping, I feel a charge go up my spine. My brain is throwing off sparks. Like a plug plugged into a wall, I said the words, but could it possibly be true? Could I be an *alcoholic?* Is *that* what my problem has been all along? After decades of individual, couple, and group therapy, meditation, yoga, all kinds of workshops, self-help books, and thirteen years in Alanon, I'm just one of *them?*

But come to think of it, as I listen to each person share, I am identifying with every single one. Even the twenty-something barefoot guy in the filthy white suit who's missing his front teeth.

But alcoholic are the *other* ones, the ones I'm still trying to recover from. To find out I'm like my mother and father—though not to the same afflicted degree—is almost too much to process. But it *would* explain why my relationships keep going from bad to worse, and even worse again.

When we return to Freddie's house, we drink coffee in his garden. As I share my revelation, Freddie smiles, happy he's found a way to please me. I thank my Dartmouth prince who has inadvertently led me to my own sobriety, and drive home.

# AMATEUR RIGHTS

EXCEPT FOR CONNECTING with Denis from time to time, I don't think much about Dartmouth. But in 2006, Arthur Fergenson, pioneering women's rights crusader, calls to tell me the forgotten women of Dartmouth are going to be adopted as honorary members of the Class of '69.

"Seriously" I say, because it sounds too good to be true.

As Arthur explains we deserve to be acknowledged, I suddenly feel seen. Though there were many in the Class of '69 who were unaware, could have cared less, or were angry when the seven of us came in the fall of '68, I am thrilled by inclusion.

"Does this mean I can come to a reunion?" I ask.

"Of course!" Arthur responds.

I wait three years for the 40th.

Everyone comes. Even Carol who lives in England, and Jane who lives in France. When I get to Hanover, Dartmouth is in full bloom. Trees look greener because my eyes have never been clearer. It's wonderful being at Dartmouth again. But it's not the first time I've come. I always make a point of driving into Hanover whenever I'm in New England, never sure why or what I continue to look for.

Though my mother would have stayed at the Hanover Inn, I want to live in a Dartmouth dorm. I spread my clothes on a twin bed, put odds and ends on the desk, and stifle an urge to decorate. With the barest of essentials, the room feels like a country club cell.

Reunion begins with dinner on the lawn across from Baker Library. Round tables set with white tablecloths, silver, and flowers for the well-heeled Class of '69 remind me of Jersey City holidays. Doing all I can to look good, I'm glad the setting sun is giving my aging face a warm, pinkish glow. Though I tend to wear black like my mother, tonight I'm wearing turquoise blue. I may say looks don't matter, but I still lean on them a lot.

Looking past the Dartmouth men I've yet to meet, I embrace the ones from Heorot and the Hop. But I'm really waiting for my fellow pioneers. Maybe because I have a daughter, some intellectual empathy for my mother, and some acceptance of myself, but when I see Binky, Nanalee, Carol, Ginny, Geri, and Jane, I hug each one like a long-lost friend I'm meeting for the very first time.

There are luncheons, dinners, play readings at Occom Pond, and dancing into the night. And because we're so much older, a memorial for the dead. But what I especially appreciate are the scheduled AA meetings at Dick's House. I'm two years sober and want to stay that way, especially at Dartmouth.

When I walk into the AA meeting, I expect to see half the class there. I'm shocked there are only two, besides myself. One with a desire to stop drinking, and another who gets up like an offensive lineman and lashes out after I share that my mother died of alcoholism at the end of my Dartmouth year.

"It's not a disease! You don't know what you're fucking talking about!" he yells, with alcohol on his breath.

Trying to stay calm, I tell myself he isn't my mother. Even though he will die a few years later exactly like she did.

## CHICK FLICK

MY HANDS DOWN favorite moment of the reunion is breakfast at Lou's with my fellow women. As I look at each one—so much older, yet somehow the same—I realize how important they are, and have always been, to me.

Binky and Carol, the two I feared and envied the most, are incredibly kind. And when Nanalee, Geri, and Ginny look at me with love, I realize I have always belonged. And then, of course, there is Jane.

"I was sure you'd been arrested that night when you were protesting against the War in Vietnam," Jane remembers. "You didn't come home. In fact, we never really talked about your anti-war activities. And I knew practically nothing about your experience in your fraternity, except you directed the play that won the first prize in the fraternity contest."

As I listen to Jane, I wonder where I was.

"As for your mother's death, I remember seeing you distraught and you telling me you had to go home because your mother was dying. You left immediately and took nothing from the apartment. I don't remember your return. I knew your mother was an alcoholic, but that's all. And you certainly didn't tell me about the terrible time you spent at home before and after your mother died. In fact, you practically never talked about your family or your past. I didn't even know you had done summer theatre at Dartmouth in 1968. You must have compartmentalized your life, and the most intimate details you shared only with Denis."

No, Jane. I didn't share them with Denis. I didn't share them with anyone.

"But I have wonderful memories of the time we spent together," Jane remembers, smiling. "The long chats in the evening, watching the snow fall, and listening to the snow plows at night. You were a lovely roommate and all my memories of sharing an apartment with you are totally positive. It's just a shock to realize you were going through a very painful period."

It's a shock to me, too.

## INTERNATIONAL DISTRIBUTION

IN 2010, AFTER living forty-two years in the nation of Manhattan, a confluence of events blasts me off the island. Lucy moves into her own apartment after graduating from Barnard, a college my mother would have approved of; I am able to sell my Music Together business because it has some value; the rents of a changing Manhattan are sky high and I can't bring myself to move to another borough, even Brooklyn; I'm three years sober and see more of life's possibilities; another relationship has ended because I am still more grounded in fantasy than fact; and Molly, our thirteen year old cairn terrier has end-stage liver failure that I swear is not from drinking. Once again, I am freed by death. But where does one go after forty-two years in Manhattan?

Paris, of course.

I haven't been to Paris since my trip with Murray because I have been waiting thirty-six years for a man to be smart enough to take me. But at sixty-one, it's time to take myself. I put my belongings in storage and move to the City of Light.

Though living in Paris doesn't heal my first sober heartbreak—a mostly email romance with a long sober man named Peter—because it carries the emotional weight of every maternal rejection and paternal betrayal, moving to Paris is a brilliant move. If New York tends to feel like the unavailable man who can't commit, Paris is the man who always loves me.

I rent a tiny, sparsely-furnished, sixth-floor apartment in an ancient building in the Marais which would be perfect if not for the woman above me. A middle-aged, chain-smoking drunk whose butts litter the old wooden staircase, she comes home every night and plays Dean Martin's *Ain't That a Kick in the Head* into the wee small hours. As I lie in bed, I imagine her falling asleep with a Gauloises in hand, burning down our sans fire escape building and consider buying a rope ladder. But other than familiar nighttime danger, I love every Parisian moment.

I write all morning in a neighborhood café. In an effort to make lemonade, I've printed all of Peter's and my emails and am organizing them into *Subject: Nice Meeting You: A Cautionary Tale of Internet Romance.* God forbid I simply accept pain and suffering. I must find meaning.

At noon, I walk along the Seine to an AA meeting at the American Cathedral and sit with people from around the world. Grateful for sober perks, I not only have instant friends wherever I go, I can say exactly how I am and no one answers back.

After the meeting, I have lunch with a friend. Then I spend the afternoon alone, walking Paris streets without a map. Going from one arrondissement into another, I visit museums, sit in parks, and go into churches. I am as happy as can be.

Living in Paris has Dartmouth perks as well. I visit Jane who lives in Tours with her husband, Michel. Talking for hours in her farmhouse kitchen, I remember why I love her. I also hop the Eurostar to London and visit Carol who graciously walks me around Hampstead Heath.

How tempting it would be to stay in Paris. Older women are appreciated here. It's okay to have bags and sags and lines. But Paris is more expensive than New York, and I miss the sounds of my own country. So, after a snowy Paris Christmas with William and Lucy, I return to New York to figure out what Peter always called "the empty next."

## HOLLYWOOD

BECAUSE I DON'T own a home or have a lease, I can go anywhere. Why not California? How bad could Los Angeles be? William has lived there since he graduated from Pomona and I no longer compare LA to New York because they're two different planets. Though my world will always begin and end in Manhattan, LA has warm weather and palm trees. I've loved palm trees since my mother took me to the Palm Court to eat pink petit-fours. So, after spending two weeks with Lucy and my dearest friends, I fly to the City of Angels on 1/11/11 on American Airlines flight #1 because it just turns out that way.

As the plane rises out of Newark, I look down at gray and gloomy Jersey City and wonder if I'm going to LA because it's my fantasy home, the place where my black and white and in-color friends lived out the stories I dialed into my heart. After all, my favorite movies and TV shows were shot in LA on studio lots and desert locations. Hollywood is where Fred and Ginger float, dancing cheek to cheek, beyond worry and care.

## TRANSFER

THOUGH THE NEW Yorker in me always misses New York, I take to Southern California like cream cheese to a bagel.

Life on the left coast is not like life in the fast lane of New York. Writing comes more easily, and uncovering the layers of my past is less frightening. Whether west coast life really is or not, it always feels like vacation.

As I walk on the wide Santa Monica beach, I surrender to the mighty Pacific. My feet hit the sand and my body relaxes. I slow down in a way I never thought I could. I like the feeling. After subletting a friend's apartment for six months, I lease a rent-controlled apartment with a palm tree outside my window.

Though I think about earthquakes everyday—I'm always asking people what to do if and when one happens—schlepping my belongings west to live in a sunnier and more peaceful place is an act of kindness towards myself.

## BACK TO ONE

BECAUSE MY FATHER had three brothers and no sisters, it made a coincidental kind of sense that my first husband also had three brothers and no sisters. My second husband had two brothers, no sisters, and three sons. My life tends to feel a lot like Dartmouth, and I like it that way. I suppose it's some kind of progress that Jason, the man I meet and marry in LA, not only has no brothers and no sons, he has two sisters—one of them his twin—and two daughters.

Whoa, Nellie.

When Jason finds me on match.com, it's nice to be found. Relaxed enough to consider someone's pursuit, I'm amazed how much we have in common. We both love Buddhism and all things Pema Chodron; he has what I snobbily refer to as "an east coast sensibility" because he was raised in New Rochelle, a suburb of New York; his father was twenty years older than his mother, just like mine; his father died when Jason was nineteen, and he also quit college and moved into Manhattan to dance; and he's a documentary film editor, so like me, he knows a good story. But what I like best about Jason is he wants to be free of the pain of his past, his defensive projections, and his over-reactions. We are a good match—as far as I can tell—even though he has two daughters.

As I listen to him go on, and on, and on about his oldest daughter in particular, I feel threatened, jealous, and confused. Not just because he relied so much on her during and after an unhappy marriage, but because she relies so much on him. I'm at a loss to understand. Father-daughter closeness scares the hell out of me. It comes with a terrible sense of foreboding.

I don't know how to navigate. By the time Lucy was four, John and I weren't together. I never saw my daughter grow up with her Daddy, perhaps to the detriment of us all. As for her stepfather, though he was loving and supportive, the ending of our marriage was worthy of high Jersey City drama and only caused more pain.

My first up close and personal encounter with a father and his oldest daughter is also fraught because she's a gifted actor who was allowed to go to theater school. She was encouraged by her mother and her father. As I watch her put herself and her body out in the world in a way I never could—going from one role to another—I am crossing a minefield.

Ancient fears roar back. Certain I will never mean as much to Jason as his daughter—as if there is an either/or—I feel an unspoken competition between a wife and daughter that must end in the betrayal of one.

Betrayal is all I know. A father who never protected me from his raging wife, a father who betrayed me with his perversion of our love. A mother who betrayed me by never protecting me from her husband until the damage was done, a mother who could only exit her untenable life by drunkenness and dying. And the husbands I cast to fulfill my scripted prophecy. Sometimes I feel like a six-year-old without the wherewithal to understand.

But because I believe the psyche finds situations that hold the seeds of its own healing, I let myself learn. That a father can love his daughter, and a daughter can love her father without the grievous suffering of either one.

## FULLSCREEN

JUST WHEN I think I've reread all of Dr. Whitlock's letters, I find another one. It's dated July 6, 1969. Clearly, he doesn't know my mother is dead.

> By now, almost anything could have happened
> with your mother, and I'm not sure how to deal
> with it. Certainly, feeling guilty about it will do
> no one any good. That's a little like feeling guilty
> about someone having pneumonia - unless you
> caused it by taking the person out in a rain storm
> needlessly. As for the daughter of the family, there
> would not have been much you could do about
> forcing her to a doctor either.

It's a week before I leave for the dance festival. Before my last fuck and fuck you Dartmouth.

> So far, you've had a great deal going for you. The
> chances have fallen your way - and you've had the
> courage and conviction to use them. I admit there
> is a potential danger of going right for the M.A.,
> that something will stop the B.A., but as long as
> you get the advanced degree, you will have lost
> nothing really.

The *advanced* degree? What is he talking about? A memory starts to surface that's about to torpedo my well-structured story.

> On the Cafe La Mama situation, an open invitation
> is a somewhat treacherous thing. I'd find out what
> it entailed before I took that route. In many ways,
> it would offer the kind of excitement you seem to

> be looking for, and they do some good stuff as well
> as junk. Again, you want to decide pretty openly
> and clearly if that is the sort of world you want to
> enter.

Oh, I remember La Mama Plexus. The company comes to the Hop to perform *The Last Chance Saloon* and after the show, Michael Brody, the lead actor, tells me to look him up in New York. I do and we have lots of sex. But the relationship doesn't last long. La Mama is too far out there for my strait-laced self and I don't do drugs.

> When you chart out what you're going to do, make
> sure you realize what may happen to your present
> college credits when and if you try to get back in
> for the degree. I doubt Dartmouth would smile on
> you for leaving after you spent so much time try-
> ing to win what they have now agreed to.

Wow. I wasn't being kicked to the curb after all. Dartmouth was willing to circumvent my bachelor's degree and throw my credits into an M.A. so I could stay. Just not like the men. Not in the crusaded way I had to have it.

## SEQUEL

A WEEK BEFORE the 2016 presidential election, my sister calls. We don't talk very often, but she's just come back from a visit with our brother in Virginia—the brother I rarely speak to or see—and wants to tell me about it. As she talks about the fun they've had together, I hold the phone an arm's length away to protect myself from the envious details. About to say a disembodied goodbye, I hear her mention a letter.

"Robbie was taking an *American Heritage* out of his bookcase and found a letter Mommy wrote to Besta," she says. "It's not finished, and I didn't really read the whole thing, but it's about Mommy's moods and depression."

I wonder why she hasn't read it. I've spent my life trying to understand our mother. All I know about Gloria Larsen Lobban is she was a very sick and abusive alcoholic; she loved New York and the arts; she was generous to friends and family with material gifts; she loved Besta and her trip to Europe; she hated Catholics and herself; and she was always angry at my father and me. Except for the time she ditched the Carrier Clinic and said how hard it was to be human, I don't really know how she felt about life. I have a vague recollection of her going to a psychiatrist, but clearly it didn't help.

"I can't wait to read it," I say, hanging up the phone.

I run to the computer to email my brother who responds within the hour.

"I will mail original to you on Saturday," my brother writes without a hello. "Not finished signed or dated. Address please?"

I'm shocked my brother wants to send me the original. I only asked for a scan to a text or a picture with his phone. Maybe he doesn't want our mother in his house.

When the letter arrives a few days later, it's packaged like a letter Christie's just sold to the highest bidder. As I open the big white envelope, I feel like I'm exhuming my mother from her grave. A blood red GLL dances at the top of a bright white, unwrinkled piece of Crane's stationery. A red border looks as if it's trying to contain what's inside. The letter, written in my mother's beautiful half-script and half-print hand, is incredibly preserved. It looks like it was written in anyone's last ten minutes. But it's dated April, 1963. My mother is thirty-nine and has no idea she'll be dead in six years.

Dear Besta,

When I hung up the phone a few minutes ago, I burst into tears and cried for a long time. It was unexpected, and somehow a relief. The weather is oppressive and my chest always hurts when it gets close and is about to rain. It was hot last night and Bob and I were both restless and tired this morning. When I finish this, I shall take a bath, the medicine, and get dressed.

Dr. Elwood is understanding, but firm. He has faith in my determination even if I don't always. I'm just tired and discouraged with feeling badly most of the time and it is difficult to keep up with everything. Yesterday I was cross with everyone and apologized later. The window washers, plumbers, and exterminators all came at the same time.

I tried to get someone to meet me in New York because I was desperate to be with someone who could make me forget myself. I went and had lunch alone, and then saw "Auntie Mame."

I am sure I saw you at the Press Conference. Did you have on a flowered hat? I thought the President looked tired. Of course, TV can be misleading.

Last night I watched the movie, "The Man," a story of the paraplegics that I've seen many times before. It always makes me wonder if their struggle is worth it. It only seems to be if someone cares enough for them, to make them keep trying to live and think clearly.

My mother's cries for help overwhelm me with sorrow. I hear the depth of her despair. How she wants to be better, but doesn't know how. How she calls her best friend Besta, as if she needs to be taken care of, too. Struck by her loneliness, I wonder what would have happened if my mother had mailed her letter. I wonder if she would have survived.

# TEARJERKER

I CANNOT WAIT to vote for Hillary Rodham Clinton. After more than two-hundred years of men, I am desperate for a female President and have done all I can to see it happen.

On Election Day—I voted by mail as soon as I got my ballot—I buy a dozen white roses in honor of the Suffragettes and put them on the coffee table so I can see them while I watch the returns. Poised for victory, I can barely contain my excitement. But as the night progresses and the unthinkable happens, my outrage and disappointment give way to despair.

I spent my childhood telling myself the world outside my family home was a kinder, fairer place. It always gave me hope, something to live for. But when an extremely-qualified Hillary Clinton, who has spent her life serving her country and its people, loses to Donald Trump, an incompetent narcissist who is not only accused of sexually assaulting multiple women, but takes pride in it, any remaining vestige of my childhood coping skill vanishes forever.

The morning after the election, the daughter who rejected Dartmouth outright writes to the mother who once put a "Children for Choice" sign in her four-year-old hand so she could march in the Pro-Choice March on Washington. I wanted her to know from the get-go. *No one* has the right to tell a woman what to do with her body *or* her life.

## SUBJECT: I LOVE YOU

Dear Mom,

I love you so much. You will see a woman become president in your lifetime because we have to. Your support of Hillary woke me up to seeing how important it is to teach my female students they can be whatever and whomever they want to be. No boy or man gets to say otherwise. I realized I wasn't dedicating enough of my energy to supporting and raising up the girls I teach. Thank you, Hillary. Thank you to all the women in my life. My girl friends who support and make me who I am. And thank you, Mom, for being a living example of the fact that no matter what is done to you, no matter how many times someone tries to take away your worth or make you feel small, you can always find, receive, and give love to others. I love you very very much and wish I could give you a big hug today.

Love,

Lucy

PROGRESS, I THINK, blinking back tears.

# VERTIGO EFFECT

I TALK TO Denis now, his Irish black hair, tinged silver and gray. As we sit and drink coffee under his giant magnolia in the garden of his Beverly Hills home, he remembers our Dartmouth year with nostalgic affection.

"Jewels, you were a singular member of the Magnificent Seven!" my old Romeo says, smiling his mischievous smile.

If I remember correctly, four of the Magnificent Seven were dead by movie's end. But I savor the compliment because Denis continues to charm.

"You were full of fire," Denis says. "You were so much fun."

"I *was?*" I say, finding it hard to believe.

Denis says he's writing a memoir about his time at Dartmouth and asks for details about my year there. He says he'll make me famous. Sucking on the tit of our mutual grandiosity, I notice he still calls me shitbird, and I wonder why I let him, why I answer to a name so subordinate and small. When every time I hear it, I feel a bit diminished.

"Stop calling me shitbird," I say, as tamped-down rage rises to the surface. "I went through initiation just like you. I'm not a shitbird. I'm a *brother.*"

"Okay, Jewels," Denis says, laughing.

Suddenly, I realize I've been trading my comfort for his. I've let him call me a name whose definition is "a completely useless individual who is unaware of his/her own complete uselessness" because it has always felt like male endearment. Relinquishing the moniker that's made me feel special at my own expense, I feel the earth beneath me quake.

## IT'S A WRAP

IN 2017, I fly east to visit Dr. Whitlock. It took five years to become brave enough to confront him about his wayward tongue. He said he didn't remember it, and that it couldn't have happened. I questioned my sanity for all of five seconds and stopped writing him for ten years. So, though we have known each other for fifty-one years, I haven't seen him in about twenty-five. I may not have even googled to see if he was still alive if the Coen Brothers hadn't named George Clooney's character Baird Whitlock in *Hail Caesar*. But I'm so glad they did. Hanging onto old resentments is too punishing to myself.

After rereading his letters, I actually can't wait to see my old advisor and friend. I want to thank him for all the times he tried to help me, and for caring every step of my way. At the time, I couldn't take in his concern. When parental love is intertwined with abuse, it's too dangerous to acknowledge my own need.

Baird lives in Belfast, Maine, with Joan, his wife of many years. The wintry morning, bright and breath-steaming cold, reminds me of a clean slate. As the sun bounces off barren winter trees, I am once again sustained by the beauty of a bright New England day.

Ninety-two-years-old, Baird bounds out the door as I'm walking up the steps. He greets me with a hug.

"You're so old!" I blurt out, because I'm shocked by how he's aged.

"You're not so young yourself!" Baird shoots back, laughing.

As I follow him into his house, I'm amazed he moves like he did when he was forty-two, and I was barely seventeen. Ever thrilled by life and learning, Baird looks up at Joan, coming down the stairs like his bright-eyed bride. When Joan greets me with a hug, I'm grateful I can finally feel their touch.

We have tea and cookies in their sun-filled living room and talk for hours, catching up on our families, our travels, and our lives. Then I tell them I'm writing a book about my year at Dartmouth.

"Believe it or not, I saved all your letters," I say to my old pen-pal. "Thank you for trying to help me."

Baird smiles his all-knowing smile. Suddenly I'm sitting in his Elmira College office. He's smoking a pipe and leaning back in his chair, about to give full weight to what he's going to say.

"Going to a college of all men wasn't the wisest of choices," Baird says, arching an eyebrow and looking deep into my eyes.

Gasping at his bluntness, I choke on a laugh. "You think?" I say, as if I agree.

As the room fills with laughter at my expense, I pick up my cup for the comfort of tea and consider a cookie. But then, I think for myself.

You might be right, Baird. Leaving the safety of women and going to a college of all men might not have been the wisest of choices. But it was absolutely necessary.

## FOLLOW SHOT

I AM CONSTANTLY surprised by how often Dartmouth pops up in my life. In 2017, as I'm leaving one of Denis's parties, one of his friends stops me and says hello.

"How do you know Denis?" he asks.

"Denis was my boyfriend at Dartmouth," I say, flaunting our connection. "I was one of Dartmouth's first women."

"Oh," the man says. "Did you know anyone in the theater department?"

"Of course," I say, a bit surprised because this is not the usual response. "That's why Dartmouth let us go there. We were all in the theater department."

"Did you know Rod Alexander?" he asks, and I wonder why.

"Yes, Rod was the head of the Drama Department."

"Did you know what happened with his daughter, Adrienne?" he asks.

"Why? Did he abuse her?" I say, without thinking.

"How did you *know?*" he asks.

"I don't. I just had a feeling," I say, not wanting to ask how he knows.

"So you believe her?" he asks, like he might not.

"I do," I say, heading for the door.

## MATCH CUT

> I know what it is like to endure the jail cell of the spirit and the emotional prison of an abusive childhood. And I know how to survive. I also know how to go beyond childhood circumstance, from being branded as the black sheep, a rape and incest victim, to complete freedom. What might have become a bitter childhood became that which grew me.
>
> - *The More Love Club* by Adrienne Alexander

TWO WEEKS LATER, I'm on my way to a coffee shop in Sherman Oaks to meet the daughter of the man who helped me into Dartmouth. Adrienne was easy to find. We have mutual friends on Facebook.

"If you ever want to talk," I message her, "I would love to meet for coffee. We sadly have some things in common."

But now that we're meeting, I'm not so sure. I'm afraid talking will be triggering for us both. Even with all the work

I have done, the past gets more and more real and I'm always afraid I won't be able to handle it when it does. But it *is* exciting to be meeting someone who knows what I'm talking about. Especially in the context of Dartmouth. And who knows? Maybe our meeting will be helpful. Maybe I'll be reassured. After all, Adrienne has published her book about abuse and she's still alive.

From the moment we meet, Adrienne and I can't stop talking. I tell her about my Dartmouth year and how desperate I was to keep up with the men. I confess how badly I wanted a Dartmouth degree. When she tells me she was in Dartmouth's first official class of graduating women, I am jealous and awed.

"Did my father ever touch you?" Adrienne asks, snapping me out of sibling rivalry hell.

"No," I say, taken aback, "but he did make a show of my breasts. He staged this moment in *The Miser* when Eric Forsythe had to practically drool over my breasts."

Adrienne nods, understanding. But as wonderful as it is to be affirmed, I also feel sad. Any thought the fault might somehow have been mine—maybe I was being overly sensitive—vanishes once and for all.

As Adrienne and I trade stories of abuse like boys with baseball cards, we note we have many things in common. We both paid a price for being criminally special to the first men in our lives. We suffered from the jealousy and abandonment of our mothers. We had broken, then better marriages. We have wonderful children. We love the theater and love to sing. And we're dedicated to thriving. Lynn Lobban and Adrienne Alexander, two women in their sixties, sexually abused by their fathers, went to Dartmouth College, became working actors, married, had children, wrote books, sitting together in a booth at Nat's Early Bite on Burbank.

"How did your family react to your book?" I have to ask, because my siblings don't want me to speak my truth.

When Adrienne talks about sibling rage and disinheritance, I'm sorry I asked. "But you're alive!" I say, because that has to be the takeaway. Adrienne survives.

But then our paths diverge. As I'm finishing my healthy green omelet, Adrienne says her father was an alcoholic.

"I had a feeling he was," I say, because I did. I just didn't want to know.

"He also told me he was sexually abused when he was a teenager in the Navy," she adds.

"Really?" I say, envious because I don't know if my father was sexually abused and might qualify for what I call the get-out-of-jail-free card. Though the majority of those who are sexually abused do *not* become abusers, too many do. I will never know if my father was acting out of his own traumatic experience, or if my mother might have been acting out of hers. I always wondered if her alcoholic uncle abused her, or if someone in my father's family abused him. It would have been nice to feel compassion for their wounds.

And then, Adrienne starts to speak lovingly of her father and our paths finally divide. She expresses her appreciation for his contribution to Dartmouth's theater, and I nod in agreement because it's true. But too much talk about the positive aspects of abusive fathers is too challenging for me. When we get the check, I am ready for goodbye.

"We have to meet again," Adrienne says, as we walk into the sunshine of a California day.

"Yes," I say, though we have yet to meet.

We acknowledge the power in being seen, hug each other, and go our separate ways. But I'm completely overwhelmed. I have to sit awhile in my car because Dartmouth and my childhood have just converged. Though I feel incredibly empowered after swapping stories with a beautiful survivor who so lovingly understands, I also feel disheartened. Not just because there are so many fathers who hurt their little girls, but because I don't feel one-tenth of Adrienne's compassion.

## WIDE ANGLE LENS

HEALING FROM EARLY trauma is a lifetime's work. I know because I try everything to get free. Sixteen years after my mother's death, a couple therapist suggests I go to the cemetery and talk to her.

"I know you had a disease," I say to my mother in the ground, "but the way you treated me wasn't fair. Your life was not my fault."

I am vaguely aware of some anger, but my good girl self can only break down.

"I love you, Mommy," I sob, "but I have to say goodbye."

If only it had worked.

Thirty-nine years after my mother's death, and twenty years after my father's, I trudge again to the cemetery. This time I'm talking to them both, making amends in case anything was my fault. As I sit beside the Lobban headstone, covered in weeds and sorely needing tending, I apologize for not understanding how sick they both were. I confess I have been dragging them behind me in a shit show of blame.

"I forgive you both," I sob, "and I hope you forgive me."

If only *that* had worked.

But five days before Christmas in 2017, something shifts inside me. As I'm writing at a faux-marble table in the corner of the 18th Street Coffeehouse, and with Bing Crosby singing *God Rest Ye Merry Gentlemen* in the background, I relinquish all hope for a childhood do-over. Crying, I let myself know how much I needed my parents to love me, and how much I still need to love them.

## REMAKE

IN THE RUN-UP to the 50th Dartmouth Reunion a lot has changed. I've lived in California for eight years, I'm in the middle of writing a memoir, and my third marriage is echoing aspects of my childhood that may portend its end.

Though I have some apprehension about going back to Hanover just weeks before the 50th anniversary of my mother's death, I cannot wait. Not everyone shows up for this one. Age has brought badly-timed challenges to more than a few, and reunions are not for everyone. Not everyone wants to revisit the past or note the passage of time. But I love a good reunion. And the 50th is like winning the Dartmouth lottery.

After Friday lunch with the Class of 2019, I head to the Hop to watch a reenactment of The Parkhurst Takeover. As present Dartmouth women play past Dartmouth men, I am grateful for the unspoken message. Sitting on a panel about 1960's activism, I tell a theater full of people how I fought against the war, but chickened out of jail. I listen to an ROTC alum—a man whose presence I once vehemently opposed— talk about his feelings and realize we were, and always are, just struggling human beings. And in a seismic shift, I feel compassion for Dean Seymour.

I visit Heorot and watch brothers younger than my children play on the lawn. The basement, laid low by beer pong, is a disgusting sight. My young brothers assure me—like kids reporting to their mother or grandmother—that the house is going to be renovated.

When the list of the dead is read in Rollins Chapel, it is ten years longer. Arthur Fergenson reads a poem; Glee Club alums sing *Dartmouth Undying,* filling the chapel with the beauty of male harmony; I sing John Wallowitch's *This Moment* because it's all we ever have; and for the very first time, I sing *Dear Old Dartmouth,* Dartmouth's alma mater. Tearing up alongside alums, spouses, partners, and female pioneers, I feel the granite in my body.

There are meals in the tent, dinners on the lawn, and Saturday night dancing. But what I'm waiting for is the traditional walk with the Class of 2019 at the start of commencement. Since I don't see an honorary degree in my Dartmouth future, I figure this is as close as I will ever get to getting a Dartmouth degree.

I wear a teal armband to protest sexual assault on Dartmouth's campus and beyond, and a reunion hat to shield me from the sun. I watch men and women receive degrees in equal measure and marvel at the accomplishments of the honorary degree recipients, including Yo Yo Ma who addresses the graduates.

> You will be powerful. And when you are, do not abuse your power. Ever.

> Remember, always, that you are a human being first. It's a truth embedded in the very foundation of your liberal arts education. Practice your humanity daily. Practice that truth. Let it power your decisions, let it inspire your thoughts, and let it shape your ideals. Then you will soar. You will fly. And you will help others soar and fly.

As the incomparable cellist plays Pablo Casals' *Song of the Birds,* I think life cannot get better than this moment on the

Green. But then President Hanlon gets up to speak about the importance of the arts.

> ...and in 1962 Dartmouth pioneered a new model for performing arts centers across all of higher education with the opening of the Hop. Not long after, the Dartmouth theater department served as the earliest pathway for women on this campus, some of whom are seated amongst you today as proudly adopted members of the Class of 1969.

If Kammy and Nanalee weren't jumping up and screaming, I might have missed the moment completely. Because it is the last thing I expect. After fifty years of crying in the wilderness, Dartmouth's first women are publicly acknowledged.

## EDITOR

AFTER I SURVIVE the fiftieth anniversary of my mother's death, it's time to stop clinging to the bottom of her scotch-stained nightgown. At seventy, it isn't just pathetic, it finally feels wrong.

I've carried my mother and father my entire life. Every man I have ever loved, lived with, and/or married has been a reflection of one or the other. Though I swore I would never be like my mother—I'd have a career and get marriage "right"—in an effort to best her, I've had to change partners and the dance ends up the same.

Drawn to accomplished men with familiar flaws, I have dragged every marriage into therapy in an effort to fix us all. But I have not always been honest. When a man is your solution, you don't want to alienate him by speaking the full weight of your truth.

I have always been in awe of women brave enough to leave a marriage simply because they are unhappy. I needed the catalyst of another man the first time because I couldn't tolerate the pain of breaking up my family. The marriage was empty, but I could not leave simply for myself. My second marriage exploded in my face, though I would not give up on it until anyone in their right mind would. Leaving a marriage because it's for my own well-being is new.

"It's okay, Lynn," a voice whispers. "You have nothing to prove. Do what's best for you now. Life is so short, sweetheart."

I wonder if it's my mother.

# REEL

Let them go.

They're gone.

They already left.

You were too busy to notice.

You were too busy untying the knots they left you in.

You've unraveled.

Let them go.

If you want to fly, you've got to lighten your load.

Dump the cargo.

Drop being right.

Unclench your fists.

Open your hands.

Float them into the blue.

Free them.

Free yourself.

## HERO'S JOURNEY

LEAVING A THIRD marriage is not easy. At my age, many women would make the most of a challenging companionship with someone they love. But when a force propels me forward, I go whether I understand or not. At the end of February 2020, I leave my marriage and once again put my belongings in storage.

When I began writing this book, it was not my intention to find love and in-my-heart forgiveness for my mother. But I have, and I am profoundly grateful. So, it makes sense to wonder if writing about my marriages might lead me to finding love and forgiveness for my father. It's a panic-inducing enterprise and I don't know if I'm brave enough, but I want to be free before I leave the planet. The only problem is, I want to write about this in Paris, not in a fucking pandemic.

When the coronavirus crosses the Atlantic, my planned, paid for, and set in motion trip grinds to a halt. I deny the reality as long as I can because it's my first reaction to anything scary. But after six months in Airbnbs, I finally surrender. I rent a small apartment five blocks from the Pacific Ocean, and take everything out of storage. Unable to run to Paris, New York, or anyplace else, I am forced to live like I did as a child in Jersey City. Sequestered, scared, and watching a shitload of television.

But because the pandemic mimics my childhood, I hit an emotional bottom I didn't know was there. It hurls me into yet another program because it doesn't take a village, it takes a small metropolis.

I start zooming and calling into ACA—Adult Children of Alcoholics and Dysfunctional Families—meetings. I went a few times over three decades ago and hated it. The meetings brought up too much pain and way too many feelings. But in the midst of unfolding global tragedy, I am ready to peel off my skin.

## OPENING NIGHT

THOUGH I HAVE often scoffed at the idea of an inner child, I have always known she was there. I just didn't want to know her. She was this dark, disgusting, faraway, angry annoyance who would only get in my way. In fact, I credit my somewhat successful life—if you don't include men and marriage—to the fact I disavowed the wounded and traumatized child inside. I crammed her into an airless box and pushed her to the back of a dark closet. I knew she'd be quiet because speaking her truth would bring injury. She'd never trust because even I could not be trusted. And she would never feel the full weight of her feelings because her feelings would be the end of us both.

But as I wade into the ACA waters, I let my little girl—and my angry and gloriously determined teenager—speak. As they share their shame and sadness—raging and grieving with those who understand—I begin to accept and even love myself. At seventy-two, I begin to find wholeness.

## BELOW THE LINE

I lie at the bottom of everything dark and scary.
In quiet moments she hears me.
She feels the pulse of my whisperings,
glimpses my light through the cracks she chisels.
I lie in wait to embrace her,
unfettered, untarnished, and untouched by human hands.
Long buried and longing,
awaiting her beneath the numbness,
the false thoughts and illusions,
I have always been here.

## ANGLE

THIS ISN'T THE first time I have written about sexual abuse. I started in 1991, telling myself I was writing a one-woman show so I would never again have to audition. *Invasion of Privacy*, a series of monologues about incest and alcoholism, was going to be a meaty acting opportunity, a gift to myself.

I sent ten pages to the Public Theater. They asked for the full script, but when I didn't hear back, I never followed up. I sent ten pages to New York Theater Workshop and was invited into their Monday playwriting group, but I politely refused. "I have therapy on Mondays," I told them, unable to admit I was too scared to feel shame in front of strangers.

Ten years later, I organized a reading. I rented the Jose Quintero Theater and brought in actors because being onstage by myself was too scary. My acting teacher, Elizabeth Browning, directed. Seventy-five people came. I remember Arthur Whitman, a teacher at Village Community School where my kids were in school, sitting in the audience long after the reading. "I don't think I can move," Arthur said. "I feel like I need an ambulance."

He wasn't the only one. My body twitched for three full days after I shared my truth.

Six years after that, in 2007, I tried again because every time I shared my story, someone shared theirs, often for the first time. I crafted the monologues into what I called a "cabaret play," and named it *Quarter to Three*, referring to the night my mother caught my father in my bed. Five actors performed the monologues while I sang Sinatra songs—*One for My Baby, You Make Me Feel So Young, Someone to Watch Over Me, Night and Day, How Little We Know, I Remember You, Willow Weep for*

*Me, Dream, Anything Goes, I'll Be Seeing You, Don't Like Good-byes*—as commentary and relief. The show ended with me singing *Always* to Molly Camp, who played me as a child. In that staged moment, I believed I loved that vulnerable child. Offstage, I didn't have a clue.

Though *Quarter to Three* was a personal triumph, after four performances, I felt like collapsing. Even after an encouraging review.

> Lynn Lobban's *Quarter to Three* is an autobiographical account to hell and back. With brutal honesty Lobban tells of a childhood fraught with neglect, abuse, pain, fear, and distortion in a seemingly perfect family setting. Ironically in her play everyone is given a voice—parents, maids, dogs, television characters, and even her stomach— while she herself is muted by an unspeakable reality and a twisted damaging love. And although everyone is vocal, none of the voices step up to help. In the end, it is her own voice that saves her.
>
> Obviously not a day at the beach, what would recommend that you not miss this audacious work? Almost every aspect of the production. You can start with a stellar cast that breathes life into the characters who shaped Lobban's life and a story so heartbreaking that it occasionally takes your breath away. Intertwine that with Sinatra songs

(thus the title) viewed with a totally new perspective, providing the escape hatch a desperate little girl needed, and then intersperse sophisticated humor at just the right moment. The result is a mesmerizing masterpiece where every action, thought, and emotion are one hundred percent believable.

*Quarter to Three* is so powerful and effective at addressing an all-too common problem you can only pray that this is just the beginning. It should become a public service production available to children as a cautionary tale, adults as a beacon of hope and inspiration, offenders as an awareness of the consequences of their actions, and to all humans as a celebration of the human spirit and desire to survive. Grateful viewers will be awestruck by Lynn Lobban's courage in presenting her story.

Even after Laurie Lawson's generous review, I couldn't go on. Certainly, it was gratifying to shine a light on abuse and be graced with the privilege of hearing other people's secrets, but I couldn't handle the shame. I just wasn't ready. I barely am now.

# RELEASE

EXPERIENCING AND EXPRESSING every dark and angry feeling about what was done to me, I begin to forgive the first man in my life. Though I will never forgive his crime, nor deny the lifelong effect it has had on me, I can finally consider the complexities of the man.

I can respect my father's skills as a surgeon, and be grateful he healed many people. I can consider the trauma he suffered in World War II as he tried to save ravaged soldiers. His drunken and repetitive stories about his four years as an Army Colonel in the Philippines drove me crazy as a child, but I now see his own PTSD and unfinished business. Finally, I can accept that my father, like my mother, was an alcoholic who suffered from every hideous aspect of the terrible disease.

As I reassure the frightened child within that she can't be hurt again—that I love and will never leave her—I can let myself know how much I loved my father and how much I needed him to love me. I can acknowledge that when he stopped being my Daddy, something in me died. I can accept all that was, and will never be.

# REVIEW

LIVING IN THE male-centric world of Dartmouth, I wanted to be one of the boys so I could feel safe. So I could be powerful. So no one could ever hurt me again.

I let the male gaze define me. Whether a man wanted or approved of me was a measure of myself. I believed men were more important. I dismissed childbirth and raising children as some lesser contribution. I thought the greatest authors, inventors, composers, doctors, scientists, artists, teachers, and leaders were men because women were simply not as good. I never imagined they were being stifled and ignored, written and left out of books.

My Dartmouth year most likely forged me into the feminist I became. I joined the National Organization for Women, subscribed to *Ms.* the moment it came out, and marched on Washington for the Equal Rights Amendment. I fought for equal pay and will forever stand up for reproductive rights. I raised a son who takes the equality of women for granted, and a daughter whose confidence in the female future always makes me smile.

Happy to be one of the girls, I hear the strength in higher pitches and know the power there. The bravest warrior is not the one who muscles through, but the one who shares her wounded heart. As I listen to a stream of women speak truths of sexual violation, I am outraged and amazed I have never been alone. When I imagine a world run by women, I think it will be a kinder and more peaceful place.

Though I cried in the wilderness of men and myself, I am freed by the telling of tales and my truth. In the picked-up sticks of memory and blank pages, my life and my body are my own. Forgiving myself for mistakes and misperceptions, I feel compassion for anyone who didn't get the chance to become what they might have been. My heart breaks in two.

# CREDITS

ONE OF THE lies I told myself in order to survive was that I didn't need help. I could do things alone. But as I look up the definition of encourage—"to inspire with courage, spirit, or hope"—I realize this book would not even exist without the encouragement of a great many people.

Thank you, Denis O'Neill, Dartmouth boyfriend and forever friend. You told me to write my Dartmouth story, and your relentless enthusiasm has kept me going, more often than not.

Thank you, long-time and most loving friend, Jean Vallely Graham. My life has been more interesting because of you, and your support continues to be invaluable.

Thank you, David Groff. Your editing skills and gentle guidance have made this book as good as it could be. You have surely made me a more confident writer, and I am forever grateful.

Thank you, Lucy Lobban-Bean, for being brave enough to read an early draft of your mother's book, and William Lobban-Bean, for your wise and helpful words regarding its publication.

Thank you, Caryl Comeforo and Joan Chapman. More like sisters than first cousins, you listened to my story and only showed compassion.

And because my story has had several iterations over the years—*Invasion of Privacy, Quarter to Three,* and *Shitbird,* the original title of this book—there are many more to thank. If I have left you out, I hope you will forgive me.

Forever thanks to the late great Artie Gaffin whose friendship and loving insight sustained me as a person and a writer. Thank you to the always missed John Wallowitch and Bertram Ross, who listened to my first monologue and did not turn away; Elizabeth Browning, beloved acting teacher and friend, whose very being is encouragement; and my fellow actors who cheered me on as I dared to find my voice: Marty Vidnovic, William Berg, Laura DuBrule, Carolyn Kitay, Janine Squillari, Amanda Reisman, Lisa Milanazzo, Paul La Greca, Merrie Nell McLeod, April Feld, Brett Douglas, Beth Kaplan Bongar, Annette Kischinowsky, David Pixley, Kate Kenny, Heather Hooten, Jennica Carmona, Joy Franz, Lisa Altomare, Ruth Darcy, Lisa Morse, Marcus DeLoach, Rhonda Musak, Ruth Lembo, Sarah Keifer, Heidi Schulman, Kevin McMullan, Lois Barth, Lynn Jordan, Marla Mase, Tiffany Hodges, and Anita Wlody.

Thank you, Lucinda Garthwaite, my loving Goddard College advisor, who lessened my shame as I finished Invasion of Privacy and finally received my undergraduate degree; and thank you, Deborah Brevoort and Jacquelyn Reingold, my inspiring MFA advisors, who taught me everything about playwriting.

Thank you, Phil Bond and Kenny Bell, for welcoming *Quarter to Three* into the Laurie Beechman Theater; Elizabeth for her compassionate direction; and the amazing cast who took the stage and empowered us all: Joy Franz, David Licht, Kristin Stewart Chase, Molly Camp, Natalie Barback, and Sarah Keifer.

Thank you to everyone who took the time to read *Invasion of Privacy, Shitbird,* or one of the many drafts of this book: Deborah Ivry, Wendy Sarasohn, Susan Greenhill, Sylvia Lavietes, Molly Newman, Peter Dunne, Jason Rosenfield, Barbara Damashek, MJ Territo, Ellen Whyte, Sally Eaton Arnold, Jean Rosenberg, David Boger, Michele Brourman, Amanda Urban, Madaline Blau, Franklin Getchell, Elaine Stritch, Murray Moss, Maia Danziger, Elizabeth Kelley Erickson, Sue Gandy, Epp Hardy, Wally Wilhoit, Barbara Sieck Taylor, Jim Cowgill, Andy Kay, Deborah Jowitt, James Dobson, Lauren D'Alvia, Jennifer Pattison Rumford, Charles Morey, Art Buchwald, Che'rae Adams, Monty Silver, Gert Basson, Chris Gerelmo, Susan Harris, Stella Sortijas, Nancy Sokolow, Margaret LaClair, Barbara Ellmann, Robin Robinson, David Bushnell, Celia Lee, Michael Bofshever, Shelley Schultz, Dona Heller, Peter Schaeffer, Arthur Fergenson, Shirley Fergenson, Lisbeth Lloyd, Marcia Ross, Kate Amend, Laurie Lawson, Rosemary McNamara, Amy Blumenfield, Cassidy Boyd, Peter Hoeglund, Ann Bronston, Lloyd Noonan, Ashley Hill, Yvonne Cassidy, Katie Dunn, and last but never least, Helen Crisp.

Thank you, Sean Plottner, Lisa Furlong, and *Dartmouth Alumni Magazine* for making me a published writer; *The New York Times* for publishing my *Tiny Love Story, 7 Women and*

3,000 *Men;* and Jennifer Smith, my first agent, who did her best during an impossible pandemic.

Thank you, Baird Whitlock and Deborah Jowitt, for permission to include your letters; Adrienne Alexander for a moment of The More Luck Club; Laurie Lawson for allowing her review; *The Dartmouth* for its articles "Courtesy of The Dartmouth, Inc. Company, Inc. Reprinted with Permission;" and *The Jersey Journal* for *Fraternity Inducts Girl Robustly* and *Agudath Sholom Buys Gifford Avenue Building* reprinted courtesy of *The Jersey Journal*, Jersey City, NJ. Copyright © The Evening Journal Association.

Thank you, Jaime Wolf, for legal advice; Jennie Rosenblum and Katie Dunn for proofreading; Jess LaGreca for your patience and cover design; Jennifer Pattison Rumford for rescuing me at the end; and Palmetto Publishing for making this book a reality.

Lastly, a heart-filled thanks to the powers-that-be, human and otherwise, who have brought me to this moment. Though I tend to agree with Maya Angelou and the African-American spiritual that sings "I wouldn't take nothing for my journey now," I would be lying if I didn't say I'm glad this part of it is over. May we all find peace.

Printed in the USA
CPSIA information can be obtained
at www.ICGtesting.com
LVHW071136150923
758193LV00004B/38

9 798822 919075